DIASPORA LOBBIES AND THE US GOVERNMENT

Diaspora Lobbies and the US Government

CONVERGENCE AND DIVERGENCE
IN MAKING FOREIGN POLICY

Edited by Josh DeWind and Renata Segura

A joint publication of the Social Science Research Council
and New York University Press

NEW YORK UNIVERSITY PRESS

New York and London

www.nyupress.org

Library of Congress Cataloging-in-Publication Data

Diaspora lobbies and the US government : convergence and divergence in making foreign policy / edited by Josh DeWind and Renata Segura.

    pages cm

    "A joint publication of the Social Science Research Council and New York University Press."

    Includes bibliographical references and index.

    ISBN 978-1-4798-1876-1 (cl : alk. paper)

    1. United States—Foreign relations. 2. Pressure groups—United States.

3. Lobbying—United States. 4. Minorities—Political activity—United States.

I. DeWind, Josh, editor of compilation. II. Segura, Renata, editor of compilation.

III. Title: Diaspora lobbies and the United States government.

JZ1480.D53 2014

327.73—dc23

2013049761

This book is dedicated to Louis L. Gerson in recognition of the insightful scholarship, deep affection, and moral commitment that he has offered his adopted homeland.

Contents

Acknowledgments

We thank Steve Heydemann for instigating this project on diaspora-government relations, Steve Riskin for nurturing its progress, and the United States Institute of Peace for providing financial support, without which the publication of this book would have been impossible. The USIP hosted two meetings at which the authors presented their ideas and debated perspectives, and we are grateful to the following people who contributed insightful and diverse perspectives to those discussions: Theodros Dagne (Congressional Research Service), Rend al-Rahim Francke (Iraq Foundation and United States Institute of Peace), Mary Ellen T. Gilroy (US State Department), Feisal Istrabadi (Indiana University), Jocelyn McCalla (JMC Strategies), Bruce A. Morrison (Morrison Public Affairs Group), David Shinn (US ambassador), and Julia E. Sweig (Council on Foreign Relations). The opinions, findings, conclusions, or recommendations expressed in this publication are those of the authors and do not necessarily reflect the views of the United States Institute of Peace or the other project participants.

At the Social Science Research Council, this project was supported by staff of the Migration Program and the Conflict Prevention and Peace Forum. Teresa Whitfield initially helped us plan the project, and Eda Pepi and Lauren Shields were essential to its efficient organization. Sabrina Stein assiduously reviewed and prepared manuscripts for publication. The assistance of other SSRC staff was also crucial: Jolanta Badura conscientiously secured participants' travel arrangements, and Lisa Yanoti diligently tracked our finances. Alyson Metzger, Jonathan VanAntwerpen, and Michael Simon patiently and meticulously facilitated the book's production, along with Elisabeth Magnus, our copy editor, and Ilene Kalish and Caelyn Cobb at NYU Press. We gratefully thank all of them for their generous and persistent efforts.

We are similarly grateful for the encouraging suggestions of two anonymous reviewers of the book's original manuscripts.

Finally, we are indebted to our spouses Dee Ratterree and Adam Lupel, and to Miranda, for their affectionate and, during times of absence and stress, unstinting understanding and support.

Introduction

CHAPTER ONE

Diaspora-Government Relations in Forging US Foreign Policies

Josh DeWind and Renata Segura

When in his farewell address as president of the United States George Washington (1796) warned the American people against the dangers of foreign entanglements, he was most concerned that "inveterate antipathies" and "passionate attachments" might lead citizens to "betray or sacrifice the interests of their own country." Since then, Americans have viewed with ambivalence the connections of their fellow citizens to ancestral homelands. On the one hand, as a nation of immigrants, Americans have accepted dual affections for both nations of origin and the United States as a common and expected aspect of hyphenated ethnic-American identities. On the other hand, Americans have also regarded persistent foreign ties suspiciously, seeing them as a reflection of potential disloyalty and a threat to national security.

Adding to contemporary concerns about foreign attachments has been the steady growth, particularly since the 1980s, of diaspora populations who have sought to influence US foreign policies toward their homelands. The potential members of such diasporas include not only recently settled immigrants, whose numbers the 2010 US Census reported had reached 38.5 million and 12.5 percent of the American population, but also multiple generations of previously established American ethnic groups. Recent immigrants from countries that began sending immigrants to the United States three or four generations ago, such as Irish youths seeking employment and Jews seeking asylum, have revived ethnic groups' interests in their national origins and given new life to organizations that seek to shape US foreign policy toward their homelands. New immigrant groups from nations without a history of substantial prior settlement in America, such as Iranians or Ethiopians, have also sought to influence US foreign policies toward their homelands, starting from scratch in learning how to do so. Finally, the children of immigrants who are born into US citizenship may take up their parents' involvement in foreign policy making, as have some Cubans and Haitians, though they have done so with somewhat different attachments and goals than their parents.

Diasporas' actual or potential influence on US foreign policies toward their homelands has been greatly controversial, particularly during times of crisis or war. Often diasporas whose many members have assimilated over multiple generations into American society and established a base of social and political power, such as Irish and Jewish immigrants and their descendants, seem to exert significant influence. But the Irish diaspora, while influential in many respects, has rarely been able to trump the United States' alliance with Britain (see chapter 5 of this volume). In contrast, the Jewish diaspora has prevailed over other diasporas and, some claim, over the United States' national interests, in shaping US policies toward the Middle East (Ahrari 1987; Terry 2005; Mearsheimer and Walt 2007). While it may seem unsurprising that some relatively recently arrived and smaller diasporas, such as those from Palestine, Haiti, or Ethiopia, have had only a limited impact on US policies toward their homelands (see chapters 4, 7, and 8 of this volume), others seem to have wielded significant influence, including the Iraqi lobby, which has been credited with pushing the United States into war in Iraq (Roston 2008; also see chapter 9 of this volume).

If the impact of diasporas in shaping US foreign policies is to be understood and assessed, then the relations they create with different branches of American government, the manner in which they exert their influence, and contexts within which their goals become the goals of US foreign policy must all be examined closely. But such influence should not be assumed to be unidirectional. As much as diasporas make an effort to shape the US foreign policy, government legislators and administrators also seek to enlist diasporas in furthering American interests. In taking such an interactive perspective, the essays in this volume respond to the need for clearer understandings of how diaspora lobbies and the government bureaucrats engage with one another and how the avenues of influence go both ways and vary over time. The authors focus not only on the arenas and processes through which diasporas and the US government influence one another in the formulation of US foreign policy but also on the ways in which the resulting policies reflect and shape diaspora and US national interests and goals. To that end, each of the case studies presented in this volume explores the nature of diasporas and the history of their relations with the US government, takes into account the contexts within which diaspora-government relations have taken on prominent or diminished significance, and draws conclusions about how the lobbying efforts of relatively recent and long-established diasporas have affected US policies toward their homelands.

For inclusion in this volume, the editors selected case studies in which diaspora-government relations have been significant for the promotion, prevention, or resolution of conflicts in the diasporas' homelands. The types and levels of policy-relevant conflicts range widely to include civil violence (the Irish Troubles), confrontations between governments (Israel and the Palestinian Authority), imposed economic sanctions (Cuba), military occupation (Haiti and Iraq), and postwar factionalism (Ethiopia). The comparative pairing of cases, each with distinct political dynamics and quite different approaches of US foreign policy, has been used as an analytic tool to underscore the different mechanisms, tools, and channels through which the diasporas and the US government interact. The authors examine how diaspora-government engagements respond to these political dynamics, reflect and shape government and diaspora interests and goals, and influence the formulation of US foreign policies.

Convergence and Divergence of Interests

To draw broader insights from each of the authors' analyses of diaspora-government relations, we have organized their essays with reference to the extent that diaspora lobbies and government legislators and administrators have sought and been able to establish a convergence of interests in the design and implementation of foreign policies. From this starting point the processes by which diasporas and the US government engage with one another include not only how they try to identify mutual values and interests but also how they employ persuasion or coercion or at times ignore or override one another's interests in seeking to formulate or sustain US foreign policies.

Two basic analytical approaches to understanding convergent and divergent policy making predominate in the essays: the first views policy convergence as a result of diaspora and government representatives' identification of overlaps between what seem to be essentially objective, preexisting national and group interests and goals. The second perspective, in contrast, views convergence and divergence as the result of a shaping of national interests in the give-and-take of democratic processes, including lobbying, and sees them as involving compromises and/or the predominance of one side over the other. Whether viewed from an essentialist or a constructivist perspective, the convergence or divergence of interests emerges through mutual engagement between diaspora lobbies and the members of the US government in forging foreign policies. To understand these relations and their dynamics, the volume's essays examine not only diaspora groups' lobbying of different branches of the US government but also outreach by officials of national political parties and representatives of US government legislative and administrative bodies as they seek to mobilize the support and assistance of diasporas in promoting or implementing particular foreign policy goals.

From the essays a general conclusion becomes apparent: the influence of diasporas and the US government on one another in shaping foreign policy increases when convergent interests and goals become recognized, whether these are preexisting or constructed, and decreases when interests and goals are seen to be divergent. But a complete convergence and divergence of values and interests between multiple actors is unlikely, if only because of the great social diversity and the complexity of policy making in a liberal democracy as large as the United States. Rarely do diaspora members, other Americans, or US government officials have single or unified interests. Analysts must take into account how government policies are determined through political processes that include narrow and targeted special interest lobbying as well as broad and open public debates. In this context, competing loyalties between a country of origin and a nation of settlement need not in and of themselves be either unusual or problematic. Although the civic virtue of multiculturalism and ethnic pluralism in politics is highly debated, most Americans recognize and accept that they and/or their neighbors will retain some level of sympathy and affective ties with their ancestral homelands. Concerns arise not so much from such foreign attachments themselves as from the perception or prospect that a dedicated minority's pursuit of its own interests and goals might subordinate either the broader interests of the majority or the welfare of the nation as a whole; it is the potentially disproportionate impact of a minority group on foreign policy and national security relative to majority interest groups—political, business, military, religious, professional, and the like—that provokes anxiety. Where this is the case, democratic processes that engage diaspora and government actors to negotiate and establish a convergence of values, interests, and policies are likely to reduce such concerns and strengthen support for the resulting policies.

The "Mischief of Factions"

Although this book takes a somewhat distinctive interactive approach to analyzing diaspora-government relations, it is not by any means the first study to view the convergence or divergence of interests as central to understanding relations between the US government and groups that seek to shape US foreign policies. The history of scholarship addressing such relations has largely been focused on the concern that James Madison (1787) identified in Federalist Paper No. 10 as the "mischief of factions": that a minority group might impose its special interests in a manner "adverse to the rights of other citizens or to the permanent and aggregate interests of the community." Madison argued that even in the absence of moral or religious restraints the constitutionally based form of federal republican government, by encouraging the democratic participation of "factions," would keep any, whether a political minority or majority, from harming either the rights of others or the common good.

To what extent constitutional structures sufficiently ensure that democratic processes produce pluralistic foreign policies in the national interest has been a subject of considerable debate. American scholars have addressed the influence of "factions" from empiricist and normative perspectives. Empirically, researchers have explored whether diasporas or, more frequently, ethnic groups and their lobbies have in fact led the US government to adopt policies inconsistent with national interests. Normatively, they have focused on the moral obligation of minorities, including diasporas and ethnic groups, to subordinate their narrow interests to the broader common good. Although either perspective can be pursued independently, they tend to become combined in considerations of the nature or origin of national interests and the principles underlying democratic processes that produce policies.

The influence of the Jewish or Israeli lobby, which is widely viewed as the most powerful diasporic lobby seeking to shape US foreign policy, provides a good example of the ways in which empiricist and normative perspectives operate. Identifying containment of the Soviet Union during the Cold War as a strategic national interest shared by the United States and Israel,

Mohammed E. Ahrari (1987) sought to explain the relatively greater influence of Jewish, as compared to Arab, lobbyists on US policies toward the Middle East. Taking a similarly empiricist view of US national interests, John J. Mearsheimer and Stephen M. Walt more recently came to an opposite conclusion: "The Israeli lobby has successfully convinced many Americans that American and Israeli interests are essentially identical. In fact, they are not." As a result, they contended, the US government has adopted policies toward Israel and the Middle East that "jeopardize U.S. national security" (2007, 8). From this perspective, once national interests are identified, whether they are promoted by particular policies can be determined objectively.

Not sharing Madison's faith that the structures and processes of republican democracy result in pluralistically representative policies without moral restraints, James Petras criticized what he viewed as the Jewish lobby's imposition of minority interests on US Middle East policies and cited the normative responsibility of intellectuals, including himself, to defend democracy by exercising freedom of speech to challenge the "tyranny" of the Israeli lobby (2006, 13–16). Implicitly taking a neutral moral stance, Janice Terry (2005) similarly recognized what she considered the disproportionate influence of the Israeli lobby in shaping US Middle East policies but nonetheless accepted the policies that resulted from democratic processes as a de facto representation of national interests. From this perspective Americans have moral obligations either to oppose or accept the influence of factions.

Others who have addressed the normative dimensions of the "mischief of factions" more broadly with regard to multiple diaspora or ethnic groups have more explicitly cited the ethical responsibility of minorities to subordinate their homeland interests to those of the United States. Reflecting his personal experiences as a Polish refugee and his political commitments as a naturalized American citizen, Louis L. Gerson drew attention to the corrosive effects that the attachments of "hyphenate-Americans" both to their homelands and to US ethnic political leaders have had on the "traditional principles and objectives of American foreign policy and their own political assimilation" (1964, vii). In context of the Cold War "struggle between freedom and totalitarianism," he argued that, because all Americans have a stake in safeguarding freedom at home and abroad, they and their ethnic political leaders must take on the "responsibility and discipline" of pursuing the "priority of the general interest over particular interests of any given group" (1964, 236–37). In the post–Cold War context of increased immigration and multicultural politics, Thomas Ambrosio came to a similar conclusion after weighing the advantages and disadvantages of ethnic interest group engagement in US foreign policy. Between the two extremes of excluding ethnic groups' participation and allowing them to dominate foreign policy making, he suggested that ethnic groups have a "legitimate range of influence" so long as they recognize a "political, and indeed an ethical, obligation" to be "focused on the end goal of defining, protecting, and advancing the interests of the broader community" such as spreading democracy instead of shielding dictatorships (2002, 208–9).

Like Madison perhaps, Ernest J. Wilson III relied less on moral persuasion and more on the efficacy of democratic processes to redress the disproportionate influence of individual factions, particularly what he viewed to be the traditional predominance of the East Coast elite in formulating US foreign policy. Stressing values of democratic inclusion, he endorsed the expanded representation of diverse groups and perspectives. Beginning with the premise that increasing globalization and the emergence of multicultural politics have created a challenge and an opportunity of linking the "double diversity" of international and domestic politics, he argued that the increased engagement not only of ethnic groups but also of diverse gender, racial, religious, ideological, and other groups can contribute to "a favorable rebalancing of priorities for U.S. foreign policy" (2004a, 12). The "core contention" underlying the various perspectives presented in his book is, he said, that "principled arguments derived from diverse life experiences are valuable, indeed imperative, for the design and conduct of American foreign policy in the world of the twenty-first century" (2004b, xii).

Approaching the "mischief of factions" as an empirical question rather than a moral conundrum, some scholars have designed and undertaken research to determine whether in fact diasporas or ethnic groups have actually promoted policies that run contrary to national interests. Responding to deep concerns expressed by Peter Brimelow (1996), Samuel P. Huntington (1996), and Arthur Schlesinger Jr. (1992) that recently increased immigration and the formation of ethnic communities give Latinos "enough political clout to be effective advocates for policies favoring their countries of origin against U.S. interests," Rodolfo O. de la Garza and Harry F. Pachon (2000, 3) reviewed previous studies and sponsored, through the Tomás Rivera Policy Institute, four new investigations of related issues. After considering Latinos' expressions of patriotism in attitude surveys, participation in and support for

US military incursions in Latin America, preferences toward immigration and border control policies, involvement in foreign policy lobbying, roles in implementing US policies as foreign service officers in Latin America, and other factors, De la Garza and Pachon found no empirical evidence that Latino lobbying was adversely affecting US interests. Rather, they found that Latinos were not actively engaged in foreign policy and that there was no clear pattern in Latinos' relationships with their countries of origin. They concluded that their empirical research, as an approach toward determining whether Latino diasporas were engaged in "factional mischief," "should be seen as the first systematic effort to establish an empirical baseline against which future Latino foreign policy activities may be compared" (2000, 15).

Finally, taking a somewhat different empiricist approach, David M. Paul and Rachel Anderson Paul undertook to identify influential ethnic group lobbies, explain what factors contributed to their clout, and assess whether their influence was excessive or counter to US national interests. To determine which organizations were most influential, they interviewed forty-one government officials (members of Congress, legislative staff and aides, committee staff, and both career and appointed administrative bureaucrats) and fifteen ethnic group leaders, whom they asked to rank the influence of thirty-eight ethnic organizations. To explain those groups' relative influence, using least square regression analyses, they compared data about the groups' population size and concentration, access to monetary and organizational resources, interest in foreign policy issues, extent of assimilation (measured by English language proficiency), and degree to which their lobbying efforts sought to alter the policy status quo. Although the researchers intended their study to measure the effectiveness of ethnic lobbies empirically, they also hoped their analysis would help determine whether such influence "may or may not be a normative concern for Americans" (Paul and Paul 2009, 29).

From their investigation and analysis, the Pauls determined that, while ethnic groups clearly affect foreign policy, their influence is not undue or disproportionate, especially in comparison with that of other business, trade, union, religious, human rights, or ideological groups. While the policy makers they interviewed tended to agree that three ethnic organizations, which they identified as Israeli or Jewish American, Cuban American, and Armenian American, held too much influence, the Pauls found no corroborating empirical evidence for these evaluations other than the observation that the influence of the Armenian American lobby seemed to exceed the group's relative population size and access to resources. Mixing moral and empirical perspectives, they concluded generally that their research not only "supports the broader pluralistic ideal that ethnic groups can and should compete in the foreign policymaking process" but also, they added, "confirms the need for critical analysis of the role and influence of ethnic groups in the pluralistic universe" (2009, 213).

Although in the final chapter of this volume Tony Smith addresses these empirical and normative issues and how they have evolved historically through different periods of US foreign policy making, the essays in this volume, instead of focusing empirically on whether the lobbying efforts of diasporas have contradicted essential US interests or normatively whether they should conform to broader national interests, central as these questions have been in American foreign policy debates, approach the "mischief of factions" by asking a somewhat different but complementary question: Under what circumstances do the interests and policy goals of diasporas and the US government converge or diverge, and what are the arenas and mechanisms of engagement between diaspora lobbies and government officials that shape that outcome? Our purpose is not to determine whether the interests and policy goals of diasporas and the US government are essentially similar or in conflict but rather to understand the processes by which they have established a convergence or divergence of interests, goals, and policies. To explain these dynamics, each of the case studies in this volume takes two complementary analytic approaches. The first focuses on the nature of each of the diasporas and the broader international foreign policy contexts that shape diaspora-government interests. The second focuses on the engagements between diasporas and the US government as they have taken shape in relation to long-standing issues and specific crises or conflicts that have been crucial in shaping American foreign policies toward the diasporas' homelands. Comparisons between these case studies shed light and raise questions about how diaspora members and government officials mobilize resources and seek to influence each other in order to establish convergence or divergence between their interests and the legitimacy of their goals and policies.

The Nature of Diasporas and the Foreign Policy Context

Diaspora-government relations are shaped by the nature of diasporas and their participation in the broader context of foreign relations and policy making of the US government—issues that are explored respectively by Gabriel Sheffer and Tony Smith. As suggested by its title, Sheffer's introductory essay, "The Effects of Diasporas' Nature, Types, and Goals on Hostland Foreign Policies" (chapter 2 of this volume), defines ethno-national-religious diasporas, particularly in contrast to transnational communities, then analyzes how in the American context their nature and types motivate and structure the convergence and divergence of interests in foreign policy making with the US government. Smith's concluding essay, "Convergence and Divergence Yesterday and Today in Diaspora–National Government Relations" (chapter 10 of this volume), examines how the United States' place and role in international affairs affect the potential for convergent interests between the government and individual diasporas and limit the extent of government tolerance for diasporas' dual national loyalties.

Warning against the danger of generalizations that ignore the heterogeneity of internationally dispersed peoples, Sheffer points to the analytic utility of distinguishing between "transnational communities" and "ethno-national-religious diasporas"—the latter including the groups examined in this volume—with regard to motivations and engagements with the US government. He argues that while the identities, goals, and international activities of transnational communities are varied and can change, particularly as their members become assimilated into their host societies, ethno-national-religious diasporas persistently identify with their national homelands and, as a result, resist aspects of assimilation that might diminish either their identities or their involvements in homeland politics. While transnational communities create and recreate hybrid identities based on different social, cultural, and economic interests that extend variously within and across national borders, ethno-national-religious diasporas seek to strengthen the unity of their ethnic and national identifications with their homelands' borders and politics. Though the identities and memberships of transnational communities transform as group interests evolve, Sheffer contends that ethno-national-religious interests persist, sustained by a combination of primordial, psychological, mythological, or religious beliefs and by instrumental contacts and exchanges with their homelands.

Sheffer's main contribution in basing his definition of ethno-national-religious diasporas on their political relations with their homelands comes from its focus on the different ways in which diaspora lobbies seek to enlist US government support for their homeland-related goals, ties, and activities, which can be social, economic, or political. Although Sheffer notes the growing importance of economic issues for diasporas in both their homelands and the United States, he gives most attention to the range of diasporas' homeland political activities, which may coincide with US interests and thus benefit from US foreign policies but are likely to become increasingly problematic in winning US government support if they involve long or short-term conflicts, violence, illegal activities, or terrorism.

Refining his typology to distinguish between different types of ethnonational-religious diasporas, Sheffer suggests that those linked to existing nation-states are likely to seek the resolution or management of conflicts, while those that seek to create new sovereign powers are more likely to engage in conflict and violence against existing state regimes and thus are more likely to disrupt US foreign relations. Sheffer intends for his typology to be used, not to predict or explain diaspora-government relations, but rather to identify the basic views, positions, and needs of diasporas and the government that, through various mechanisms of foreign policy negotiation, become recognized as the basis of convergent or divergent interests and mutual influence.

In contrast to Sheffer's typological analysis, Smith's is historical and situational. He examines three stages of American foreign policy during which diasporas have played important roles. During the first stage, from 1900 to 1941, the attachments of diasporas to homelands engaged in World War I led some diaspora members to oppose both US neutrality toward the war and US support for the creation of the League of Nations. If divergence between diaspora and government interests characterized this first stage, the second stage, from 1941 to 1989, was a period of convergence brought about largely by the global implications of Cold War politics, which pitted US interests against Soviet communism. The use of immigration and refugee policies as tools to promote foreign policy interests tended to reinforce the support of growing diaspora communities for US policies toward their ancestral homelands. But in the third and contemporary stage, since the dissolution of the Soviet Union in 1989, acceptance of the rights of minorities to organize politically on the basis of racial, religious, or national identities has become increasingly common and has given legitimacy to multiculturalism in domestic politics. Smith argues that although in the first stage the primary loyalty of diasporas to the United States over their homelands was expected and required, such loyalty is no longer mandatory, and he discerns no overall pattern of either convergence or divergence of interests in diaspora-government relations. "Here we find the worm in the fruit of diasporic arguments," he warns, "based on celebrating the rights and powers of an ethnic community while omitting any corresponding discussion of their obligation as citizens of democratic states."

As the world's remaining superpower, the United States, by engaging with all nations of the world, puts greater demands on Americans to define and balance national interests in relations with other countries. This imperative in turn becomes particularly significant for diasporas, whose membership and diversity of national origins have increased through immigration, when they seek to influence US policies toward countries they view still to be their homelands. Within this contemporary context, Smith raises two questions about the role of diasporas in US foreign policy that are fundamental to the place of minority interest groups in a democratic polity: First, when can US government policy be characterized as either subservient to diasporic influence or consonant with the national interest? And second, what are the rights and obligations of diasporas toward the "reasonable construction of the common good"? While Smith points out the threats that diasporic conflicts of interest pose to national security and the extent to which legitimate security concerns have been dismissed by political commentators and in public policy debates, he does not pretend to be able to provide an authoritative or final resolution to the issues, which he believes are likely to remain with us so long as the United States has so dominant a role in world affairs. Rather, he concludes, the resolution of this difficult moral political quandary must come from citizen engagement in foreign policy debates over the relations between specific diaspora goals and national interests.

Smith's emphasis on the importance of democratic debate draws our attention to the arenas and forms of engagement through which US foreign policy is negotiated—to the mechanisms by which diasporas and other interest groups negotiate the terms of foreign policy with relevant offices and agencies of the administrative and legislative branches of government. On one side of such engagements are the organizations created by some diaspora members to pursue particular policy goals along with other Americans who have similar interests. On the other side are the elected and appointed government officials who in turn seek to carry out the foreign policy goals as understood and formulated by the particular political party or government in power. One of the goals of the case studies prepared for this volume is to examine how these engagements and alliances take shape and how their manner affects the relative influence of diasporas and the outcome for US foreign policy.

The Relative Influence of Diasporas in Shaping US Foreign Policy: Jewish and Palestinian Diasporas

One reason for comparing the relations of Jewish and Palestinian diasporas with the US government is that the conflicts between Israelis and Palestinians over population and territory in the Middle East make the diasporas rivals for US government support, a competition in which the success of the Jewish lobby in establishing a convergence of interests with the US government results in a divergence from Palestinian interests. Beyond this competition, the authors writing in this volume provide contrasting perspectives regarding the effect that lobbying is either perceived or misperceived to have on US policies and their impact in Middle Eastern affairs. At question is how to determine which party in a diaspora-government relationship has greater influence on the other and what circumstances permit one or the other to take a predominant role.

Leaders of many diasporas view the Jewish lobby to be a model for emulation because it seems to have mobilized a broad and unified Jewish American constituency and attained influence necessary to ensure the United States' unswerving support for Israel throughout decades of conflict with Palestinians. Mohammed Bamyeh seems to embrace this view when in his essay "Palestinians, Diasporas, and US Foreign Policy" (chapter 4 of this volume) he states, "The influence of the pro-Israel lobby on US foreign policy is an established, demonstrable, documented, and clear fact." Bamyeh argues that the Jewish lobby has been able to wield disproportionate foreign policy influence because the US government, since the end of the Cold War with the Soviet Union, has failed to develop an alternative and independent strategic perspective toward international relations. In other words, it is the absence of a defined national interest and a meaningful national policy that permits the Jewish diaspora to wield uncontested influence. According to Bamyeh, the fundamental question that should be asked is how the United States can formulate a foreign policy that reflects both its own national interests and its international responsibilities. Such policies will not be produced out of the "reality" of structural necessity or objective conditions, he contends; rather, they must emerge from political leadership, will, and breadth of perspective in a discussion of the appropriate role of the United States as the world's unrivaled superpower. The imperatives of a rational, coherent, and independent foreign policy will then, he concludes, guide rather than be determined by diaspora initiatives.

In contrast, Yossi Shain and Neil Rogachevsky, authors of "Between JDate and J Street: US Foreign Policy and the Liberal Jewish Dilemma in America" (chapter 3 of this volume), argue that Americans have greatly exaggerated the influence of the Jewish lobby in shaping US policy, largely as a result of their unrealistically high and characteristically "can-do" expectations that, through diplomacy and action, the United States should be able to bring about an enduring solution to the Israeli-Palestinian conflicts. They contend that, as part of the broader and conflicted Arab-Israeli relations in the Middle East, Israel-Palestinian problems are more complicated than Americans realize and are perhaps intractable to a "top-down" approach. So when American-led negotiations break down or fail to find a resolution, Americans conclude that "something nefarious must be blocking its way" and place blame on the Jewish lobby. Shain and Rogachevsky label this explanation a "theory of everything" that both overestimates and misrepresents the strength of the Jewish diaspora and lobby.

Though the authors of these two case studies disagree about the power and influence of the Jewish diaspora lobby, both seek to clarify differences between diasporas and the lobbies that claim to represent them. Bamyeh contends that the claims of lobbies generally, and of the Jewish lobby in particular, to represent diasporas or their home nations as a whole are a "construct" by a minority that seeks to exclude other opposed or simply disengaged elements of a diaspora. Shain and Rogachevsky point out that the Jewish diaspora is far from monolithic and that the assimilation of the youngest generation of liberal Jewish Americans is leading them to adopt universalistic rather than religious values. This shift in values is reflected in young American Jews' direct intervention into Israel's social welfare activities and the formation of a new "J Street" lobby, which Bamyeh characterizes as "perhaps the only inlet Palestinians may have in the lobbying game" because the organization defines itself as pro-peace rather than simply pro-Israel.

When Diasporas Shape US Foreign Policy: Irish and Cuban Diasporas

The Irish and Cuban diasporas provide examples of groups' becoming able to establish a convergence between diaspora and government policies through their use of electoral power and their members' integration into branches of government responsible for designing US foreign policy—cases in which differences between diasporas and the government are somewhat blurred and interests unified. The influence of the Irish diaspora has in large measure grown out of their long history of immigration and ethnic group integration into American society. That history, according to Joseph E. Thompson's essay "America's Role in the Northern Ireland Peace Process" (chapter 5 of this volume), has resulted in a loosely connected but electorally significant membership of forty million Irish American citizens. The Cuban diaspora is more recent and geographically restricted in its settlement, but according to Lisandro Pérez, in his essay "Cuban Americans and US Cuba Policy" (chapter 6 of this volume), its members have had perhaps an even more determinant voice in shaping US foreign policy toward their homeland, not only because of their concentrated electoral power in Florida, but also because of the absence of competition in identifying alternative national interests. Given the electoral power and positioning of diaspora members within the legislative and administrative branches of government, various US governments have adopted the interests and goals of the Irish and Cuban diasporas as the interests of the United States in formulating foreign policy, although this congruence has not always been predominant in the past and may not remain so in the future.

The long-standing support that Irish Americans have given to the independence and unification of Ireland has throughout the nineteenth and twentieth centuries diverged from the United States' national interests in building strong economic and political ties with the United Kingdom, which historically has resisted relinquishing its role in the governance of Ireland. As a result, says Thompson, both Irish Americans and officials of various US government administrations formerly assumed that, because their interests diverged, they could have little influence over one another's goals and policies, particularly regarding conflicts in Northern Ireland and political relations with the British government. Mutual disengagement began to change, however, after the British government took extreme measures to repress not only violent tactics of the Irish Republican Army but also more peaceful political efforts of moderate republicans, and this enabled diaspora organizations to mobilize broad support among Irish American citizens and congressional representatives of Irish descent for a peaceful resolution of "the Troubles." As an umbrella organization claiming to represent the interests of Irish Americans, the Irish National Caucus became a centralized source of both information and a moderate republican perspective for the US media and the government. The electoral potential of this popular mobilization was extended into the legislative branch with the formation of the Ad Hoc Congressional Committee for Irish Affairs and the Friends of Ireland, which consisted of seventy members of Congress and sought to expand American collaboration with Northern Irish moderates.

Recognizing the growing popular and congressional support for the US government's taking a role in Northern Ireland peace negotiations and the importance for Democrats of winning over Catholic voters in the coming elections, President Bill Clinton appointed a special envoy who has been widely credited with facilitating the signing of the 1985 Anglo-Irish Agreement and eventually the Good Friday Agreement, which established a basis for ending violent political conflicts in Northern Ireland. The convergence between diaspora and government policies resulted not so much from an overlap between diaspora and national interests as from the mobilization of the political power of the Irish American diaspora within both the electorate and legislative branches of government, through which diaspora interests became recognized as national interests.

Although the population of Cuban Americans in the United States comprises fewer than two million people, their concentration within Florida and their positions within the US government legislative and administrative branches have enabled them to wield perhaps an even greater influence than that of Irish Americans in shaping US policies toward their homeland, an influence enhanced by the absence of rival interests or policies toward Cuba since the end of the Cold War. Before the fall of the Soviet Union, the US government's interest in containing communism in Latin America and the Caribbean was closely aligned with the goals of Cuban refugees who sought to overthrow the regime of Fidel Castro in Havana. This congruence led various administrations to back, implicitly or explicitly, marginal or shadowy paramilitary and political activities aimed at overthrowing the Cuban government. It was the Reagan administration that urged the Cuban diaspora leaders to form the Cuban American National Foundation (CANF) as a lobby that would subsequently take the lead in shaping US policies. Over time, Pérez observes, "Cuban Americans have gone from being mere agents of US Cuba policy to being key actors and shapers of that policy." The influence of the diaspora was increased not only by the electoral power of Cubans in local and national elections in Florida but also by the election and appointment of Cubans to important posts in the US government, including, during the Bush administration, two presidential cabinet members; policy makers and analysts in the Department of State and National Security Council; four members of Congress; two senators; and more. "This level of representation," says Pérez, "blurs the lines between the diaspora and the US government" and, during the first decade of the twenty-first century, has enabled Cubans "to influence from within the formulation of US policy toward the island."

While there have been recent signs of potential modification of US policies toward Cuba with the goal of bringing about change by promoting social and economic reform as opposed to imposing political and economic isolation, the impulse seems to come more from generational shifts within the Cuban diaspora than from the government's independent identification and pursuit of alternative national interests. More recent refugees and immigrants from Cuba, many of whom have grown up during the revolution, seem to share traditional immigrants' interest in supporting the welfare of family members back home more than they share the goal of the "historical exiles" of overthrowing the revolutionary government—a less monolithic approach seemingly shared by a growing portion of the generation of Cuban Americans who were born and raised in the United States. With some "exhaustion" regarding the thus far ineffectual impact of American policies in overthrowing the Cuban regime and with Cuban Americans' initiation of debates about alternative approaches, the goals and role of the Cuban diaspora may in the future cease to be an overriding factor in maintaining the US policy of isolating Cuba. The extent to which the Cuban diaspora, through its electoral power in Florida and integration into political circles in Washington, D.C., will continue to dominate the formulation of new policies remains to be seen.

Both the Irish and Cuban cases seem to serve as illustrations of Smith's notion of "negotiated convergence," in which diasporas define US interests and shape foreign policy toward their homelands. But there are also cases of convergence in which the influence of diasporas has been limited and the US government has independently defined its national interests, as in the cases of US policies toward Haiti and Ethiopia.

When the Government Defines US Foreign Policy Independently of Diasporas: Ethiopian and Haitian Diasporas

The Ethiopian and Haitian diasporas provide cases in which their lobbies have struggled unsuccessfully to establish common interests with the US government and to exert influence over the US government in designing its policies. The lack of diaspora-government convergence in these instances seems to be in part a result of the limited resources and influence of diaspora lobbying organizations but more importantly a result of the overriding importance of alternative US national interests and goals. Considering their dim prospects of affecting US foreign policy, these diasporas' organizations have tended to intervene directly into their home country's affairs rather than to continue seeking influence through US policies.

In characterizing the relations between the Ethiopian diaspora and the US government, Terrence Lyons, in his essay titled "Diaspora Lobbying and Ethiopian Politics" (chapter 7), describes a lack of convergence in interests and policies. Diaspora lobby organizations in the United States have tended to be dominated by adherents to Ethiopian political parties opposed to the party currently controlling the Ethiopian government. Pointing to US values and the need for long-term stability in Ethiopia in order to gain leverage with US administrations, leaders of diaspora organizations have promoted US policies of democratization and respect for human rights in Ethiopia. But since the Ethiopian People's Revolutionary Democratic Front came to power in 1991, the executive branch has viewed the exile diaspora groups as extremist and out of date in refusing to seek incremental changes through collaboration with the Ethiopian government. Targeting congressional members who are involved in US policy making toward Africa and represent districts where Ethiopians were concentrated, the lobbies had some success in the House of Representatives in 2007 when they succeeded in getting approval for the Ethiopian Democracy and Accountability Act over objections of the US State Department and Ethiopian government. However, the act never reached the Senate for a vote and did not become law. Instead of shaping policy in response to the Ethiopian diaspora, US administrations gave greater priority to policies that would strengthen broader counterterrorism efforts in the Horn of Africa and would maintain a strategic partnership with the regime in Addis Ababa.

As a result of their limited capacity to influence US policies, Ethiopian diaspora organizations have pursued other strategies to affect politics in Ethiopia, including lobbying international organizations and intervening directly in Ethiopian domestic affairs by sending remittances to support parties, engaging in Ethiopian public debates, and returning home and running for elective office. Lyons concludes from this case that lobbying the US government should be viewed as only one of a number of transnational strategies that diasporas can consider in pursuing their homeland goals.

The history of the Haitian diaspora's relations with the US government presented in Daniel P. Erikson's essay, "The Haitian Diaspora: Building Bridges after Catastrophe" (chapter 8), focuses on two separate but interrelated foreign policy concerns: US relations with the government of Haiti and with Haitian migrants. Because Haiti has offered little economic or political strategic value to the United States as an ally since the end of the Cold War, American policy has been "primarily geared toward making modest, as opposed to transformative, investments in Haiti." With regard to policies toward Haitian migrants, Erikson says that US policy makers "have made avoiding a refugee crisis a top priority"—a goal that has led the government to seek, above all, political stability in Haiti and control over irregular flows of boat people and others seeking asylum and residence in the United States. To ensure stability, the United States has made promoting democracy and economic sustainability the core of its foreign policy but has done so only reactively and intermittently, thereby undermining its policies' effectiveness. Although the US government has sought to include the Haitian diaspora in its vision for Haiti's future, Erikson has found that diaspora leaders have generally assumed an oppositional stance toward US policies, which they view as pursuing US goals that are inconsistent with Haiti's and the diaspora's intertwined best interests.

The skepticism of diaspora leaders regarding US policies toward Haiti and Haitian migrants is rooted in their perception that the United States has shored up repressive, corrupt, and incompetent military and civilian governments while also discriminating against Haitians seeking asylum in the United States. Although the Clinton administration intervened to return to office President Jean-Bertrand Aristide, who had been popularly elected in part with support from the diaspora but then ousted by a military coup, the US government—along with other international donors—also withdrew financial and political support following Aristide's subsequent reelection and ended up, at the least, facilitating Aristide's second overthrow and exile from Haiti. In response to Haitians who have fled Haiti's political chaos and poverty to seek asylum in the United States, the US government has interdicted and returned the vast majority to Haiti through a program widely viewed by diaspora members as unjustly targeted and discriminatory toward Haitians. Even though diaspora members have been grateful when the United States has provided much-needed relief and development assistance, particularly following the 2010 earthquake that killed hundreds of thousands of people and leveled much of the capital city, Port-au-Prince, they have also feared and resisted the prospect of Haiti's evolution into a dependent client state and resulting loss of national sovereignty.

As a result of their differences, there has been little sustained interaction between the Haitian diaspora and the US government, although the aftermath of the 2010 earthquake did provoke greater convergence around the core goal of rebuilding Haiti. Prior to that event, Haitian diaspora organizations tended to focus their limited resources and energies in programs that intervened directly in their communities in Haiti or, discouraged about Haiti's future, in programs that advanced the welfare of the diaspora in the United States. Lacking a unified vision, resources, and, because of their dispersed settlement in different cities, the electoral power necessary to create an effective lobby, diaspora leaders have tended to operate more as individual political entrepreneurs and to rely upon American church, union, and rights organizations to represent Haitian interests to the US administration or, particularly, to the legislature, through the Congressional Black Caucus. Overall engagement between the Haitian diaspora and US government has been episodic and has lacked the "deeply woven interconnections" found in other cases, particularly of the Jewish, Cuban, Irish, and Iraqi diasporas. However, Erikson notes that "the Haitian earthquake provided a new opportunity for the country's diaspora to reassert itself as a key partner in rebuilding the troubled country."

When Diaspora and Government Foreign Policy Goals Converge: The Iraqi-Neoconservative Alliance

The success of some members of the Iraqi diaspora and some members of the US administration in together bringing about regime change in Iraq seems to exemplify the great extent to which a convergence between diaspora and government goals can determine US foreign policy. However, in retrospect, their success in taking the nation to war raises questions about the role of the media in enabling the public to monitor the arenas within which diaspora-government relations are formed and to understand the effect minority views can have on policy formulation.

Walt Vanderbush's essay, "The Iraqi Diaspora and the US Invasion of Iraq" (chapter 9), traces the collaboration between leaders of the Iraqi diaspora and neoconservative Americans, many of them linked to the Iraqi National Congress (INC) and the Project for the New American Century (PNAC), to convince the US government to wage war and bring about "regime change" in Iraq. With support from the CIA during the presidency of George H. Bush, who had sent US troops to the Middle East to force the withdrawal of Iraqi troops from Kuwait, Ahmed Chalabi, who had been forced into exile by Saddam Hussein, created the INC and then undertook a two-part strategy of winning wider American support by allying with neoconservatives and lobbying Congress. In the mid-1980s the neoconservative academic Albert Wohlsetter had introduced Chalabi to Paul Wolfowitz and Richard Perle, who had left the government during the Clinton presidency to join the PNAC. These two lobbying groups played key roles in convincing the Congress to pass the 1998 Iraq Liberation Act, which established regime change in Iraq to be the goal of US foreign policy. Then, with the election of George W. Bush, at least ten of the original twenty-five members of the PNAC took up positions within government with the intention of toughening US policies toward Iraq. Following the attacks on the World Trade Center and the Pentagon orchestrated by the al-Qaeda leader Osama bin Laden, Bush sought to have Hussein held responsible. Chalabi played a very important role in establishing Hussein's alleged culpability by providing an "inexhaustible" supply of Iraqi defectors and experts who served as informants to the media and as witnesses in congressional hearings, giving what later proved to be misleading information that was used to bolster mistaken beliefs: that Iraq had weapons of mass destruction, that because Hussein was allied with al-Qaeda he might provide those weapons to anti-American terrorists, and that, if the United States were to invade Iraq and disarm Hussein, its troops would be welcomed by Iraqis with "sweets and flowers."

In marketing the invasion and occupation of Iraq, the diaspora lobby and like-minded government officials were able to frame debates as a choice between invasion or appeasement, thus sidelining alternative perspectives and silencing voices of opposition. The INC claimed credit for placing 108 articles in the news media, including the *New York Times*, the *Washington Post*, and the *Times* (of London), during a nine-month period before the war. Despite the impression of diasporic unity given by the mainstream press in the United States, hundreds of prominent diaspora Iraqis from different social and political backgrounds had signed a petition initiated in the United Kingdom opposing both the Hussein dictatorship and the impending war, and many predicted the reception of American troops would be far different from the welcoming reception projected by the administration. According to Vanderbush, by being able to manipulate the press, the Iraqi diaspora and neoconservative officials within the administration were able to convince not only a majority of Americans but also members of the Congress that the lobbyists' goals and policies of regime change in Iraq were in America's national interest.

Arenas and Mechanisms of Diaspora-Government Relations

The essays in this collection contribute to our understandings of diaspora-government relations by examining the nature of diasporas and the strategies they adopt to influence their homelands thorough US foreign policy and by placing their relations with the US government in broader historical and contemporary foreign policy contexts. Individual case studies indicate that, where there is a convergence between a diaspora's goals and what the US government has taken to be its national interests, the diaspora's lobbying efforts can indeed influence US policies toward their homelands. When there is a distinct divergence between the diaspora's agenda and American interests, these groups have relatively little influence, particularly when specific government policies are framed by broader national agendas, such as opposing communism or confronting terrorists. More complicated and difficult to assess is how a convergence of interests has been created or, in contrast, how the US government and diasporic groups have failed to establish common interests upon which to base foreign policy goals and policies.

As noted above, the essays in this volume focus on what Sheffer has defined as "ethno-national-religious diasporas." Factors that affect diasporas' ability to establish their interests and goals as the basis of US policy include their numbers, concentration, mobilization, and integration into American society and politics. But diasporas' interests and goals change over time, particularly as the first-generation members give way to second and succeeding generations born in America and, sometimes as well, to new waves of immigrants. The nature of the ties between ethno-national-religious diasporas and their homelands varies significantly, from aiding a homeland government in reducing poverty to seeking the overthrow of an existing regime. The goals and strategies of diasporas toward their homelands, and thus their attempts to influence US policies, are also affected by whether their ethno-national-religious identity connects them to a state, as in the case of Jews to Israel, or to a stateless nation, as in the case of Palestinians, with their divided allegiance to the Palestinian Authority.

The receptiveness of the US government to the initiatives of diasporas in defining a convergence with US foreign policy interests, goals, and policies is affected by the wider foreign policy context. Broad national policy concerns have historically placed limits on the extent to which diasporas, such as those of Ethiopians or Haitians in recent years, can realize narrower homeland goals through American policies. Such was the case during the world wars in Europe and the Cold War and is even perhaps the case now, when the government is preoccupied by threats of international terrorism. Government receptiveness has varied depending on the type of policies in question, which have ranged from fixing the immigration status of diaspora members to supporting economic development, protecting human rights, or advocating for regime change in the home country. The extent of US government support has been also affected by the extent to which a policy sought might challenge broader US national interests, require American military or economic resources, or create international political risks. Within these limitations, when there are no clearly established alternative national interests, diasporas may have considerably greater influence in establishing their own goals as US policy, as with the Cuban and, perhaps at times, the Jewish diasporas. Conversely, when the government seeks support from a diaspora, it may for its own reasons adopt policies that coincide with diaspora interests, as seems to have been the case with the Clinton administration's intervention into Northern Ireland peace talks, which it hoped would secure Irish Catholic votes. When there is a congruence of goals between a diaspora and an influential part of the US government, even if not of underlying national interests, then a mutually supportive alliance can have an enhanced and perhaps disproportionate impact in shaping US policy, as was the case with the Iraqi diaspora and, some argue, the Jewish diaspora.

Regardless of their importance, the characteristics of diasporas or broader foreign policy contexts cannot in and of themselves predict the extent of convergence or divergence in diaspora-government relations or the influence that diasporas and the government will have on each other in shaping US foreign policy. Long-established and large diasporas, such as the Irish diaspora, may have relatively less influence over US government policies than more recent and smaller diasporas, such as that of Iraqis. Conversely, the US government may have limited ability to obtain the cooperation of diasporas in pursuing its own agenda, as with Haitians or Ethiopians. A more significant impact on US policy seems to result from instances in which diasporas and the government can establish and pursue convergent interests and related policy goals.

The cases of diaspora-government relations examined here provide insights into the processes by which different arenas and mechanisms are employed by diasporas and the government to negotiate and establish convergent and divergent interests, goals, and policies. Diasporas' relations with the government are forged within two major arenas of interaction, with the executive and legislative branches of government. We adopt the term *arena* because it suggests a public opportunity, even if not a physical location, within which multiple actors in addition to diasporas and government agencies can lobby and debate. The executive arena includes interactions between diasporas and offices of administration, such as the president, the Department of State, the Central Intelligence Agency, the National Security Council, and other agencies that inform and implement US foreign policy. The legislative arena includes interactions between diasporas and members of the House of Representatives and the Senate and their different foreign-policy-related subcommittees, within which US foreign policies are set in law.

Within these arenas diaspora leaders and government officials adopt particular strategies and mechanisms of influence as they aim to shape foreign policy. One of the most important of these mechanisms is diasporas' use of their electoral power and campaign donations to elect or win over public officials sympathetic to their cause. Other significant strategies used both by diasporas and by government officials include the provision of information to their counterparts and/or the media in an attempt to frame foreign policy agendas and to shape opinion. Finally, the members of diasporas and government officials can seek to influence each other through intermediaries, whether leaders of national organizations or representatives of friendly states or international organizations. Our aim in this volume is not to catalog all the interactions and mechanisms that shape the dynamics of diaspora-government relations so much as to indicate significant factors that influence policy making in addition to the nature and types of diasporas and broader foreign policy contexts.

The issues and cases that the authors address in this volume are intended, not so much to be comprehensive and to fully represent the wide diversity of diasporas, their relations with the US government, and resulting policy outcomes, as to identify some of the important factors that must be taken into account in assessing and understanding those relationships. This collection is not the first to examine the role of diasporas in shaping US foreign policy, but its analytic focus in bringing together an understanding of the contemporary nature of diasporas, historical contexts, and the individual dynamics in convergent and divergent relations between diasporas and government do offer innovative perspectives to guide researchers and policy makers in analyzing and negotiating diaspora-government relations.

References

Ahrari, Mohammed E. 1987. "Domestic Context of U.S. Foreign Policy toward the Middle East." In *Ethnic Groups and U.S. Foreign Policy*, edited by M. E. Ahrari, 1–22. Westport, CT: Greenwood Press.

Ambrosio, Thomas. 2002. "Legitimate Influence or Parochial Capture? Conclusions on Ethnic Identity Groups and the Formulation of U.S. Foreign Policy." In *Ethnic Identity Groups and U.S. Foreign Policy*, edited by T. Ambrosio, 199–215. Westport, CT: Praeger.

Brimelow, Peter. 1996. *Alien Nation*. New York: Harper Perennial.

De la Garza, Rodolfo O., and Harry F. Pachon. 2000. *Latinos and U.S. Foreign Policy: Representing the "Homeland"?* Lanham, MD: Rowman and Littlefield.

Gerson, Louis L. 1964. *The Hyphenate in Recent American Politics and Diplomacy*. Lawrence: University of Kansas Press.

Huntington, Samuel P. 1996. *The Clash of Civilizations and the Remaking of the World Order*. New York: Simon and Schuster.

Madison, James. 1787. "The Federalist 10." http://en.wikisource.org/wiki/The_Federalist/10.

Mearsheimer, John J., and Stephen M. Walt. 2007. *The Israel Lobby and U.S. Foreign Policy*. New York: Farrar, Straus and Giroux.

Paul, David M., and Rachel Anderson Paul. 2009. *Ethnic Lobbies and US Foreign Policy*. Boulder, CO: Lynne Rienner.

Petras, James. 2006. *The Power of Israel in the United States*. Atlanta, GA: Clarity Press; Black Point, Nova Scotia: Fernwood Books.

Roston, Aram. 2008. *The Man Who Pushed America to War: The Extraordinary Life, Adventures, and Obsessions of Ahmad Chalabi*. New York: Nation Books.

Schlesinger, Arthur M., Jr. 1992. *The Disuniting of America: Reflections on a Multicultural Society*. New York: Norton.

Terry, Janice J. 2005. *U.S. Foreign Policy in the Middle East: The Role of Lobbies and Special Interest Groups*. Ann Arbor, MI: Pluto Press.

Washington, George. 1796. "Farewell Address." September 19. American Presidency Project. www.presidency.ucsb.edu/ws/?pid=65539.

Wilson, Ernest J., III. 2004a. "Introduction: Framing the Discussion of Globalization, Diversity, and U.S. International Affairs." In *Diversity and U.S. Foreign Policy: A Reader*, edited by E. J. Wilson III, 1–15. New York: Routledge.

———. 2004b. Preface to *Diversity and U.S. Foreign Policy: A Reader*, edited by E. J. Wilson III, xi–xii. New York: Routledge.

Diasporas

CHAPTER TWO

The Effects of Diasporas' Nature, Types, and Goals on Hostland Foreign Policies

Gabriel Sheffer

At the beginning of the twenty-first century, diasporas, which were and are created by trans-state migration, are not vanishing. Quite the contrary: despite certain difficulties in exactly delineating their cultural and social boundaries, demarcating their structures, and determining the numbers of their members residing in various host countries, since the end of the twentieth century several new diasporic entities[1] have emerged, and numerous older entities continue to exist and be very active. Moreover, various surveys show that diasporic entities are growing in population, are organizing or reorganizing rapidly, are active in various arenas, and are using more political and economic mechanisms in both their hostlands and their "countries of origin" or homelands. They are exerting increasing influence—both positively in economic, cultural, and social developments and negatively in conflicts, terrorism, and crime—on their homelands, their hostlands, their brethren residing in other host countries, regional organizations such as the European Union, and the general international system. Hence, notwithstanding negative reactions to them and restrictions imposed on their immigration, emergence, development, behavior, and activities, which are generated mainly by stronger social and political nationalist groups and governments in hostlands, including some liberal democracies, it is clear that the capabilities and impacts of diasporic entities that permanently exist in hostlands will only continue to grow.

As a result of these developments, research on diasporas has greatly expanded. However, most books and articles deal mainly with the evident political and economic backgrounds, organization, and impacts of those growing entities on both their host and homelands. They deal with clearly observable political positions of diasporans, their hostlands, and their homelands, and with the more evident ways that diasporic entities and homeland and hostland societies and governments deal with each other and achieve their goals. For example, such studies focus on diasporic entities' and state leaders' formal agendas and public statements, noting patterns of diaspora members' donations to candidates for elected parliamentary positions, political lobbying, organizational structures and activities, use of the media, and so on.

While these analyses and the resulting descriptions are necessary, politicians, officials, and scholars should also examine the more fundamental and significant features of diasporas and the sources of their relations and influences: for example, the identities and identification of members, the consequences of the heterogeneity of these entities, members' formal and informal loyalties to their hostlands and homelands, the convergence or divergence in aims within and between such entities and their hostlands (particularly in the sphere of the relations between hostland governments and these entities), their motivations when launching aggressive activities, hostland governments' relations with the governments of these people's homelands, and the governments' changing perceptions of the severity of the conflicts in which they and other such entities are involved. For example, in the case of the US government's relations with diasporans, diasporic entities, and their organizations, which is the main theme of this volume, the purpose should be to understand the types of such entities in the United States, their organizations and mechanisms, the types and positions of leaders and members, the arenas in which they operate, the convergence or divergence of aims among their members, and their homelands' relationships with American society and government.

Diasporan individuals and entities permanently residing in hostlands are cooperating with hostland societies and governments (this is connected to the convergence features of such relationships), but they are also involved in various kinds of conflicts with hostlands' societies and governments (this is connected to the divergence features of such relationships). They may be involved in moderate disagreements or conflicts with hostlands that are the result of legitimate differences of opinion and interest (concerning, for example, the character and nature of government in the homeland), the local and international policies that homeland governments pursue (for example, policies related to nuclear power, as in the Iranian case), the economic interests that should be preferred, and so on. Yet some may be aggressive, use terrorism, or be connected to organized crime and involved in criminal activities (these are connected to the divergence aspect of the relationships). All these patterns certainly pertain to the United States and its relations with the multiple diasporic entities within its boundaries.

Diasporas and their established groups and entities in hostlands are highly heterogeneous, and sweeping generalizations about them should be qualified, especially concerning their involvement in cooperation or conflicts in their hostlands and homelands. Members of particular diasporas and diasporic organizations vary a great deal in the extent and nature of such involvements, and involvements can change over time. The perpetrators of conflictual and aggressive acts are also highly varied: for example, though it might be assumed that they would most likely be first-generation international migrants recently settled in a hostland, many belong to second, third, or even fourth generations permanently residing in hostlands.

Diasporas and Transnational Communities

Although this essay concentrates on ethno-national-religious diasporas, a comparison of them to what are called "transnational communities" facilitates empirical analysis of these entities and a clearer and better drawing of general theoretical and practical conclusions concerning the goals, challenges, and activities facing them and their hostlands, especially the United States. Essentially, there are two main academic approaches to and definitions of international communities of former and current migrants. One considers them all to be "transnational communities," and the other distinguishes between transnational communities and "ethno-national-religious diasporas."

I will argue here that despite the popularity of the first approach, which considers all diasporas to be transnational, there is a need to use the concept and term of "ethno-national-religious diasporas," which more adequately characterizes most of these entities, especially those that are relevant to the US government. However, it should be noted that members of ethno-national-religious diasporas can also be active members of what are called transnational communities. Hence I suggest the need not only to recognize the differences between these entities but also to create a theoretical and analytical synthesis between certain elements of the two approaches. I focus on ethno-national-religious diasporas primarily because all the entities discussed in this volume fall in that category.

The anthropologists, ethnologists, and, to a lesser extent, sociologists and historians who developed the transnational communities approach viewed all former and present international migrants as adopting imagined deterritorialized identities that were and are robustly influenced by postmodern, globalizing, and hybridizing trends (Glick Schiller 2007). Their main argument has been that international migrants to new hostlands exist as independent or highly autonomous individuals, groups, and communities in what these scholars regard as the new global transnational environment. These scholars have maintained that for all migrants who permanently reside outside their countries of origin their identity and consequently membership in ethno-national groups is entirely subjective and self-selected.

According to this approach, a shared ethno-national origin is merely one feature among many on which identity and membership in transnational communities can be based. Members may also share, in their own perception or in the eyes of outsiders, such characteristics as physical features, religious beliefs and affiliations with certain churches and sects, a broad regional geographical background, a language, a profession, or even only political ideological beliefs. Transnational entities are usually highly diverse and ill-defined.

By emphasizing the subjectivity, multiplicity, and hybridism of members' identities and sense of belonging, this view has challenged or even rejected entirely the significance of specific inherent ethno-national-religious identities and their connections to countries and societies of origin. Some "extremists" among these scholars have gone so far as to argue that "diasporas should be seen not as given communities, a logical, albeit deterritorialized, extension of an ethnic or national group, but as *imagined communities*, continuously reconstructed and reinvented" (Tsagarousianou 2007, 101).

Recently, however, some "transnational" theorists have given more emphasis to the importance of considering the continuing connectedness to a homeland that the concept of ethno-national-religious diaspora represents. Indeed, one well-known scholar in this field states that "diasporas are the exemplary communities of the transnational moment" (Tölölyan 1991, 5; see also Shuvall 2000; Vertovec 1997; Van Hear 1998; Faist 2000, 2007; Braziel and Mannur 2003; Dufoix 2008). Further, even some of the founders of the early transnational approach have admitted that combining all dispersed persons in the same category has proved problematic because "there are many forms of transnational processes and associations beyond migration, and migrants themselves participate in a range of transnational processes and connections" (Glick Schiller 2003, 123). Hence a second wave of views about transnationalism has emerged, and some of its adherents now draw a clear distinction between transnational and ethno-national-religious entities. They argue that sometimes individual ethno-national-religious diasporans may voluntarily become members of transnational networks but that they still maintain their original identity and therefore belong as well to the ethno-national-religious diaspora.[2]

We turn, then, to the second approach to studying international communities of former and present migrants, according to which most ethno-national-religious diasporas cannot be viewed simply as one kind of a transnational entity and are instead considered to form a special category that should be discussed on its own (Sheffer 1986). This approach, initially developed by political and sociopolitical scholars, has been based on qualitative and quantitative historical, analytical, and theoretical studies of diasporic entities and their origins, boundaries, modes of organization, and activities (including their contributions to the economic development of their hostlands and homelands, the political support they render to their brethren, and their involvement in terrorism and crime on behalf of their homelands and brethren). One of the main arguments for treating ethno-national-religious diasporas as a special category is that ethnicity, nationalism, and ethno-nationalism are not becoming obsolete, as was once predicted, but are instead persisting and becoming stronger all over the world. In most states and among most people who have migrated out of their homelands and reside in host countries, ethno-nationalism significantly affects how events in the homelands of dispersed persons influence them in their hostlands, and how dispersed persons in turn influence developments in their homelands and hostlands. Accordingly, the following is a brief comparison of transnational communities and ethno-national-religious diasporas.

Features of Transnational Communities

Transnational communities tend to be informal, loosely organized or non-organized networks of widely dispersed persons and groups. Since persons who regard themselves, or are regarded by others, as forming these entities are not necessarily of the same ethno-national origin, they have in common some other characteristics that in their own perception or in the eyes of the general public and politicians in their hostlands determine their belonging to such networks. Thus they may have in common religious beliefs and affiliations to a religion or a sect ("Muslim," "Buddhist," "Catholic"), or a regional geographic background ("African," "Latino," "Arab"), or a language ("Francophone," "Chinese speaking"), or a set of ideological beliefs ("communist," "anticommunist," "jihadist," "Green"). Only some of those who might be placed in these categories actually consider the network to be a community to which they belong. Thus, for example, not all Cubans in the United States would regard themselves as members of a Latino transnational network, and not all Iraqis or Palestinians who reside outside their countries of origin would regard themselves as members of an Arab or Muslim transnational network. Many of them would instead regard themselves as basically members of a specific ethno-national-religious diaspora (e.g., Cuban, Iraqi, Palestinian) that has certain connections with a broader transnational network.

Some of these networks, but certainly not all of them, are influenced by postmodern epistemological trends and ideas, as well as by various actual aspects of globalization, such as the ease of migration, current sophisticated communication systems, individualism, neoliberalism, and spreading hybrid cultures. Members of transnational communities that are not based on noticeable distinctive physical markers can relatively easily change their cultural, religious, and social identities, affiliations, and loyalties and integrate up to the extreme point of full assimilation into hostland societies. What ties together these persons, and hence also their networks and organizations, are mainly their cultural, religious, political, or economic interests—a pattern that differs from the patterns of belonging in the ethno-national-religious diaspora category.

Because members of these entities are influenced by constantly changing factors, the boundaries of transnational communities are not clearly drawn, fixed, or stable. Most of these entities and their members who permanently reside in hostlands experience continuous processes of cultural hybridization that cause substantive heterogeneity of the larger entity and also of smaller subgroups residing in the same country, region, or city. Consequently, they tend to integrate or assimilate into their host societies, and their memories of their ancestors or of their "original homelands" are not very significant for the transnational community's continued existence as a coherent entity in their hostlands. Even when transnational movements are influenced by strong historical memories or genetic ties, as in the case of Muslim and African transnational movements such as the Islamic Jihad, the influence of postmodern developments and ideas, ideologies, and political goals predominates.

Features of Ethno-National Diasporas

The category of "ethno-national-religious diasporas" includes all the diasporas discussed in this volume—the Ethiopian, Haitian, Cuban, Iraqi, Irish, Jewish-Israeli, and Palestinian. Hence, the rest of this essay will focus on this category. An ethno-national-religious diaspora is a formation of people who are united by a shared ethno-national cultural, social, and political origin and identity and who permanently reside as minorities in one hostland or in a number of hostlands located away from their original, actual or imagined, historical homeland. There is a difference between these entities and irredentist groups permanently residing in adjacent states to the homeland who have not migrated from their place of original permanent residence. Even if some observers and activists regard such groups as diasporas, irredentist groups are not discussed in this essay as they have not emerged as a result of migration from actual or imagined homelands.

Ethno-national-religious diasporas emerge out of voluntary and/or forced migration from their homelands to one or more host countries. Diasporans may also experience secondary and even tertiary migration from one hostland to another. The members of these diasporas maintain their ethno-national identities, which are sometimes buttressed by religious beliefs. These identities are based on an integrative/synthetic combination of shared genetic factors, memories of historical origins, actual and perceived connections to a country of origin and its people, adherence to a cultural ethno-national-religious background, and psychological and instrumental factors (Sheffer 2003, 79; Sheffer 1996).

Whereas those considered to belong to transnational networks do not necessarily identify as such, there is no great gap between ethno-national-religious diasporans' identity and their own public identification. These days, as a result of the reawakening of nationalism and ethnicity, such diasporans are not so shy or reluctant to publicly identify as belonging to these entities and to proclaim their contacts with their homelands, and in certain cases it is even becoming fashionable to do so—as in the case of the Colombians, Iranians, and Turks, as well as the Ethiopians, Haitians, Cubans, Iraqis, Irish,

Jewish-Israelis, and Palestinians, which are at the center of the discussion in this essay and volume. Such self-identification helps the diasporans to define the boundaries of these entities, increases their solidarity, and facilitates fund-raising and political activities in their hostlands.

The strategies used by diasporans for coping with their complex situations in their hostlands include various degrees of integration (allowing them to operate seriously within their hostland but at the same time to maintain a separate identity and identification), acculturation (blending into the hostland culture but maintaining their own ethno-national culture), communalism (maintaining themselves as a separate entity but promoting social, political, and economic integration), corporatism (having representative organizations that are recognized by the hostland governments and by the social-political systems there), autonomy (maintaining a certain degree of integration but at the same time acting primarily in accordance with their own cultural, social, political, and economic background and interests), establishment of coalitions (with other diasporas or sociopolitical organizations), and isolation (going it alone). Most members of ethno-national diasporas select a combined communalist and autonomist strategy, typically following the relevant rules of both homeland and hostland (Sheffer 1996, 39; 2003, 9–10).

Diasporas can be categorized as *historical* (such as the Jewish and Armenian), *modern* (such as the Italian, Irish, and Polish), or *incipient* (such as the Turkish and Pakistani, and even some reawakening Scandinavian diasporas in the United States), as well as *state-linked* (made up of those who have a state in their homelands) or *stateless* (made up of those who have no state in their homeland, such as Basques, Kurds, Palestinians, and Romas) (see Sheffer 1986, 2003). Incipient diasporas, which are composed of recent migrants, become established entities in the cultural, social, political, and economic systems of their hostland as a result of their members' determination to maintain their ethno-national identity, maintain contacts with their homeland, establish adequate organizations, activate these organizations, maintain close contacts with other members of the emerging entity, and establish and remain ready to protect the borders of the entity. When these diasporas eventually succeed in establishing themselves as permanent entities, they become historical diasporas.

In most cases, the cores of ethno-national-religious diasporas are relatively united, even though core members are not necessarily totally homogeneous socially or politically, and even though some members, despite their connections to their homelands, may be critical of either the government there or certain social groups. Most cores of diasporas are well organized and can act together efficiently.

This solidarity of ethno-national-religious diasporas is one of the main bases for their cultural, social, political, and economic long-term survival. Although certain historical diasporas that still exist today, such as the Chinese, Indian, Jewish, and Armenian, have changed over the centuries, these are ancient entities that have overcome acute threats to their identities and hence to their existence, identification, and behavior. In fact, they have survived planned and spontaneous attempts to annihilate them totally, assimilate them, or fully integrate them into hostland societies. Their core members are capable of existing as distinct organized communities in today's globalized postmodern world in which there have emerged expectations that ethnic minorities and diasporas will totally disappear, either through full assimilation or through a return to their homelands. In contrast, transnational communities may dissolve and disappear for ideological, social, or political reasons.

Another important characteristic of diasporans, especially of core members who are not fully integrated into their hostlands, is that they maintain constant and intensive contacts with their homelands, whether or not these are independent states. They create elaborate trans-state communication networks that permit and encourage multiple exchanges of money, political and diplomatic support, and cultural features with their homelands and with other segments of the diaspora wherever these exist. They are deeply involved in their homelands' affairs and in the affairs of various hostlands where their brethren reside, and their networks facilitate the organization and promotion of activities in cultural, social, economic, and political spheres. In turn, such activities create a potential for friction with both homelands and hostlands and are related to highly complex patterns of divided, dual, or ambiguous loyalties to these countries. In some cases such friction can catalyze involvement in aggressive, terrorist, and criminal activities. Further, under hostile circumstances in their hostlands, or in view of noticeable problematic situations or significant social, political, and economic developments in their homelands, some members of ethno-national diasporas consider returning or actually return to their homelands. This was and is the case, for example, with the Irish, Jewish, Turkish, and even Japanese diasporans. In some cases, like that of the two hundred thousand Brazilian Japanese diasporans who have returned to Japan, return has created the background for clashes with certain elements in their homelands.

On the basis of the above description, the current processes of globalization and economic liberalization do not seem to cause total assimilation, integration, or hybridization of members of ethno-national-religious diasporas, and cores of both established and incipient diasporas do not face major threats of an eventual total disappearance. Because of their geographical dispersal within their hostlands, migration to other hostlands, or return to their original homeland, these diasporas' geographic and demographic boundaries are constantly changing, yet these boundaries are still quite clearly drawn and can be maintained and protected to an extent by diaspora members. In fact, current trends of globalization, liberalization, and multiculturalism strengthen rather than weaken many ethno-national diasporas because they provide members with additional cultural, ideational, economic, social, political, and communication resources that help them sustain their existence.

In summary, despite certain similarities between transnational communities and ethno-national religious diasporas (such as the facts that members of both reside in various countries and that they maintain contacts with other people belonging to the same entity, share certain views, and establish organizations), differences in their origin, identity and identification, ideology, boundaries, connections, organization, and patterns of behavior suggest that some clear distinctions should and can be made between these two types of dispersals. Nonetheless, some of the members of ethno-national-religious diasporas can be and are active in transnational communities as well.

Diasporas in the United States

The following discussion focuses on diasporas and diasporans that are simultaneously involved and active in the social, political, and economic arenas in the United States and in their homelands, especially in those homelands that are engaged in internal or international conflicts, including conflicts with the US government (e.g., the Cuban, Iraqi, Jewish/Israeli, and Palestinian diasporas). This part of the essay assesses the main current goals, patterns of development, and organization and mechanisms of diasporas' involvement in their relations with the US government regarding the two types of conflicts—conflicts in their homelands and in the United States.

New wide-ranging social, economic, and political developments in the United States (and in fact, all over the world), and especially the recent economic slowdown, have various significant implications for diasporas and their converging and diverging relations with the United States and with their homelands. These include not only a vastly increasing number of diasporas and diasporans in the United States, despite efforts to reduce the number of illegal immigrants entering the country and to control the number of legal immigrants, but also the increasing social, political, and economic power of the cores of various diasporas, which augments their ability to protect their members and act on behalf of them and their homelands. These developments have come about partly because an increasing number of diasporas now have representatives in local and national political positions in the United States and support candidates for various offices in the US Congress and state political organizations. Yet another reason for this development is divided or dual loyalties, especially among members of incipient diasporas, whose main orientations and interests are directed toward their homelands. In fact, their positive and negative activities vis-à-vis their homelands are increasingly resourceful and effective. Consequently, diasporas have become more demanding and active in their attempts to promote their own and their homelands' interests.

There is a particular need to follow such new trends in the views, policies, and activities of militant members of established and emerging diasporas. To a certain degree, these trends depend on policies that the US administration is and will be pursuing related to immigration, integration, and activities of organized and incipient diasporas. In view of the current administration's sympathetic and tolerant views and positions concerning ethnic issues in general, and the African American population and some but not all diasporas in particular, organized diasporas and individual diasporans have greater direct access to the White House itself and to the government administration. Therefore they can more easily attain their goals and obtain certain advantages for themselves and, when urgently needed, also for their homelands. In other words, there seems to be an increase in the number of core diasporas and diasporans with interests that converge with the interests and policies of the US government.

The following are the most evident goals that diasporas in the United States try to accomplish and that create divergence and some conflicts (the diasporas cited as examples are the ones that are discussed in later chapters of this volume):

1. Facilitating the immigration of their relatives to the United States. This is currently a concern of Iraqis, Palestinians, and Ethiopians.

2. Preventing the expulsion from the United States of their relatives who are here illegally. This is a concern of most of these diasporas, probably except for the Irish.

3. Achieving basic social, political, and legal legitimacy and recognition from the American society and government. This applies especially to Ethiopians, Palestinians, and Iraqis.

4. Influencing policies and activities vis-à-vis the diasporans themselves and their homelands. Although in certain cases (e.g., the Cuban diaspora) and for some political reasons relations of some diasporas with the presidency have weakened, most diasporas (e.g., Ethiopian, Palestinian, Iraqi, Irish, Jewish/Israeli) are gaining more direct access to the president, Congress, and the administration.

5. Establishing coalitions with important political forces, including other diasporas. This is the case especially with Jews and Israelis, Palestinians, Ethiopians, Iraqis, and Cubans.

6. Achieving greater freedom for economic activities both in the United States and in their homelands. This applies to the Ethiopians, Iraqis, and Palestinians.

7. Getting additional political, diplomatic, and economic legitimacy and support for their homelands and for divergent groups within diasporic entities. This applies to all diasporas discussed in this volume.

Convergence and Divergence of US Government and Diaspora Aims Concerning Conflicts

Various studies, including those presented in this volume, show that most of the more acute conflicts in which diasporas and diasporans are involved are those occurring in their homelands rather than in the United States. This implies a degree of convergence in the basic interests and goals between many members of such diasporas and US society and government. Consequently, diasporas are deeply involved in conflicts that are also of interest to the US government. There are of course conflicts in diasporas' homelands in which the United States is not deeply interested or intensely involved. Diasporas' capacity to achieve their goals in such conflicts is much more limited than in cases when their interests converge with those of the American government.

The conflicts in which the United States is both interested and involved and that afford diasporas a greater chance to influence the American government are of two kinds. First are conflicts of long-range strategic importance to the United States. What drives the US government to become deeply involved in such conflicts are primarily American ideological concerns and political and economic interests but not necessarily the wishes and needs of the relevant diasporas. Examples include the Iraqi and the Israeli-Palestinian conflicts. Second are conflicts of short-term significance to the United States. It is likely that because of realistic attitudes toward long-term US involvement in complicated and costly conflicts like those in Iraq and Afghanistan, future American administrations will prefer to be engaged in short-term conflicts in which diasporas have been or will be implicated. For example, this has been the case for US involvement in the Libyan conflict.

In the past, the United States' involvement was motivated by a desire fundamentally to resolve some of the more acute long-term conflicts. Now it seems that the US interest will be rather to participate in such conflicts' management, which means, for example, achieving the end of fighting, beginning and pursuing mutual talks by the participants, and economically supporting sides that are willing to negotiate, all of which might eventually lead to the conflict's resolution.

The most prevalent cause of conflicts in which individual diasporans, groupings, and entire communities are involved, and the motivations for related involvement by the US government, are the expulsion of diasporan brethren from their entire country of origin or from a certain part of that homeland. Some, but not all, of the various Palestinian diasporic organizations clearly exemplify this diaspora's goal and involvement and the US reaction. Next are the struggles for separation and independence in homelands. Two of the best-known cases in which the United States has been involved are the Irish and the Israeli-Palestinian conflicts. Another case has been that of the Basques, involving the Euskadi Ta Askatasuna (Basque Homeland and Freedom), which was supported by certain segments of the Basque diaspora in the United States. Yet another has been the Armenian case, in which the Armenian diaspora in the United States has been quite deeply involved and active.

Diasporas became involved in these homeland conflicts because of cultural, political, social, and economic discrimination and deprivation of their kin in their homelands. The Cuban diaspora fits this category. Legal and political persecutions in homelands have also been conflicts causing diaspora involvement. The Ethiopian, Iraqi, and Cuban cases fit this subcategory. Cuban Americans have been involved in most developments in their homeland since Castro's revolution, and they are still very interested and involved in what is happening there. Finally, cultural, social, political, and economic discrimination in the United States, bordering on blatant racism, has motivated diasporans to address such issues. To an extent the Haitian, Ethiopian, and Palestinian diasporas are all combating such discrimination in the United States.

The most salient observation regarding ethno-national diasporas' involvements in conflicts is that state-linked diasporas (including all the diasporas discussed in this volume, except for the Palestinians) try to promote the resolution and management of such conflicts and "invest" less in encouraging conflicts than stateless diasporas do. This is because state-linked diasporas that want to help the struggle in the homeland and change the regime must coordinate their activities with their homeland government and maintain reasonably good political relations with the US administration. In contrast, certain groups in stateless diasporas such as the Palestinians may be more aggressive, demanding, and ready to fight for the achievement of their main goal, which is a sovereign state in their homeland. This was also the case for the Jewish diaspora before the establishment of Israel as an independent state, and for the Armenian diaspora's activities before Armenia gained its independence.

The following significant factors determine the goals and the intensity of diasporas' activities and of US government reactions. The first factor is the nature and severity of the conflict—the more acute the conflict, the greater the readiness of diasporas to get involved, but the more reluctance the US government will show. The second factor is the US government's perception of the severity of such conflicts and, mainly, of their impact on American interests. If the perception is that such conflicts are of major American interest, US involvement will be quicker and more intensive. The third factor is the sort of relations that exist between the US administration and the governments of the diasporas' countries of origin. Where relations are reasonable and there is a possibility for a rational dialogue between the two governments, the United States will be ready to get involved in attempts to resolve the conflicts, but where relations are tense and there is no immediate acute

American interest in limiting or resolving such conflicts, the US administration will try to keep a distance. Finally, the greater the intensity of the contacts between the US government and social actors in the diasporas and in their homelands—the closer the interests and relations with these actors—then the greater the degree of expected US involvement.

Diasporas' expanding activities in the economic sphere are bound to create clashes and even conflicts with US society and government. That diasporas have recently been more involved in economic issues pertaining to both the United States and their homelands is linked to the greater ability of most diasporans to earn and raise money in the United States. In turn, this enables diasporans to get involved in a variety of projects that the US government needs to know about in order to control them and avoid severe conflicts and damage, whether within the United States or in the diasporas' homelands. These economic matters pertain not only to the relations between competent diasporans and their homelands but also to recent developments in the United States itself. Thus members of diasporas donate substantial sums of money in support of candidates for the US presidency and for congressional, state, and local legislative offices. This has been very noticeable in the last American elections, in which, for instance, the Jewish diaspora supported Barack Obama and, as usual, both Democratic and Republican candidates for Congress. Simultaneously, diasporas' remittances to their families and relatives in their homelands have been increasing, notably for the diasporas discussed in this volume, except perhaps in the Irish and Jewish cases. Diasporas' expanding economic activities are also connected to their increasing tendency to invest money in social and economic enterprises in their homelands rather than to donate it to governments and official organizations. This has been the case particularly with the Irish and Jewish diasporas, and to an extent with the Iraqi and Haitian diasporas. Finally, in certain cases, diasporas financially support rebellious individuals and groups in their homelands. This has been the case with the Iraqi, Cuban, and Palestinian diasporas. All these matters that are becoming main issues in diasporas' activities should be of concern to the US government.

Diasporas' Violent and Criminal Activities

Some organized core diasporas and individual diasporas promote conflict and violence in their homelands as means of furthering their various self-interests. They do so by politically and financially supporting the relevant rebellious or criminal groups in their homelands and by lobbying and pressuring the US government. At the same time it should be noted that in certain cases both organized diasporas and individual diasporans contribute to the management or resolution of conflicts in their homelands and try to solve conflicts between their homelands and the United States. It seems that now the US government is aware of these intentions and activities and is acting to avoid troubles for itself.

The deeper causes and consequently the more immediate motivations that lead ethno-national-religious diasporic entities to launch or support violent and terrorist activities in either their homelands or host countries have not changed much during the last decades, even as globalization and "glocalization" have intensified (Sheffer 2006). Most deeply rooted conflicts involving terrorist actions that diasporans carry out or support are intended to achieve national, nationalist, or communal goals in their homelands or host countries. The religious beliefs of these groups, including Palestinians and Iraqis, are only secondary and supportive elements of their identities and thus also are only secondary in determining their goals and the actions they take to achieve them, including support of or participation in terrorist activities. But terrorism by a transnational religious entity such as al-Qaeda is usually motivated by an absolute belief that an otherworldly power has commanded and sanctioned the application of violence and terror for the greater glory of the faith. It is uncertain how many diasporans have been and are totally motivated by such a belief, but it is pretty clear that their numbers are small, even though dangerous.

As far as their goals in these matters are concerned, there are certain similarities between transnational and ethno-national-religious diasporic entities, both state-linked and stateless. Yet the difficulty in establishing the similarity between ethno-national-religious diasporas, such as the Jewish, and transnational communities, such as the Muslim, is connected to the general debate about the role of religion in shaping the identity, identification, and behavioral patterns of ethnic entities in general, and particularly the diasporic groups that are discussed in this volume. The recent extreme terrorist activities, including 9/11, that have been launched by al-Qaeda and other Sunni and Shiite Muslim transnational groups and organizations have drawn unprecedented attention to such groups. Politicians, scholars, and other observers usually refer to such entities as homogeneous diasporas. However, in most instances terrorism and other violent actions are carried out not by highly organized homogeneous "Muslim," "African," "Latino," or "Asian" diasporas but rather separately and autonomously by members of transnational entities and organizations, such as al-Qaeda.

Therefore the US government should more attentively examine and clearly differentiate the motivations and purposes of various Muslim, Asian, and African groups whose origins are in different nation-states or perceived homelands. However, it is difficult to determine whether the activist members of combative fundamentalist Muslim groups, such as those comprising North African and Asian ethno-national diasporans, are motivated by "pure" religious sentiments or mainly concerned with the political and cultural rights of their co-nationals in their homelands and host countries. This should particularly be taken into account in view of the tendency to lump together all diasporic and transnational entities' motivations and purposes when they engage in terrorism.

A further relevant distinction should be drawn between those groups that target their violent activities at their homelands and those that act against hostlands. Thus transnational entities and organizations, such as al-Qaeda, mostly target host countries. But ethno-national-religious diasporic entities and organizations, such as those of the Iranians, only occasionally carry out or support terrorism in their host countries, including the United States.

Still another distinction to be made is that between state-linked and stateless ethno-national-religious diasporas. Because of their multiple interests in host countries and their complicated relations with their homelands, state-linked diasporas are more reluctant to use violence and terrorism to promote their interests either in hostlands or in homelands. The major reasons for the use of terrorism and violence by state-linked diasporas are related to the origins and nature of the conflicts and the capacity of the diasporas to deal with them. Stateless diasporas are more inclined to use violence and terrorism and to disguise what are primarily political and social motivations by offering cultural and religious explanations. Stateless diasporas are mainly interested in supporting the struggle of their kin in the homeland to gain independence there—as was the case with the Armenian and Jewish diasporas before the establishment of "their" independent states in homelands.

Various reliable estimates (see US State Department Reports on Terrorism, 2004–present; Johnston 2008) show that tourists are increasingly involved in terrorist activities, as are refugees and asylum seekers. However, the kinds of dispersed persons who have been most likely to carry out recent terrorist activities, not only in the United States but all over the world, are first, members of ethno-national-religious diasporas, and second, members of transnational religious dispersals.

Twenty-five groups that have been involved in conflicts or rebellions and have espoused terrorism in either their homelands or host countries have been linked to ethno-national-religious diasporas. They have performed terrorist acts in addition to nonviolent tactical activities such as lobbying, propaganda campaigns, and legal protest marches and demonstrations. Furthermore, out of the fifty most active terrorist organizations and groups, twenty-seven either constitute segments of ethno-national-religious diasporas or are supported by such diasporas. About twelve organizations using terrorism have proven links to ethno-national-religious diasporic entities.

In sum, it seems that, except for al-Qaeda and a few other militant organizations that are essentially culturally and religiously motivated, the most active and supportive movements and organizations of terrorist actions are ethno-national stateless diasporas. The next most violently active movements and organizations are those that try to improve cultural, political, and economic conditions in their homelands.

All governments, and especially that of the United States, should pay greater attention to diasporas' criminal activities, since these have become causes for conflicts between diasporas and hostlands. Diasporas' involvement in criminal activities, again both in their countries of origin and in hostlands, is of course not a new phenomenon. For example, the well-established Italian and Irish diasporas were involved in such activities. However, the collapse of the Soviet Union, the end of the Cold War era, the rapid and far-reaching development of global communication systems, and the increasing number and activities of diasporas have prompted a new wave of organized crime involving diaspora members on both international and local levels. Diasporans have been recruited to participate in such organizations and have cooperated with such networks out of their own initiative. They have joined together to help their comrades in their criminal activities in both homelands and host countries and to enhance their personal and collective economic interests.

Worldwide criminal networks benefit from their origins in diasporas or from their connections with diasporas. Actually, organized diasporans, or those having close ties with their brethren in the diasporas, allow criminal operators a certain degree of freedom of movement, access to information, "ready-made" networks of communication, political assistance, cover, and social backing. Like other businesses, international criminal activities require enforcement and coverage mechanisms, which diasporic networks can easily provide. Increased migration, much of which stems from states with weak economies and political instability, has created a large demand for both financial support and larger global networks. In many cases, such networks become particularly prominent where immigrant groups are not fully integrated into their host societies.

These connections create mutual benefits for diasporans and for their brethren in their homelands. Despite attempts by various governments to prevent such criminal activities, because of the extensive availability of sophisticated communication systems it is difficult to determine which diasporic and criminal networks contribute to such activities.

The principal activities of these networks are drug trafficking, illegal arms trade and supply, human trafficking and smuggling, especially of women and children for prostitution and servitude, and money laundering. Some criminal networks that are operating in or have connections with diasporas, including those in the United States, are the Italian Mafia, Russian networks, Chinese networks, and Israeli networks. Lately, various Latin American networks have expanded their interest and activities beyond drug production and trafficking and have become involved in money laundering and production of counterfeit goods; Nigerian networks are active in drug trafficking and sophisticated fraud schemes; smaller but very active are the Albanian networks; also active are, among others, Somali, Cameroonian, Iranian, Armenian, Chechen, and Sudanese (involved in the conflict in Southern Sudan) networks.

The following, then, are the main conclusions concerning diasporas' violent, illegal, and criminal goals and activities. First, most existing diasporas are not tightly knit entities that collectively pursue any single aggressive strategy, and especially not terrorist or criminal activities. Second, nobody should generalize and suggest that all core members of diasporas are involved in terrorist and criminal activities or support them. In fact, in most cases, such as the Irish, Jewish, Palestinian, Iraqi, Turkish, Basque, and Kurdish diasporas, only a relatively small number of individuals and small groups of core members support or participate in such activities. Third, in most cases, terrorism is not a permanent strategy but a temporary tactic. It is intended to achieve mainly social and political goals, and when these are achieved the diasporas' tactics change. Fourth, in most cases the use of terror as a tactic is confined to relatively short periods of crisis in homelands, host countries, or other states where their brethren reside. Hence, the use of terror and violence does not transform certain or entire diasporic entities and groups into warrior communities. Finally, many diasporic entities and groups are engaged in activities intended to enhance the cultural, civic, and economic well-being of their own communities, their host countries, and their homelands. Therefore, stigmatization of entire diasporic entities is unwarranted and should be avoided because it creates a permanently hostile environment that can make the lives of most diasporans even harder than they usually are and can push these people to use more dangerous tactics and means.

The ability of hostlands to deal with the terrorist and criminal activities of diasporas depends on the integration of such diasporas into the hostland. The more integrated a diaspora is, the easier it should be for the hostland society and government to deal with it. But much also depends on hostland-homeland relations. The closer and better such relations are, the more easily the hostland can deal with such issues. Close political and diplomatic relationships and security cooperation make it easier to identify the groups, organizations, and individuals involved and to try and stop them. When homelands are involved in such activities, it is much more difficult for the hostland to deal effectively with them. Some hostlands, including the United States, use international organizations and networks, such as the United Nations, to help stop terrorist and criminal activities in their states and in other states with which they have close connections and relations.

Mechanisms for Diasporas' Influencing the US Government

The degree of convergence or divergence between the basic views, positions, and needs of diasporas and hostlands plays a significant role in determining the influence of one side on the other. But it varies from one diaspora or hostland to the next because of differing integration of diasporas into their hostlands and loyalty toward these hostlands. It also varies because of differing relations between hostlands and homelands. According to the essays in this volume, for example, a high degree of convergence has existed between the United States and Northern Ireland ever since the Good Friday Agreement; and the earthquake in Haiti, by stimulating US aid, has led to a greater convergence between the United States and Haiti. Next on this end of the spectrum are US-Israel relations. US-Palestinian relations (except for Hamas) are becoming friendlier. On the other end of the spectrum, the most problematic relations are those between the United States and Ethiopia, Iraq, and Cuba.

To an extent, convergence or divergence in these cases depends on the degree of diasporas' integration into the United States, the maintenance of their ethno-national-religious identity, and the strength of their connection to their country of origin. All these factors determine the specific mechanisms that the United States and each diaspora are using to promote their own interests. The more convergence between the US government, the diasporas, and their homelands, the more diasporas employ moderate and civilized methods to persuade the government to promote their interests. On the other hand, the greater the divergence, the more radical and aggressive the diasporas' activities become.

Certain diasporas have become more conscious of what other diasporas in the United States and elsewhere are doing to attain their own and their homelands' goals, and because of the relative ease of communicating with other diasporas and the availability of information about diasporas and their organizational and behavioral patterns, there is a great similarity in the variety of mechanisms and arenas that all these diasporas are using. In the United States most diasporas use the following tools:

1. Lobbying of Congress, the president and the administration, governors, state senates, and even local mayors and municipalities. Lobbying is easier now because diasporas are increasingly financing the electoral campaigns of US politicians.

2. Persuading their known and active members to vote as groups for candidates that seem sympathetic to them and to their homelands.

3. Raising funds to support candidates in congressional, municipal, and local elections.

4. Mobilizing public demonstrations and gatherings, which are covered by the local, state, and national media and are intended to influence the general public and politicians to pursue certain policies in support of the diasporas; also the use of print and electronic media, radio, television, and conferences.

5. Providing information to all those who are interested and involved in policy making and execution.

6. Organizing trips for politicians and bureaucrats to the diasporas' homelands, and, in the homelands, organizing trips and activities for local politicians and bureaucrats to the hostland to coordinate either peaceful or combative actions.

Let us turn now to the tools used by governments in general and the US administration in particular to promote and protect their interests vis-à-vis diasporas and their homelands. As far as the US government's internal interests are concerned, recently it has mainly tried to track the intentions and the legal activities of the diasporas and, consequently, to establish and maintain direct links and dialogues with diaspora leaders and activists. The primary purposes have been to ensure that the diasporans behave according to the US laws, rules, and customs and to promote diasporans' integration into US political culture.

The three most controversial issues with which the United States must deal are diasporas' terrorist and illegal activities, their involvement in the economic and financial sphere, and illegal immigration into the United States. The US government has tried its utmost to stop or at least to control these activities. As long as there are no major problems in these areas, the relations between the United States and the diasporas will be similar to the relations between the United States and its other citizens.

Similarly, so long as there are no major controversies or divergences between the diasporas' homelands and the United States, the latter will use regular political and diplomatic means of communication and persuasion with both the diaspora and its homeland. However, if for various reasons these relations become tense or acute conflicts develop between the two countries, then among other political, diplomatic, and economic means, the US government will probably try to enlist the relevant diaspora organizations and their leaders to promote its interests in solving the conflict. This has been the case for example, with certain Jewish, Iraqi, and Palestinian groups and organizations.

Assessing the Effects of Diasporas on the US Government

One of the most difficult tasks facing analysts of relations between governments and various social, political, and economic groups, organizations, and individuals is determining the actual effects of their public statements and activities. Even when statements of demands and activities of individuals and entities are correlated with positive government responses to these statements and actions, correlation does not necessarily indicate causation. Without clear firsthand statements by senior policy makers that they were influenced by specific actors or actions, it is extremely difficult to ascertain the sources of impacts on policy making and implementation. This basic general theoretical observation applies to diasporas' influence not only on the policies and activities of hostlands but also on their homeland leaders, governments, and organizations that are involved in these matters.

By the same token, it is difficult to distinguish between the influence of diasporas and direct relations between host and homeland governments: for example, either specific impacts of the Jewish diaspora on the US government's policies since the 1980s or the Israeli government's influence during the same period. The extent of the Jewish diaspora's influence is questionable not only because we can generally assume that the US and many other hostland governments are inclined to make independent decisions concerning activities that would promote their own interests, but also because US administrations increasingly have direct and effective contact with the Israeli government. Since the late 1980s, nearly all the policies and actions of the United States regarding Israel and the conflicts in which Israel is involved have been directly related to the contacts between the Israeli and US governments. The same is true of the direct links between the US government and other diasporas' homelands discussed in this volume, including the Palestinian, but excluding the Cuban diasporas.

Nonetheless, the essays in this volume suggest that under certain circumstances and regarding certain spheres of action, leading activist diasporans and well-organized and connected diasporic entities and organizations can and actually do influence US foreign, economic, and security policies. Additional studies are required, but the following observations can be tentatively offered.

The articles in this volume indicate that under certain circumstances diasporas can influence the formulation of internal and external policies of the US government. For example, when diasporas are fully aware of their own needs and goals, they follow very closely and inventively the political mood and policies of the US administration and, when they notice a lacuna in the relevant US foreign policy, they try to step in and may have an effect on the formulation of policy and even on its implementation.

Furthermore, the success of diaspora efforts to influence governmental policies and actions depends on whether the relevant diasporans and their organizations do not contradict evident US interests. It is pretty obvious that the chances of getting positive and supportive reactions from the US administration are much better when the United States' and diasporas' interests and goals converge. Recent examples for this pattern include both the Jewish and Palestinian cases (see chapters 3 and 4 of this volume).

Diasporans' success in influencing the US government depends not only on their ability to coordinate between the main actors in the homeland as well as various persons and institutions in the United States but also to neutralize opposition in the homeland and the United States. Occasionally doing so depends on establishing coalitions with other diasporas or ethnic groups in the United States. What is happening now in the Jewish American diaspora serves as an interesting example. Recently formed Jewish groups such as J Street promote policies that diverge from those of the veteran and dedicated pro-Israel lobby the American Israel Public Affairs Committee. This may create certain difficulties for rightist Israeli governments in achieving their goals (see chapter 3 of this volume).

The voting patterns of organized diasporas' members in American national, state, and local elections may produce the background for diasporas' successful influence on elected officials regarding policies toward diasporas and their interests both in the United States and in their homelands. Thus, despite some problematic positions of Cubans in the United States, and the wariness of the US government toward some of those positions, cooperation between Cuban Americans and the current US administration has reinforced policies to change the Cuban regime, although by no means through the use of force (see chapter 6 of this volume).

Individual leaders and activists may have greater influence and produce more and better results for diasporas or for their homelands than established diasporic organizations. Although this observation does not contradict the undeniable significance of organizations not only for successful lobbying but also for diasporas' continuous survival and achievements in all spheres, this is particularly the case when such diaspora leaders are friends of the US president, the secretary of state, senators and congressmen, and administration officials, or when they have personal as well as professional contacts with such politicians and officials. However, even when diaspora leaders have no such intimate relations with politicians and government officials, a great deal depends on their personalities and modes of operation vis-à-vis these figures. The Iraqi case is a good example of this pattern (see chapter 9 of this volume).

Moreover, the ability of diasporas to influence the decisions and actions of the US government depends, of course, on their ability to successfully lobby in Congress and the administration. As the literature on the Jewish diaspora's ability to influence the US government has proposed, this diaspora has shown considerable ability in lobbying successfully. However, these alleged accomplishments have also attracted substantive criticism and opposition (e.g., Mearsheimer and Walt 2008). Various diasporas have devoted much time and energy to studying the Jewish diaspora's alleged triumphant lobbying and are following some of its patterns in addition to relying on their own skills and innovations. Other diasporas, including some discussed in this volume, have successfully developed their own mechanisms to influence the US administration. To an extent, the thriving lobbies that many believe are mainly responsible for diasporas' influence on the US governmental policies depend to a great extent on their ability to "use" media and communication networks to launch public campaigns that gain the attention and consequently the support not only of American politicians and officials but also of the general public. Such was the case with the activities of the Ethiopian diaspora in 2005 (see chapter 7 of this volume). During many decades this was also true of the influence of the Jewish diaspora, and it is becoming also the case with the Palestinians. These diasporas have succeeded in attracting the media's attention.

There are some basic preconditions for the effective influence of ethno-national-religious diaspora entities and individual diasporans on the United States and other host governments. The various positions of diasporas in the United States and their influence on American society and politics would improve especially if the US government would study and recognize the identity and identification of the members of diasporas; the degrees of their integration into American society, politics, and economy; the depth and intensity of their relations with their homelands; their cultural inclinations and needs; their connections with other diasporic entities of the same ethno-national-religious background residing in other hostlands; and other factors discussed above. Further study of these aspects of the relations between diasporas and the US government could lead to better insights into various sensitive issues pertaining to divergence and convergence between their aims.

The analysis in this essay suggests significant topics for further academic studies about diaspora-government relations. First, scholars should recall that diasporas are multifaceted and heterogeneous and should focus not only on their core members and core organizations but also on peripheral members and organizations, for these may be the most dangerous troublemakers for the United States and by the same token for other hostlands. Moreover, researchers should study the internal and external problems troubling diasporas and their members and the role of trans-state diasporan communication networks in addressing them. Researchers should also explore the extent to which diasporans, especially younger and better-educated radicals, are alienated from American society and politics as well as from the main sectors in their homelands. These persons may pose the most acute threats to the United States by initiating or becoming active members in groups or organizations that are involved in illegal activities in the United States or in their homelands. Attention should also be given to the activities of diasporas' fund-raising and investment organizations and of their main lobbies. It would be helpful to learn more about the connections of diasporic individuals and organizations to transnational communities in order to understand their links with ethno-national diasporas in other countries. Attention also should be given to the possibility of turning diasporas into mediators between their homeland and the United States. Finally, to balance the picture drawn in this essay about the connection of diasporas to conflicts and clashes with their American hostland, it should be emphasized again that many diasporans are engaged in activities that are intended to enhance the cultural, civic, and economic well-being not only of their own communities but also of their host- and homelands. One should be careful to avoid stigmatizing entire diasporic entities and thereby fostering a hostile environment that could worsen the lives of diasporans and diasporas and risk pushing them to adopt more dangerous tactics and means vis-à-vis the United States.

Notes

1. I am using this term because not all of these persons form communities.
2. As discussed in Sheffer (2013).

References

Braziel, J. E., and A. Mannur. 2003. *Theorizing Diaspora—A Reader*. London: Wiley.

Dufoix, S. 2008. *Diasporas*. Berkeley: University of California Press.

Faist, T. 2000. *The Volume and Dynamics of International Migration and Transnational Social Spaces*. Oxford: Clarendon Press.

———. 2007. "Transnationalisation and Development(s): Towards a North-South Perspective." Working Paper 16. Center on Migration, Citizenship, and Development, Bielefeld, Germany.

Glick Schiller, N. 2003. "The Centrality of Ethnography in the Study of International Migration." In *American Arrivals: Anthropology Embraces the New Immigration*, edited by Nancy Foner, 99–128. Santa Fe, NM: School of American Research Press.

———. 2007. "Beyond the Nation-State and Its Units of Analysis: Towards a New Research Agenda for Migration Studies." In *Concepts and Methods in in Migration Research*, edited by K. Schitterhelm, 39–72. Conference Reader. www.cultural-.capital.net/reader/concepts-and methods.pdf.

Johnston, W. M. 2008. "Incidents of Mass Casualty Terrorism." May 12. www.johnstonarchives.net/terrorism.

Mearsheimer, J., and Walt, S. 2008. *The Israel Lobby and U.S. Foreign Policy*. New York: Farrar, Straus and Giroux.

Sheffer, G. 1986. "A New Field of Study: Modern Diasporas in International Politics." In *Modern Diasporas in International Politics*, edited by G. Sheffer. New York: St. Martin's Press.

———. 1996. "Whither the Study of Ethnic Diasporas? Some Theoretical, Definitional, Analytical and Comparative Considerations." In *The Networks of Diasporas*, edited by G. Prévelakis, 37–46. Nicosia: Cyprus Research Centre.

———. 2003. *Diaspora Politics: At Home Abroad*. Cambridge: Cambridge University Press.

———. 2006. "Diaspora and Terrorism." In *The Roots of Terrorism*, edited by L. Richardson. New York: Routledge.

———. 2013. "A Conceptual Framework for Understanding the Roles of Diasporas in Intrastate Conflicts." In *Nonstate Actors in Intrastate Conflicts*, edited by Dan Miodownik and Oren Barak, 84–105. Philadelphia: University of Pennsylvania Press.

Shuval, J. 2000. "Diaspora Migration: Definitional Ambiguities and a Theoretical Paradigm." *International Migration* 38 (5): 41–57.

Tölölyan, K. 1991. "The Nation-State and Its Others: In Lieu of a Preface." *Diaspora* 1 (1): 3–7.

Tsagarousianou, R. 2007. "Reevaluating 'Diaspora': Connectivity, Communication and Imagination in a Globalized World." In *Sociology of Diaspora*, edited by A. Sahoo and B. Maharaj, 101–17. New Delhi: Rawat Publications.

US State Department. 2004–present. Country Reports on Terrorism. www.state.gov/j/ct/rls/crt/index.htm.

Van Hear, N. 1998. *New Diasporas: The Mass Exodus, Dispersal and Regrouping of Migrant Communities.* London: UCL Press.

Vertovec, S. 1997. "Three Meanings of Diasporas." *Diaspora* 6 (3): 277–97.

Competing Convergent
or Divergent Interests?

CHAPTER THREE

Between JDate and J Street: US Foreign Policy and the Liberal Jewish Dilemma in America

Yossi Shain and Neil Rogachevsky

For years, the two-state solution to the Israeli-Palestinian conflict has preoccupied writers, diplomats, and politicians throughout the world. Policy and diplomacy have followed suit. Notwithstanding the failure of the Oslo Peace Process, the international community has continued its efforts over the last decade to solve the conflict: international conferences like the 2008 Annapolis conference, White House ceremonies and conversations, third-party mediated meetings, shuttle diplomacy by top American envoys, Tony Blair taking up residence in Jerusalem as the envoy of the "Quartet," the Saudi Initiative of 2002, and Secretary John Kerry's recent "shuttle diplomacy" between Jerusalem and Ramallah, to name a few. These efforts have not borne much fruit. Why? Is not the two-state solution within the interest of all parties? Some have said that the only missing ingredient is a serious American push. Above all, the US president must be able to marginalize the hawks in Israel and diminish the influence of the hard-line "Israel lobby" at home.

That the Israel lobby is a powerful obstacle to peace is an important opinion in America and Europe and has long prevailed in certain sectors of the Arab world. No matter who is in charge in Washington or Jerusalem, no matter the diplomatic processes as well the changing currents in Middle East affairs, the failings of the peace process as well acrimony or difficulties in other parts of the Arab or Muslim world are often attributed to the obstruction of the Israel lobby. Movie director Oliver Stone's comment in July 2010 that the "Jews" direct US foreign policy in ways contrary to the national interest was an extreme but by no means unique expression of this viewpoint.

The Israel lobby explains everything: why the United States invaded Iraq, saber rattling about Iran's nuclear program, why no American president has succeeded in bringing about a Palestinian state, why there is "Muslim rage" against America, and why misery persists in the Arab and Islamic world. In this sense, the narrative of the power of the Israel lobby serves as a "theory of everything." In the United States, the theory of everything has not attained the power it enjoys in the Arab world or among some Europeans or Latin Americans, but it nonetheless serves as an important, and sometimes decisive, argument for the failures in the Middle East. Many American Jews have been affected by the widening role of this theory of everything in public discourse. Jews have been accused of sacrificing their liberal values for the sake of Israel. This charge puts them on the defensive regarding their loyalties.

To those who believe that the Israel lobby holds up progress in the Middle East, the election of Barack Obama in 2008 seemed to portend a real opportunity. Finally, it seemed to them, a president had been elected who would not be indebted to so-called "hawkish" Israel supporters like AIPAC. In his Cairo speech of June 2009 Obama ignited hopes of a new start in the Middle East by promising he would be more evenhanded, expressing as much support for the plight of Palestinians as for Israeli security concerns. Previous American administrations had paid lip service to a settlement freeze at various times. Obama would demand a settlement freeze without exceptions. In the person and policies of Barack Obama it seemed that the pro-peace camp had a supporter as never before.

Obama's opportunity would be enhanced by support from a new lobbying organization within the American Jewish community itself. J Street, the self-styled "pro-Israel, pro-peace" lobby, was created to great fanfare in 2008. Its chief purpose, according to founder Jeremy Ben-Ami, was to support President Obama's Middle East policy in the face of any opposition from the traditional lobby, AIPAC. "Our number 1 agenda item," Ben-Ami told the *New York Times Magazine*, "is to do whatever we can in Congress to act as the president's blocking back" (Traub 2009). With a serious pro-peace president, along with new institutional mechanisms to shepherd the process through the corridors of American power, the peace camp believed that a breakthrough toward a Palestinian state and broader regional peace was imminent. Furthermore, the majority of Jews supported the renewed vision of peace expressed by the Democratic Party establishment. Democratic Party pollster Mark Mellman showed at the time that "support for Israel is a critical element of Jews' voting behavior" in the United States and that Jews remained fiercely loyal to the Democratic Party even when broader domestic support for the president's agenda was eroding (2009). Republican hopes for a "Jewish migration" to Mitt Romney in 2012 as a consequence of his purportedly more pro-Israel stance similarly failed to materialize.

In a more fundamental way, however, hopes for a breakthrough on Israel-Palestine have been dashed. In Obama's first term, America's shifting and ultimately tepid policies on settlements, Jerusalem, direct negotiations, and other issues seemed to indicate that the issue had gone onto the back burner, just as it had done for his predecessors. As a consequence of the Arab revolutions, some commentators have argued that resolution of the conflict would have beneficial effects elsewhere. Yet in practice, and despite John Kerry's shuttle diplomacy, the issue has mostly faded as a priority as American attention has focused on Libya, Egypt, Syria, and now Iran.

As we write in the fall of 2013, it seems that the Israeli-Palestinian conflict will frustrate the aims of the Obama administration, just as it has done to his predecessors. Cognizant of this fact, the theory of everything has tried to account for the failure. Setbacks have intensified the rhetoric about the Israel lobby. In April 2010 John Mearsheimer, coauthor of *The Israel Lobby*, a renowned blueprint for the theory of everything, gave a speech in Washington, D.C., dividing the American Jewish community into "righteous," "ambiguous middle," and "new-Afrikaners." The implication was that traditional supporters of Israel were perhaps not only misguided but also immoral. Meanwhile, Palestinians often argue that setbacks in the peace process (or to Palestinian aims in that peace process) are the result of Obama's "caving to the Jews." According to an internal memo of the Fatah faction of Mahmoud Abbas regarding the policy of Obama's first term, "Obama couldn't withstand the pressure of the Zionist lobby, which led to a retreat from his previous positions on halting settlement construction and defining an agenda for the negotiations and peace" (*Ha'aretz* 2009). This irrefutable theory of everything cozily explains all failure.

The idea that the Jews retain great power over US foreign policy in the Middle East is not new, and certainly not restricted to those who are obsessed by the influence of Jews, or anti-Semites. This view has been encouraged by the character of the Jewish community in America and its strong ties to Israel. At various moments over the last few decades, analysts have described growing rifts or tensions between Israeli and American Jewry. In 2001, Professor Egon Mayer and some colleagues released a controversial study (Mayer, Kosmin, and Keysar, 2001) of the American Jewish community in which he portrayed mutually reinforcing trends of increasing secularity, decreasing attachment to Jewish religious and communal institutions, and a weakening sense of Jewish identity among large parts of American Jewry. He also noted decreased attachment to Israel. At the same time, Steven Rosenthal published a monograph called *Irreconcilable Differences*, saying that the alliance, which had been strong in the seventies, had been suffering repeated shocks since the eighties. Liberal Jews, he claimed, were becoming more alienated from the state of Israel because of a new wave of right-wing policies thought to run counter to the values of American liberalism.

All of these developments were swept aside by 9/11 and the second Intifada, during which American Jewry, across all denominational and political divisions, mobilized behind Israel. The unprecedented unity of American Jewry in the first years of the twenty-first century can be attributed to this great crisis at home and abroad and wouldn't have been possible without such a crisis. Even many who hadn't given much thought to their Jewish identity stood up to be counted in those years. Lawrence Summers, current chief economic adviser to President Obama and then president of Harvard, declared in a widely noted speech that he could no longer remain complacent in the face of the virulent anti-Semitism that had manifested itself not only in the Middle East and Western Europe but even on American college campuses, including his own.[1] Summers had described himself as "Jewish . . . but hardly devout" (2002), but the times demanded such a response.

Similarly, in 2001 Jonathan Rosen wrote in the *New York Times* that 9/11 had been a road-to-Damascus moment for his American and Jewish identity. The attacks had awakened Rosen, a secular Jewish American, to the threats to Jewish security and the dangers of anti-Semitism, which he had previously associated with a different continent and a different era, Europe of the 1930s and '40s. The attacks on Jews and Israel during these years were not limited to physical violence; they included psychic violence of the most debilitating kind, including attempts at delegitimizing Israel as a state.[2] And, in those few post–9/11 years, Jews of all stripes took note.

Many secular, unaffiliated, or even "hidden" Jews could not articulate the nature of their attachment to Israel or explain what compelled them to act upon it, but they instinctively understood the nature of the threat to Israel and to themselves, and many of them came out in large numbers to express their solidarity with Israel through participation in mainline Jewish organizations' fund-raising drives, rallies, and other events, or through new grassroots groups sprouting up and building new networks, many of them existing primarily if not entirely in cyberspace. Many felt that they had no choice about their involvement.

This rallying around Israel in the early part of the 2000s expressed recognition of the Israeli and Jewish security dilemma. The fact that Israeli reality is never fully "normal," and that existential threats are always looming—and certainly Jews are always sensitive to them—perpetuates a special kinship bond among Jews worldwide vis-à-vis Israel. In this respect no Jew—that is, no person for whom his or her identity as Jewish is important and who cares (at minimum) about the mere survival of the Jewish people in North America, Europe, or elsewhere—can erase the memory of shared suffering or ignore current threats. In that respect the well-being of Jews in Israel is vital for Jewish survival—especially since Jews in Israel are fast becoming the largest and most distinctive segment of the Jewish people in our time. Of the thirteen to fourteen million Jews in the world today, almost half currently live in Israel. Threats to Jews in Israel are de facto threats to Jews everywhere.

That solidarity moment, too, has now passed. In the last years of the Bush administration and the first part of the Obama administration there has been another "mood swing" in which liberal Jewish Americans have increasingly expressed doubts about their relations and kinship ties to Israel, not least because of their exposure to the charge of the theory of everything. No piece captured this mood swing better than Peter Beinart's much-discussed essay in the *New York Review of Books* "The Failure of the American Jewish Establishment" (2010). In the piece and a subsequent book *The Crisis of Zionism*, Beinart chastises the American Jewish establishment for being out of touch with the views of younger American Jews and calls for a "new American Jewish story" (2012, 8). Young liberal Jews, Beinart claims, are less instinctively attached to Israel than their parents and grandparents. They reject Jewish-Israeli particularism and are instead committed to universal values and human rights. According to Beinart, establishment voices like AIPAC and the Conference of Presidents have been pushing away young Jews by supporting hawkish Israeli policies. "For several decades, the Jewish establishment has asked American Jews to check their liberalism at Zionism's door," writes

Beinart. "Now, to their horror, they are finding that many young Jews have checked their Zionism instead" (2010).

While Beinart's critique is hard hitting, we offer this counterquestion. Is it possible, given the condition of Judaism in America today, for Jews to "check their Zionism" and still remain Jews? In our view, this is becoming more and more difficult. Periodic discontent notwithstanding, Israel is now the most important element of liberal Jewish identity and mobilization in the United States. Israel is perhaps the only viable denominator in liberal American Jewry guaranteeing Jews continued communal life qua Jews. The Holocaust, which once served this function for liberal Jews, is no longer privileged Jewish property. Jewish ethnic traits have mostly disappeared among Jewish liberals. Liberal synagogues and schools face declining rates of enrollment and attendance. A Pew Survey on American Jewish demographics released in October 2013 which found that 58 percent of American Jews and 71 percent of non-Orthodox Jews are functionally "assimilated"—that is, do not practice outward expressions of Jewish identity—could not come as a surprise to anyone who has followed liberal American Judaism in recent decades (Pew Forum 2010). There remain, of course, great Jewish American writers and Yiddish revivalism, but Jews too have long since lost their cultural monopoly on these, and, more significantly, they prove ephemeral. Rates of intermarriage, meanwhile, are as high as ever, and Jewish suburban life is no longer a powerful draw.

For good or ill, Israel has emerged as the fulcrum of all world Jewish affairs. Whether political, religious, or cultural, all Jewish issues necessarily involve Israel because today the Jewish state contains all of Judaism in its noisy diversity. In this respect, only Israeli-related affairs are able to galvanize non-Orthodox Jewish identity and activism. If, then, American liberal Jews could indeed check their Zionism at the door, they would risk checking their Judaism as well.

Indeed, while Beinart gloomily forecasts a situation where young liberal Jews are disengaged from Israel because of its changing character as well as policies with which they disagree, all evidence points in the other direction. Frustration of some liberal Jews with Israeli policies notwithstanding, liberal Jews (who continue to identify as Jews) have hardly checked their Zionism at the door. Demographers and political scientists—most recently Theodore Sasson (2010)—have shown that the forms of American Jewish identification with Israel have indeed changed, but not weakened, over the last few decades. While in the seventies and eighties Jews still expressed support for Israel through large umbrella organizations like the United Jewish Appeal, more recently Jews have moved to issue-specific support in their donations and direct social and political engagement. American Jews, whether politically liberal or conservative, religious or secular, have sought to fashion Israel in their own image. The flourishing of "American friends of" Israeli schools and universities, settlements and yeshivas, developing towns, hospitals, political parties, civic movements, religious institutions, and museums is indicative of this development. Even in the Great Recession of 2008–9, in which Jewish philanthropy suffered immensely, Jewish involvement in Israeli causes remained high. Criticism of Israel by American Jews does not dispute this trend and may even confirm it. Sasson notes that the "critical orientation of diverse sets of American Jews toward Israel and their disengagement from centralized fundraising do not indicate alienation but rather the opposite: More American Jews care sufficiently about Israel to seek to influence her" (2010, 192).

Beinart identifies two poles of American Jewry: religious Jews, "deeply devoted to the state of Israel," and liberal or secular Jews committed primarily to human rights and universalistic values(2010). But he doesn't explain what exactly is Jewish about this commitment to universalistic values absent Israel and whether this commitment would be powerful enough to mobilize and sustain American Jewish identity. As much as he dreads the prospect, Beinart tacitly assumes that there could be liberal Jewish life in America without an Israeli component. The aforementioned Pew report would seem to dispute that optimistic assessment. In fact, *only* Israeli-related affairs now permit energetic communal affairs among liberal Jews. Without Israel, there are few barriers against total assimilation and even fewer outlets for social and political activism.

For American Orthodox Jews, it is altogether a different story: in principle, the failure of Zionism would not spell the end of their Judaism. Their confident practice of religious ritual ensures communal continuity and affinity, although here, too, Israel helps. Modern Orthodox American Jews are very engaged with Israeli affairs, and their concerns are often an extension of religious Zionist concerns in Israel. Even the traditionally anti-Zionist Haredi, who long believed that Zionism was blasphemy, and mostly followed the dictum *Dina-de-malchoota-Dina* ("The law of the land rules") in their countries of domicile, are now totally enmeshed with the state of Israel.

Transnational ties between the ultra-Orthodox in America and Israel have become so intense in recent decades that they are part and parcel of every aspect of Israeli life. Air travel to Israel from the United States is now dominated by the ultra-Orthodox, prompting some secular Israelis to fly on the Sabbath to avoid prayers. There is hardly a domestic social or political debate in Israel in which the ultra-Orthodox do not participate, hoping to gain accommodations from the state and shape it in their own image. This means, however, that they are to some degree co-opted by Zionism, exemplified by new Haredi units in the military and, most recently, the effort of politician Ya'ir Lapid and his Yesh Atid Party to expand the draft to Haredis. Even if their version of Judaism rejects basic tenets of traditional Zionism and modern state institutions, the fact that Haredis in Israel now mostly speak Modern Hebrew rather than Yiddish shows that they have not been immune from Israeli influence. Their participation in high and low affairs of state inevitably makes them take part in the Israeli project.

What about liberal Jews? As has often been said, the "greatest enemy" of the Jews in America is their success. Although they continue to crave integration into all aspects of American life, and often achieve it, many remain concerned with Jewish survival and the perpetuation of Jewish identity. The high rates of Jewish assimilation show that this is not so easy. Yet this is an issue of the liberal society more broadly. In liberal societies, identity begins at home, and Jews must find Jewish mates or non-Jews who adopt a Jewish way of life. The immense success of the Jewish dating site JDate among liberal Jews reveals that the desire to perpetuate Jewish identity remains strong. Once married and seeking to participate in communal Jewish life, young Jews quickly discover that the options for "nonreligious" participation are always dominated by Israel. Usually advocating political liberalism, young liberal Jews then have the opportunity to express their principles by trying to influence the domestic and foreign affairs of Israel. Like Orthodox Jews, they hope to shape the country in their own image. Liberal institutions such as the New Israel Fund and the advocacy group J Street, founded in 2007, have sprung up and indeed flourished as a result of these concerns.

JDate and J Street are the twin pillars of American Jewish liberalism today. JDate represents Jewish particularism: keeping the tribe going. J Street represents Jewish universalism: making the tribe conform to a universal liberal ideal. JDate is fairly self-explanatory: find a Jewish mate. J Street has had a more difficult time setting its boundaries. Its spokespeople have declared that one should criticize Israel policies but without hostility, and indeed with love, for the Jewish state itself. Whatever the plausibility of J Street's approach, it is subject to clear pressure to remain pro-Israel. Was it perceived to be anti-Israel or "post-Zionist," it would be quickly marginalized (as post-Zionism is a marginal phenomenon in Israel), and its clout would be damaged in Washington. To be sure, some American Jews have openly embraced "post-Zionism," prominent Jewish intellectuals like the late Tony Judt among them. But these individuals carry a flag with no army—can Jews as a group be rallied to post-Zionism? Thus far, at least, the influence of "post-Zionism" within the American Jewish community has been negligible.

For the JDate and J Street crowds, religious affiliation tends to be to the more liberal streams of Judaism. Some, but not very many, more observant Jews use JDate to look for a prospective *shidduch* (matchup), and a few participate in J Street. There is, of course, a correlation between strict Jewish religious observance and nonleftist politics. But liberal Jews in America cannot ignore the growing influence of orthodoxy on Jewish affairs and practices in the diaspora and especially in Israel. This paradoxically forces liberal Jews who want to remain Jews to be even more engaged in Israeli affairs, for the battles to determine the future of Jewish practice and belonging are being fought not in Brooklyn or Los Angeles but in the streets of Jerusalem and Tel Aviv, and in the yeshivas and liberal Jewish learning centers of Jerusalem, along with the Supreme Court and Knesset of Israel.

Debate over a new conversion bill in the Israeli Knesset in the summer of 2010 again proved that battles about the future of Judaism and Jewish identity are fought in Israel. The controversy erupted when the member of Knesset David Rotem introduced a conversion bill in the Knesset aimed at allowing non-Jewish Russians in Israel to convert, while at the same time granting the Orthodox rabbinate the exclusive power to certify conversions. Uproar in the diaspora ensued, as Jews from liberal streams feared it would invalidate their own processes of conversion. Prime Minister Benjamin Netanyahu said the bill threatened to "tear the Jewish people apart" (Barak 2010) and appointed the head of the Jewish Agency, Natan Sharansky, to come up with some kind of compromise. Paradoxically, the uproar in Israel served as an at least potentially fruitful opportunity for Jews around the world for dialogue on vexing communal issues.

Diaspora interest in the issues raised by the Israeli conversion bill, though perhaps noteworthy for the unusual intensity of response in the diaspora, is surely not new. For the past two decades, the so-called "Who is a Jew" or conversion issue has been the catalyst for diaspora-Israeli antagonisms, but also, as Natan Sharansky noted at the time, for conversation and dialogue (*Yediot Ahronot* 2010). More broadly speaking, the influence of ultra-Orthodox Jews in determining laws in Israel has brought them into direct contact (if only in confrontation) with liberal Jews. An earlier "Who is a Jew" controversy, which erupted in 1988, remains the best illustration of this fact. At that time, the Orthodox parties in Israel demanded changing the "Law of Return" (which allows all Jews the right to immigrate to Israel should they choose), in accordance with a stricter interpretation of Jewish conversion, which would invalidate some of the conversions performed by conservative and reform rabbis in America. In response, subsequently, leaders of organized American Jewry declared an open revolt against Israel. Ultra-Orthodox leaders, however, supported the effort. This was the first time that the bitter hostility between American non-Orthodox leaders and the New York–based Lubavitch Hasidic movement—led by the late Rabbi Menachem Mendel Schneerson—was injected into the Israeli arena with such ferocity. The Lubavitchers' ardor and money ignited Israeli religious zealousness and the move to change Israel's legal definition of who is a Jew. It left an indelible mark on the future direction of Israeli politics and society. Dr. Ismar Schorsch, head of the Conservative Movement, commented: "This is an American affair which the Lubavitcher Rebbe is forcing upon Israel. . . . Israel is the battlefield" (Shain 2007, 81).

We see, then, that disagreements of American liberal Jews with Israeli policies actually serve as a catalyst for communal activism, at a time when other forms of communal activism, religious and cultural, continue to decline. If American Jews can dispense with Israel, as Beinart claims, then he should explain how else they might mobilize as a community within the United States. Liberal involvement in Israel, on issues of particular domestic legislation and on foreign policy through institutions like J Street, reveals that liberal American Jews *require* Israel, if only to kick around.

Liberal Jews in America and others who claim that Israel should "end the occupation" usually do not believe that this would harm Israel. They rather believe that Israel, a country with a powerful military, could handle the compromise. In fact, they say, the resolution of the conflict would be good for Israel for moral and demographic reasons.

Whatever the changing views in Israel, a significant portion of the Israeli electorate and its leadership subscribes to this view as well. These include President Shimon Peres, former prime minister Ehud Barak, head of the opposition Tziporah Livni, as well as former prime ministers Rabin and Ehud Olmert. As prime minister, Ariel Sharon, the lifelong hawk, led the disengagement from Gaza, much to the chagrin of many on the Israeli right and supporters in the diaspora. Sharon came to believe that the Israeli presence in the West Bank would damage security over the long run. Whatever his private thoughts on the matter, current prime minister Benjamin Netanyahu has himself said that Israel would recognize a Palestinian state under certain conditions. With the possible exception of Naftali Bennett's new Ha'beit Hayehudi Party, withdrawal from territory remains consensus opinion.

Yet trying to resolve the Israeli-Palestinian conflict has not been easy. Shlomo Avineri, the doyen of Israeli political scientists, has argued that even though the two-state solution is the only viable option, it may not be viable at the present moment. No agreement could be reached, he asserts, on Jerusalem, refugees, security, and settlement evacuation. Avineri (2010) claims that even if an agreement could be reached the American role would be only as a guarantor rather than as an initiator: "The solution is likely to come from the ground up, not from the top down."

Perhaps no other world conflict has received as much attention as the Israeli-Palestinian one, and every president feels compelled to get involved, no matter what other geopolitical issues are at stake. Yet as Barack Obama has learned, focusing on it, especially in diplomacy, is a sure path to frustration. This is not to say, of course, that American involvement in Israeli-Palestinian, or Israeli-Arab, affairs has always been futile. American administrations have surely played a part in settling some aspects of the Israeli-Arab conflict when conditions were ripe—though perhaps not always as critical a part as some think. When Israel signed a peace agreement with Egypt in 1979, as Fouad Ajami explained, "It was initiated by the two parties and blessed by a cornered America" (1981, 163). The Palestinian question, meanwhile, was not decisive to Egypt. "For him [Sadat] the question was not Palestine, but Egypt" (163). When King Hussein of Jordan signed his peace treaty with Israel in 1994, the Palestinian issue was secondary. American involvement, important though it was, was by no means the decisive factor. Even the Oslo Agreement, purportedly initiated by President Clinton, was initially drafted in secrecy in Norway by Israelis and Palestinians. Despite all of this, the view that "American involvement is paramount" remains prevalent in Washington and in the region. Though tempered by the recent storms in the region, the much-suffering American diplomat still nobly believes that goodwill and energy should be enough to get a deal done.

President Obama had rebuked his predecessor President Bush for getting involved in the Israeli-Palestinian issue only late in his presidency. By contrast, he would be there from day one. The inevitable letdowns have promoted the theory of everything. All frustrations from other arenas that accompany American involvement in the region, from Afghanistan to Iraq, the war on terror and the Arab revolutions, Muslim anger at America, and even the occasional rift with European allies, are often viewed through the prism of the unsolved Israeli-Palestinian conflict. America expects, and is expected, to break all impasses, and when it does not, something nefarious must be blocking its way.

But can anyone remember the last time America was able to bring about an enduring solution to ethnic conflict in the Middle East, or, in fact, anywhere? What America should do in the Middle East is in fact an enigma. It is no longer true (if it ever was) that resolution of the Israeli-Palestinian issue would help America further its other goals in the Middle East. For American goals in the Middle East are themselves now decidedly unclear.

The difficulties of the conflict, combined with the belief in its inherent solvability, concentrates undue attention on the power of the Israel lobby. If this compares to any other situation in American politics, it would be to the Armenian lobby, which recently suffered a significant blow. In 2009, Armenia and Turkey signed a peace agreement with the assistance of Secretary of State Hillary Clinton. For years, the understanding in America, and elsewhere, was that the Armenian lobby dictated the terms of US-Armenian relations and the terms of discussion between the United States and Turkey. This view was widely held in Turkey, in Armenia, and in the media and scholarly worlds. Some Armenian Americans consider the new peace agreement treason and a betrayal of the nation and memory of the Armenian genocide. Raffi Hovannisian, an Armenian American who became Armenia's first foreign minister, echoed the frustration of the Armenian diaspora: "The signing of the two diplomatic 'protocols' between Armenia and Turkey might indeed constitute the latest entry in the ledger of crimes committed, and covered up, against the Armenian nation . . . with a small group of improperly elected leaders apparently racing toward a forsaking of both identity and interest"

(Hovannisian 2009). But few on Capitol Hill, or in the White House, paid any attention to these opinions. The opportunity was there, and it was seized. When conditions are ripe, peace treaties can be signed, lobbying notwithstanding. The same applies for the Israeli-Palestinian conflict and other now intractable issues in the region. If the situation permits it, diplomatic inroads may be made. We are still in the process of discovering whether the ongoing Arab revolutions will present such a "ripe" moment, or, as is regrettably more likely, a further geopolitical hindrance. Yet even if there were a breakthrough, the theory of everything might be difficult for some diehards to leave behind. For friends and foes of the Jews, as well as the Jews themselves, "Jewish Power" has always been an attractive proposition, long before Jews obtained even a semblance of it. But with a perplexing reality in the Middle East and elsewhere, one should say to Americans, Europeans, Arabs, Muslims, and Israelis: dispense with the theory of everything. No one really knows what to do in the region. The theory is confusing, and we are already confused enough.

Notes

A version of this chapter appeared as "Between JDate and J Street: US Foreign Policy and the Liberal Jewish Dilemma in America," in *Israel Journal of Foreign Affairs* 5, no. 3 (2011). Reprinted with permission.

1.   On anti-Semitism on US campuses, see Bombardieri (2002) and Wohlgelertner (2002).

2.   See the exchange on the subject between Lind (2002) and Garfinkle (2002).

References

Ajami, Fouad. 1981. *The Arab Predicament*. New York: Cambridge University Press.

Avineri, Shlomo. 2010. Speech given at Rabin Center, Tel Aviv, July 27.

Beinart, Peter. 2010. "The Failure of the American Jewish Establishment." *New York Review of Books*, June 10. www.nybooks.com/articles/archives/2010/jun/10/failure-american-jewish-establishment/?pagination=false.

———. 2012. *The Crisis of Zionism*. New York: Picador.

Bombardieri, Marcella. 2002. "On Campuses, Critics of Israel Fend Off a Label." *Boston Globe*, September 21.

Garfinkle, Adam. 2002. "Israel Lobby (Part II)." *Prospect Magazine,* September.

Ha'aretz. 2009. "Fatah Memo: We Lost Hope in Obama for Caving to Zionist Pressure." October 13.

Hovannisian, Raffi. 2009. "An Open Letter to the Armenian Nation." *Armenian Weekly*, October 12. www.armenianweekly.com/2009/10/12/raffi-hovannisian-an-open-letter-to-the-armenian-nation-protocols-and-preconditions/.

Lind, Michael. 2002. "The Israel Lobby." *Prospect Magazine,* April.

Mayer, Egon, Barry Kosmin, and Ariela Keysar. 2001. *American Jewish Identity Survey: An Exploration in the Demography and Outlook of a People.* New York: Graduate Center of the City University of New York.

Mearsheimer, John. 2010. "The Future of Palestine: Righteous Jews vs. the New Afrikaners." April 29. Palestine Center, Washington, DC. *MRzine*, April 30. http://mrzine.monthlyreview.org/2010/mearsheimer300410.html.

Mellman, Mark. 2009. "The Jews and the Democrats." *Hill*, October 7. http://thehill.com/opinion/columnists/mark-mellman/62091-the-jews-and-the-democrats.

Pew Forum, Religion and Public Life Project. 2010. "A Portrait of Jewish Americans." October 1. www.pewforum.org/2013/10/01/jewish-american-beliefs-attitudes-culture-survey/.

Ravid, Barak. 2010. "Interior Minister Yishai: Absence of Conversion Law Poses Danger to Jewish People." *Ha'aretz*, July 18.

Rosen, Jonathan. 2001. "The Uncomfortable Question of Anti-Semitism." *New York Times*, November 4.

Rosenthal, Steven T. 2001. *Irreconcilable Differences: The Waning of the American Jewish Love Affair with Israel.* Hanover, NH: Brandeis University Press/University Press of New England.

Sasson, Theodore. 2010. "Mass Mobilization to Direct Engagement: American Jews' Changing Relationship to Israel." *Israel Studies* 15 (Summer): 173–95.

Shain, Yossi. 2007. *Kinship and Diaspora in International Affairs.* Ann Arbor: University of Michigan Press.

Summers, Larry. 2002. "Address at Morning Prayers, Memorial Church, Cambridge, Massachusetts, September 17, 2002." http://president.harvard.edu/speeches/2002/morningprayers.html.

Traub, James. 2009. "The New Israel Lobby." *New York Times Magazine*, September 13. www.nytimes.com/2009/09/13/magazine/13JStreet-t.html?pagewanted=all.

Wohlgelertner, Elli. 2002. "Take Back the University." *Jerusalem Post*, August 9.

Yediot Ahronot. 2010. "Sharansky, US Rabbis Discuss Conversion Bill." June 14.

CHAPTER FOUR

Palestinians, Diasporas, and US Foreign Policy

Mohammed A. Bamyeh

Palestinians have never had any influence of any kind on any US foreign policy. By contrast, pro-Israeli interests have until recently had an unusual level of influence on all significant US policies on the Israeli-Palestinian conflict, as well as on US approaches to larger issues pertaining to the Middle East as a whole. That one may respond to this assertion by pointing to occasional disagreements between US and Israeli policy makers only confirms the point: for such observations question only why there was not *complete* convergence of all policies. The complete omnipotence of the pro-Israeli lobby especially in the past three decades, and the complete absence of any Palestinian influence, are hardly theoretical propositions. That lobby has routinely been able to get almost *all* of Congress to issue declarations of unquestionable fidelity to Israel, even at points when Israel was identified by the rest of the world as an aggressor. There are very rare exceptions in which the Israel lobby does not get its way. I will later discuss the specific nature of three such exceptions—the sale of AWACS aircraft to Saudi Arabia in the 1980s; President Bush's withholding of loan guarantees to Israel in 1991; and the much more recent failure to persuade Congress to approve President Obama's initial request for authorization to launch a punitive attack on Syria in September 2013. But the general rule is that the lobby almost always gets what it wants, and more completely than is possible to explain in terms of any rational US policy goals. The clearest example from recent times is the Obama administration's otherwise unfathomable staunch opposition to the Palestinian statehood bid at the United Nations, a position that went not simply against a vast majority of world opinion but also against expressed US policy principles themselves on the conflict. That US diplomacy in that case appeared so hostile to a Palestinian effort to assert, if only symbolically, their right to statehood cannot be explained by any rational US interests. Further, such an expression of this vehement hostility as the subsequent withdrawal of the United States from UNESCO after that organization admitted Palestine cannot be explained away as a simple enactment of a congressional mandate to do so. For here the question becomes: Why did Congress decide, with virtual unanimity, to pass such a mandate even as the official US position recognized the right of the Palestinians to an independent state?

The Obama administration, which was initially reputed to be the "least friendly" of US administrations to Israel in decades, entered office on the auspicious note of withdrawing the nomination of Charles Freeman to head the National Intelligence Council, entirely because of pressure from the pro-Israeli lobby. That same administration also began its career immediately after the Gaza war that ended in January 2009 and that resulted in the destruction of the entire infrastructure of civil services for a desperately poor and completely besieged part of the world, the death of 1,500 people, the maiming of thousands more, and the dislocation of most of the population. By any standard of imagination it was a war crime, denounced everywhere in the world, *except* in the United States. Then president-elect Obama, aiming to strike a note of conciliation with the Muslim world, found it advisable to register his disapproval by staying completely silent rather than making any statements. In his first foray into the conflict, he publicly demanded a freeze on Israeli settlement activities in the occupied territories as a condition for meaningful negotiations—a position that again appeared perfectly logical, given its conformity to the vast majority of world opinion and an acknowledgment of the status of a key long-standing obstacle to any realistic conception of peace. Within a few months, Obama retreated from that position and essentially adopted the Israeli government position, more or less like all other presidents before him. But in this case, this alignment was with the position of the most right-wing government in Israeli history, filled with ultra-nationalists who dreamed of a Jewish state purified of all Arab presence and religious fanatics of the kind that one would be horrified to see sitting in the governments of neighboring countries.

I do not wish to go on proving what others have demonstrated so well (Mearsheimer and Walt 2007). The influence of the pro-Israel lobby on US foreign policy is an established, demonstrable, documented, and clear fact. There can be no sharper contrast to it than the absence, even demonization, of *any* Palestinian perspective. This disparity in influence suggests two elementary propositions: one concerning the Palestinian struggle, another concerning US foreign policy. For the Palestinians, their cause cannot be pursued on the basis of simple "realistic" arithmetic, since that kind of straightforward "realism" means that they have no hope. Edward Said was discerning enough to observe that the Palestinian cause had to be carried out as a "willed" struggle, rather than one that obeyed the calculus of realism.

Indeed, the most energetic moments of Palestinian mobilization and activism were historically associated precisely with their most desperate situations. The 1936 revolt against the British authorities pitted a largely peasant population with little prior experience with mass mobilization against the British Empire at the height of its power. The modern emergence of an organized Palestinian national mass movement took place in the aftermath of the 1967 War, when Arab leaders who had adopted the Palestinian cause as their own suffered a crushing defeat, and when all of historic Palestine ended up under Israeli jurisdiction. And when Israel marginalized that chapter of Palestinian history as it pushed the PLO far away to Tunisia in 1982, it was confronted with a completely surprising Palestinian intifada in 1987, whose genesis defied everything sociologists knew about the "determining circumstances" of social movements (Farsoun and Landis 1990).

This lesson has to be kept in mind because it is what the Palestinians themselves know about their cause. There is no absence of "realism" in the familiar (and narrow) sense of the term, but struggles of this kind have never been resolved by realistic people—indeed, they cannot be. It is for this reason that elsewhere I argued that ethical questions rather than realpolitik need to be foregrounded if one really wants a solution, since willed struggles are driven not simply by conflict over material resources such as land or water—although these are important—but by a deeper ethical sense of being aggrieved and a victim of profound injustice. That is why the Palestinians cannot really be "taught a lesson," as has been the hope of countless Israeli campaigns. Their cause is just.

I have explored the social psychology of this willed determination elsewhere, arguing that its main origins are traced to a common conception among especially diaspora Palestinians that their dispossession is (1) temporary, (2) unjust, (3) unchosen, and (4) accidental (Bamyeh 2003). These standpoints led to a heavy investment in institutions and practices of memory: that is, the production of town and village histories, the maintenance of extended family networks in the diaspora and even of former class positions, an educational and familial orientation of children to the original homeland, and the building of a globally connected civil society that to a certain extent became integrated into the PLO and also helped support the Palestinian Authority. The PLO itself, as I have argued before, may be regarded as a diaspora organization, especially in its first two decades. As such it exemplified for much of its history the influence of the diaspora perspective on Palestinian politics.

Yet the division of Palestinian political energies between diaspora and nondiaspora elements should be placed in proper context. It is true that for much of its history Palestinian struggle rotated around two slogans, *sumud* (steadfastness) and *'awda* (return), corresponding to the perspectives of nondiaspora and diaspora Palestinians respectively. Yet in practice there was little need in Palestinian politics to prioritize one slogan over the other. The long periods of absence of any peace prospects obviously created no compulsion for seeing Palestinian struggle as anything other than integral. *Sumud* was conducted with an eye to the demonstrated fate of the diaspora, and *'awda* corresponded well to the belief that its best hope consisted of a successful *sumud* strategy. Only at Oslo in 1993 could one identify, for the first time in Palestinian history, some hints that a choice might have to be made between these two perspectives. But even then such a choice was delayed, as all important issues, including the status of refugees and the right of return, were conceptualized as end points of what turned out to be a hopelessly stalled process.

There is no evidence that the input of the Palestinian diaspora into Palestinian politics differed in any substantial way from that of nondiaspora Palestinians. All factions of the PLO, as well as Hamas, were and are active both in the diaspora and in the occupied territories. The inflow of diaspora capital into the occupied territories has helped strengthen local civil society, foster economic development, and alleviate the recurrent hardships attendant to a life under countless blockades and harassments.[1] Apart from the question of the right of return, significant as it is, there are no other political issues pertaining to the Palestinian cause that are specifically associated with the diaspora.

While the role of the diaspora in Palestinian politics has been significant, it is a mistake to overstate that role or suggest that the diaspora is a complicating factor in the ongoing struggle. Indeed, persistent attempts by various Israeli governments between 1967 and 1993 to create an organizational divide between diaspora and nondiaspora Palestinians have failed in spite of the massive coercive and other resources at the disposal of the Israeli state. Such efforts involved Israeli insistence on negotiating only with a select leadership of the population living under its occupation and only over local issues, while rejecting any dealing with the PLO. The reason for such a failure is clearly associated with absence of any real incentive for any Palestinian leadership, anywhere, to cement a national divide in exchange for the next to nothing that was always on the table.

In addition, the diaspora, while a crucial factor in maintaining Palestinian identity and organized presence worldwide, never played a complicating factor in the conflict. The most intense periods of violence are associated with local resistance resulting from the frustrations of the Oslo process on the ground, and not with any input by diaspora elements, whose cause—namely the right of return—was simply being postponed. In fact, the onset of Oslo showed how the typical diaspora response to the prospects of a resolution was a hopeful but restrained attitude, not a rejectionist or obstructionist stand. The diaspora investment in Palestine after 1993 was in fact largely economic, educational, and developmental. There was little evidence of any effective diaspora incitement to the symbolic politics of martyrdom, which evolved later under purely local conditions.[2]

Palestinians in the United States

In the United States, diaspora Palestinian communities are of relatively recent origins. They tend to commingle in the larger sea of migrant Arab and Muslim communities in US suburbs and also to foster the familiar pattern of investment in practices of memory that is perhaps a defining feature of modern Palestinian identity. In addition, they contribute to civic organizations with charitable mandates in the occupied territories, including the Jerusalem Fund for Education and Community Development and the Holy Land Foundation (one of the largest Islamic charities in the United States until it was shut down and had five of its officers jailed in a 2008 retrial for alleged ties to Hamas).

While incidental migrations to the United States are documented as far back as a century ago, sizable Palestinian migration to the United States began only after 1965 and gained more momentum only after the Gulf War of 1991. Currently, the Palestinian population in the United States is estimated at about 250,000, although US census data (disputed for a variety of reasons) put the number at 72,000 (Cainkar, Abunimah, and Raei 2004; Arab American Institute 2006). This population tends to be concentrated around certain metropolitan areas, notably Chicago, Detroit, New York, San Francisco, Cleveland, Houston, and Jacksonville. Cainkar, Abunimah, and Raei (2004) note that the lure of the old country looms large among such recent migrants, and many, including longtime residents, say to interviewers that they do not intend to stay in the United States permanently. Since Oslo, one can document a pattern of "circulatory migration," with families or their children being sent back to spend some time in Jordan or the occupied territories. The Palestinian census of 1997 found that seven thousand Palestinian residents of the occupied territories (excluding East Jerusalem) were born in the United States. Remarkably, 83 percent of those were under the age of nineteen, compared to 43 percent of all other Palestinian residents of the territories who were born outside Palestine (Cainkar, Abunimah, and Raei 2004).

Following Douglas Massey's seminal work on patterns of Mexican immigration, Cainkar, Abunimah, and Raei (2004) found that many Palestinians in the United States likewise prefer to keep strong ties to Palestine—even when their mobility is hampered by economic realities—and think of the economic opportunities offered by life in the United States as a means to provide better for an eventual family life in Palestine itself. These expressed strategies become easier to understand if we keep in mind that individual Palestinians tend to define themselves largely in terms of their family links and obligations, which are now transnational in scope. Hardships brought about by the Israeli occupation have only strengthened family and social bonds among Palestinians, since the traditional structure of mutual bonds and obligations became an even more indispensable means of survival.

"Circulatory migration" is of course only one of the manifestations of modern immigration in general, and it seems to be connected to the fact that communication technologies as well as the structure of globalization processes in which immigration is implicated allow for continuing and varied links. Thus a "diaspora" here is more than a sum total of a dispersed population; it is an essential and continuing feature of modern Palestinian identity. Of course, diasporic consciousness among Palestinians is historically novel, and it may indeed be compared to the very old conception of Jews as diasporic people. That is to say, while being diasporic defines the experience of the majority of Palestinians and is now a defining feature of Palestinian national identity, compared to Jews Palestinians had little time to translate that diasporic consciousness into institutional formats, although their accomplishments in that regard remain quite impressive—one need only mention the PLO between 1967 and 1993, for example, as the ultimate organizational embodiment of the Palestinian diaspora.

That there is an active Palestinian diasporic civil society and political organization is clear, as well as the fact that especially in the United States this civil society lived under the shadow of government intimidation and paranoia even before the events of September 11, 2001. Antiterrorism laws in particular have done much to push charitable activity underground, as such laws have made little distinction between humanitarian support, community development, and direct support for the political or military program of militant organizations. The prosecutors of the Holy Land Foundation case, for example, conceded that a "substantial amount" of the organization's funds went to worthy causes. Yet the Foundation seemed to have had some natural ties to what is generically called "Hamas" (which is still a substantially charitable organization that only recently entered politics and even more recently became defined by militancy). The blanket repression of everything else that the Holy Land Foundation did showed little understanding of the complex web of social affiliations, in which certain participants, as one would expect under circumstances of unresolved national conflict, have militant sentiments. On the other hand, one effect of this repressive environment has been the increased expectation that Arab and Muslim community organizations and public intellectuals should do more to counter pervasive negative images. For more than a decade, US universities have been hard pressed to meet increased demands for knowledge about Muslims in general, and the demand for Arabic courses in particular has been rising faster than available expertise can meet it. To these new facts, associated with the increased publicness and salience of Islam in American life under hostile conditions, one may add another demographic factor whose real impact is still hard to measure. The eventual return to the United States of hundreds of thousands of troops who had been serving in Iraq, some of whom I saw in my own classes later as seekers of deeper knowledge about peoples and traditions they confronted but did not understand, will likely crystallize into a new stock of knowledge about the Middle East in general. Finally, one must add the potential knowledge impact of the recent Arab revolutions, which are said to have inspired the Occupy movement in the United States and also to have awakened a hitherto dormant interest in peoples who were once regarded as too distant from our ways and values. The status of Palestine remains an integral part of this more general, evolving knowledge about Islam and Arabs.

Since especially the late 1960s and early 1970s, the US government's perspective on the conflict has generally seemed beholden to sources of advice that are substantially friendly to Israel, and alternative views have been routinely suppressed. Such alternative views can prosper little in the lopsided context of a nonexistent Palestinian lobby and a formidable Israeli one. It seems, in fact, that the only entry Palestinians may have in the lobbying game for now is through a perhaps more balancing influence exercised by a different *Jewish* group, such as J Street (which defines itself as "pro-Israel" but also "pro-peace").

The reasons for the absence of an effective Palestinian pressure group vary, although the relative newness of Palestinian communities in the United States is certainly a factor. Diasporic Palestinian political energies have been largely invested in building the PLO and Palestinian civil society in exile, as well as in cementing social bonds and maintaining a sense of Palestinian identity within a globally dispersed community. Much of this has had to be done from scratch, amid challenging conditions that included loss of property and livelihood in Palestine, the need to provide for extended families, and the novelty of Palestinian diasporic life. Investing in lobbying seemingly distant institutions as US Congress seemed for a long time not only unrealistic, given the vastly superior resources and entrenched influence of the Israeli lobby, but also a wasteful distraction from the task of rebuilding a Palestinian society in exile. Building pressure groups apparently required strategies and skills that were quite distinct from those of building resistance movements whose primary aim was seen to involve mobilizing Palestinian society, where the tasks were realizable and clear, rather than influencing US foreign policy, where the likelihood of success seemed remote.

In addition, mobilizing Palestinian identity in diaspora conditions entailed the cultivation of new leadership that was quite distinct in approach, and sometimes in social origins, from traditional, pre-1948 forms of leadership to which Palestinians had been accustomed. As in much of the Levant, pre-1948 Palestinian society was to a substantial degree led by a class of notables who came from well-established families, each with strong roots in a particular city or town. Elements of that leadership pattern survived in diaspora conditions, but such conditions proved conducive to the emergence of nontraditional, new leadership that did not correspond to the old class structures of Palestinian society.[3] This new leadership was initially less connected to the structures of global and even regional power, and its base was the refugee camps that became the focus of political life of the new Palestinians activist class. Only after 1974, with Arafat's speech at the United Nations, did the political energy of this new class begin to manifest itself in diplomatic relations in an international arena beyond the Arab world. However, at that time US-Israeli relations had consolidated into a form of strategic alliance solidified by Cold War calculations, and the Israeli lobby was ascendant.

Given these circumstances, Palestinian leadership found it far easier to seek access to US policy makers through surrogate sources, such as Arab governments that had good relations with the United States. This was indeed the preferred and seemingly only realistic strategy, given the organizational difficulties in the United States and the prohibitions against the PLO as a terrorist organization that were in effect until Oslo. Yet that strategy involved two major shortcomings. First, access to the United States through foreign governments reached at best only the executive branch, leaving no impression on a Congress that remained, as critics have long held, an Israeli "occupied territory" immune to any countervailing pressures. In fact, one of the few anticorruption undercover operations aimed at members of Congress, the so-called operation Abscam (short for "Arab scam") in 1980, targeted *only* the handful of members of Congress who were likely to be sympathetic to Arab voices, in effect silencing whatever alternative perspective, meager as it was, might have been taking shape in Congress.

The second shortcoming of the strategy of relying on surrogate Arab allies had to do with the fact that, nationalist rhetoric aside, the interests of the Palestinian diaspora had no natural convergence with the primary goal of most governments, which was their own survival, as Michael Hudson (1979) has long demonstrated. The politics of legitimacy did mean that Arab governments of all stripes had to rhetorically uphold the Palestinian cause as sacrosanct, but they ignored it in practice, since its resolution or lack thereof did not fit neatly into their goal of survival as new regimes that lacked rootedness in society and relied for survival on a combination of authoritarianism and foreign alliances. That was especially the case after Nasser, for whom populism seemed to work for a while in making the regime appear somewhat more rooted in society and more independent of the games of the great powers. But populism alone did not alter the basic structure of the dilemma of the old Arab regimes, and Nasser's defeat in 1967 refocused his own energies, as well as those of other Arab governments, given that all of them were historically novel and rootless, on the task of ensuring their own survival through the imperatives of global alliances. That orientation left little room for an earnest and systematic pursuit of a resolution of the Palestinian cause, which was left to the Palestinians alone. Palestinians themselves knew that, and the rapid consolidation of the PLO after 1967 is the greatest manifestation of that growing awareness. Yet the PLO itself had to find allies wherever it could, and whatever factions within it (for example, the Popular Front for the Liberation of Palestine [PFLP]) saw a revolution against Arab governments as part of the larger struggle to liberate Palestine found themselves in a distinct minority. The one hope for a change in this state of affairs has resided in the long-term dynamics of the Arab Spring: if it produces, at the very least, governments more sensitive to local public opinion, their strategy will have to take more seriously the fact that such opinion is almost entirely sympathetic to the Palestinian plight.

From its beginning the cause of Palestine enjoyed an enormous symbolic significance throughout the Arab and Muslim world, and its symbolic status only increased over time. That status had something to do with ethics of decolonization and a widespread perception, across much of the Third World, of Palestine as an emblem of the unsettled account with colonialism. From an anticolonial Third World perspective, the tragedy of Palestine was that it had succumbed to settler colonialism precisely at the point when other colonized peoples were gaining their independence. In addition, Palestine had always enjoyed an element of religious significance due to its status as a holy land, for Muslims as well as non-Muslims. And Israel had always appeared to almost all peoples of the Middle East as an imperial, Western implant that had nothing to do with their traditions and as an unwelcome disruption of a common regional civilization. The founders of Israel themselves saw Israel as largely part of the "West"; David Ben-Gurion, for example, moved to Palestine in 1915, when the Arab population was a vast majority, but never bothered to learn Arabic, even though he learned seven other languages. His dictum, that Israel exists in the Middle East only geographically, is now a position so commonly accepted in Israeli culture that very few Israelis read or watch Arab media or literature, know Arabic, or express interest in the Arab culture surrounding them on all

sides. And Israel's policies of occupation, dispossession, and vastly disproportionate violence have done little to encourage the people living all around it to
regard it as anything other than an imperialist, foreign implant.

All these associations gave the Palestinian cause an aura of regional and
even global prestige that was most registered in public opinion, though it
rarely resulted in meaningful governmental action. Still, that aura contributed to the rapid international recognition that the PLO received almost
everywhere in the 1970s (when the United States and Israel became isolated in
their refusal to extend that recognition). In the United States, this aura meant
that in principle Palestinians could ride the wave of other groups, especially
Arab and Muslim, that were beginning to take organizational form in the
1980s, notably through the Arab American Anti-Discrimination Committee
(ADC) and the Council on American-Islamic Relations (CAIR). But even
though such groups were sympathetic to the Palestinian cause, they had to
cater to a broad spectrum of issues affecting their communities, which mainly
concerned problems they faced in the United States. Palestine thus remained
an orphan, the object of universal sympathy by those who had other urgent
tasks to worry about and who calculated that fostering Palestinian interests in
the formidable landscape of a hostile Congress would take all their energies
and likely deliver little in the way of results.

US Foreign Policy

That we could document the influence of the pro-Israel lobby does not fully
explain, I think, its success, given that it has complicated other US interests—for example, US relations with the entire Arab and Islamic worlds; the
persistent disruption of regional stability in the larger Middle East that this
conflict has caused; and the divergence of US views on this conflict from
the views of virtually all of its own other allies, including most European
countries. Willingness to pay such a price is probably not easy to explain by
successful lobbying alone, or by the alternative explanation that the relationship between the United States and Israel is one of "strategic alliance," since
the purpose of such an alliance is far from clear, especially in a post–Cold
War world. And compared to Israel, the United States has had far more useful regional allies from a materialist point of view: the oil-producing Gulf
countries, for example, have always been willing to deliver more tangible and
necessary goods without coercion or force.

Overall, it is clear by now that the continued struggle for Palestine has exacted an enormous strategic cost on the United States—one that can be measured, for example, by the resulting collapse of all old Arab regimes within a decade of 1948; their replacement with anti-Western or otherwise unstable political arrangements; the failure of the so-called Baghdad pact in the 1950s (which would have established the equivalent of NATO in the Middle East); a series of catastrophic regional wars; and the universal resentment toward the United States that one finds almost everywhere in the Middle East outside Israel. All the peoples of the Middle East have suffered tremendous human disruptions because of the continuation of this conflict. But strategically speaking, the United States has also paid an enormous price for its lopsided policy.

It may seem therefore difficult to explain, from a purely rational perspective, why such a price is paid, given that alternative paths and policies are possible. It has been suggested that there is no clear payoff for the United States for resolving the Israeli-Palestinian conflict. However, the question of "payoff" can be assessed in various ways. If one attends to the question of the "strategic cost" of the conflict rather than immediate results—which would themselves be tremendous—the argument for active and evenhanded policy becomes obvious. That means that US "interests" here are decided not simply in old-fashioned terms of realpolitik but also in terms more appropriate for current global realities, where public sentiments and open, less conflict-laden zones are as much legitimate policy goals as diplomatic relations and formal state-level agreements.

Rather than asking *why* irrational policies are followed, it may be more fruitful to ask *how* they are followed. The "why" question presupposes a purpose, but the "how" question focuses on the dynamics of policy rather than its purpose. Therefore, the "how" question would be the more appropriate one to ask when it appears likely that the policy has no plausible strategic purpose or, relatedly, where the policy is supplied to the government from without. In this case diaspora organizations become more relevant, since they function as sources of policy only in the *absence* of policy. This becomes evident when we consider how in all instances in which AIPAC did *not* get its way, that was largely because the US government had been committed to a specific policy with rational foundations focusing on tangible interests or comprehensible strategic goals (rather than on a dogma of "strategic alliance"—largely fruitless—with a pariah state). The well-known episode of the sale of AWCS to

Saudi Arabia, which is often cited by defenders of the Israel lobby as evidence that it is weaker than we tend to think, proves actually the point that lobbying is less effective when it goes against a clearly defined and pursued policy of the United States. Saudi Arabia, and the Gulf region in general, is not Palestine. The United States had identified Saudi Arabia in particular as a country worthy of specific commitment already in 1945, and that commitment remained thereafter immune from counterlobbying pressures. The Gulf region, in general, was over time deemed too important for US interests to be left to the oscillations of lobbying initiatives. Palestine, by contrast, had nothing to give and held no comparable interest. Thus the US government was (and still is) able to pursue a policy independent of the lobby where it actually has a policy (in the case of Saudi Arabia and the Persian Gulf) but succumbs to the lobby where it feels no specific urgency to develop its own policy (Palestine).

The same argument applies to another famous episode of lobby failure, namely President Bush Senior withholding $10 billion of loan guarantees to Israel in 1991 in an effort to stop Israeli settlements in the occupied Palestinian territories and thereby pave the way for peace talks. But that rare episode, too, marks a moment in which the United States did finally (and briefly) commence a serious drive to resolve the Israeli-Palestinian conflict, as part of the larger arrangement for the Middle East as a whole following the Gulf War of 1991. The Madrid conference (which eventually led in a convoluted way to the Oslo Accords) emerged out of that drive and was possible only because the United States exercised enough pressure on Israeli prime minister Yitzhak Shamir to begin a peace process. So that moment in US history, too, was associated with a new policy (later abandoned) that regarded the whole Middle East as a region ripe for reconstruction, with the Palestinian issue being a hurdle that needed to be overcome along the way. We also need to keep in mind the specific environment of US triumphalism that produced that episodic elaboration of policy independent of the lobby—namely the eviction of the Iraqi army from Kuwait, the demands of the regional alliance built by the United States to accomplish that goal, and the overall sense of American confidence about playing a unique role in the world following the end of the Cold War. The abandonment of that project shortly thereafter (for various reasons that are beyond our scope here) also meant the end of an interest in policy and thus the return of the Israel lobby to the center stage of US policy making regarding Palestine shortly after the election of Bill Clinton.

The last and most recent example of lobby failure concerned President Obama's effort to get Congress to approve US military strikes against Syria in retaliation for the latter government's use of chemical weapons against rebels on August 21, 2013. The record here is not actually clear, since Congress was relieved from having to vote while it was being lobbied by AIPAC to support Obama's use of force. In this case we had an exceptional condition, in which both the lobby and the administration were going against a strong public sentiment opposing any intervention, a sentiment that was also substantially informed by public weariness after two long, expensive, and apparently pointless wars in Afghanistan and Iraq. Without such a resolute public sentiment that Congress would have found difficult to ignore, a sentiment rooted in recent national experience, the outcome might well have been different. This case shows how strong opposing public sentiment can complicate and even defeat the effort of the strongest lobby, even when its effort is allied to the administration's expressed goals. But this sentiment is not what one typically encounters in the United States regarding the Israeli-Palestinian conflict, where the Israel lobby almost always gets all that it wants.

The abandonment of the effort to forge a coherent US strategy on the Israeli-Palestinian conflict after the Madrid conference in the early 1990s marked the lack of a holistic strategy and sense of meaning behind being a superpower.[4] I have commented at length elsewhere on this post–Cold War lack of strategic purpose (Bamyeh 2000). There I traced the loss of a sense of coherence to the end of the Cold War, which deprived the United States of a strategic perspective that had made it possible for policy makers before 1989 to see all local conflicts in the framework of an all-encompassing global conflict with a clear enemy. That of course did not mean that local conflicts before 1989 were necessarily as interminable as the global conflict, nor that they were easy to resolve when that larger conflict was over. Rather, it essentially meant that local conflicts during the Cold War had to have a controlled character. Even as local protagonists had their own agendas, the pursuit of those was not allowed to endanger a larger global strategy. Thus Middle East wars before 1989, devastating as they were, had clear beginning and end points. Even when local leaders or groups acted on their own, they had to keep in mind the larger calculations of their global allies, who had an interest in limited and clearly controllable conflicts rather than poorly defined adventures. Thus even though atrocities that fit a larger game plan were allowed or tolerated, something like the pointless slaughter in Gaza in 2008–9 would not have been permitted during the Cold War, nor would the equally point-less summer war with Hizbullah in 2006 (nor, for that matter, would we have had the Iraq War, probably the most pointless war in history).

Much of the above may appear hypothetical and speculative. But the underlying theme is that underneath every such recent conflict we can detect lobbying pressures much more clearly than during the Cold War—when pressure groups knew that they could not violate or exceed the limits imposed by a strategy of a global struggle. Lack of alternative points of view, therefore, is simply another way of saying that we have no grand strategy. It means that the preferences of the most effective pressure group *become* the policy. Hence our own interest in studying the connection between "diasporas" and US for-eign policy, which would have been a less compelling theme if we had some-thing like the Cold War, namely a condition requiring a strategic, long-term, consistent global perspective that would encourage all diaspora and lobbying efforts to conform to it. Thus to say that US policy tends to gain solidity, clar-ity, and purpose when it "converges" with the interests of a diaspora commu-nity appears to answer the wrong question. For the question should be how a foreign policy may be formulated so that it is holistic and rational, while allowing for the right amount of diaspora inputs. In such a case, "conver-gence" becomes an issue of how a diaspora community may help in fulfilling a rational objective (for example, investing economically, socially, and politi-cally in a peace process that is actually going somewhere). Alternatively, a "convergence" may appear to take place because there is really no policy other than what powerful interests happen to dictate at any particular moment.

The real question, then, is not how diasporas influence US foreign policy but *why* some of them have been able to do so with such impunity. And if I am right that they do so because they fill in answers to the knowledge void created since 1989 when the United States ceased to know with certitude why it should be a superpower, then the possible solutions become obvious. One is to simply accept this state of affairs, so that if you feel that a certain pres-sure group is influencing US foreign policy in an unwholesome way, you cre-ate an alternative pressure group to try to pull foreign policy in the opposite direction. In either case, whatever policy emerges would be a reflection of the power of one pressure group or another rather than an expression of a holistic strategy or national interest.

A second solution is to provide a superpower with a real, and new, purpose that would have the effect of giving a meaningful and rational context to foreign policy as a whole. This of course requires will, leadership, and breadth of perspective. But it is not something that "reality" is going to produce out of some structural necessity. The Obama administration aroused great expectations at the beginning entirely because Obama represented the prospect of nothing more than *going back* to 1989 and making the decisions that should have been made then. But it is easy to see how this redirection of policy away from both the catastrophic neoconservative course of 2001–8 and the unfocused haze of 1993–2000 may be derailed, for such redirection relies less on objective conditions than on willed qualities. The latter include leadership (meaning here defiance of powerful special interest groups when they seek to undermine a rational policy) and breadth of perspective (meaning highlighting of long-term global benefits rather than short-term political and electoral gains).

Thus far, the clearest foreign policy merits of the Obama administration, especially when it comes to the Middle East, have consisted in guarded attempts to correct the previous administration's worst mistakes. Paramount here is the quality of leadership, by which I mean relative independence of policy from pressure groups. This was exemplified in one sense by a new approach to the Muslim world and the attempt to address "Muslims" directly and in a way that gave some credence to some of their grievances. It was later evident in a somewhat confused but eventually accepting response to the Arab revolutions—easy to formulate when the revolutions targeted unfriendly regimes as those in Libya or Syria, but more painful to the Israel lobby especially in the case of Egypt (even though Obama did little there other than acknowledge the certainty of the fall of Mubarak in 2011, only to later accept the Israeli, and Saudi, argument that it should live with and continue to provide aid to the military after its takeover in July 3, 2013—in violation of a US law that prohibits aid to militaries involved in coups). But at the beginning of the Arab Spring uprisings in 2011, US positions on them were apparently taken independently of lobby pressures, benefiting from the fact that lobbies, like all observers, were caught off guard by those grand historical developments and had difficulty making sense of them initially.

Therefore, it seems to me that focusing on the role of "diasporas" in US foreign policy addresses the wrong question, and for two reasons. First, "diaspora" politics create foreign policy only in the *absence* of such policy. The policy toward Cuba, for example, may be a relic of the Cold War, but as such it could be made sense of *in that context*, and the mobilization for it by a segment of the Cuban community in the United States thus could at least appear then to conform to rather than to undermine a larger Cold War strategy. A new policy toward Cuba could have been proposed once the Cold War ended, but it had to be postponed for no reason other than the absence of a new and coherent world vision—so that the old policy, now representing *only* the perspective of a lobbying group, remained and assumed an even more fanatic form. This means that rather than fixating on diaspora influences as being a problem, which in some sense they can be, we ought to devote attention to the very meaning of a superpower in a post–Cold War age in which there should really be no enemies, since there is no *global* conflict. That discussion, then, becomes the basis for a more rational approach to the world. And when we have that, then diaspora initiatives of all kind may be guided by the imperatives of a rational, coherent, and independent enough foreign policy rather than be allowed to determine it.

Second, the term *diaspora* in connection to foreign policy is highly misleading. What we are talking about in effect is not a diaspora community acting in unison but pressures applied by organized segments that may in effect represent a minority—albeit a powerful minority—within diaspora communities. That the organized Iraqi opposition managed to present itself not only as representatives of an Iraqi diaspora before the 2003 war but even more as the legitimate mouthpiece of all Iraqis corresponded less to any social or political reality than to the coincidence of the viewpoints of a select segment of an exile Iraqi intelligentsia and a bold new imperial experiment envisioned by neoconservatives. But analytically, it is a mistake to speak of the "diaspora" as the actor in that case.

This suggests, just as in the case of the powerful Israeli lobby, that a "diaspora," when "mobilized" for instrumental foreign policy aims, is really a construct based on *excluding* other elements of the diaspora, which often may be its majority, that either are opposed to what is being done in their name or, as is more likely the case, are unengaged. A diaspora, therefore, does not influence foreign policy. An organized pressure group may do so in the name of one diaspora or another. To the extent that it succeeds, we must suspect that the reason lies in the prior absence of a rational foreign policy and the curious fact that a world power as important as the United States has been languishing for more than two decades with no sense of direction. Only an intelligent will can supply that sense of direction and purpose. A will of this kind may or may not yet reside in Washington. But it does reside elsewhere in the world, wherever the resources for a struggle against injustice consist largely of one's will to struggle. Such struggles, of which the Palestinians' is a great example today, can only go on.

Notes

1.	For a study of the likely contribution of the diaspora to the economic health of a Palestinian state, see Hijab (2004). For some trends, see Hanafi (2000).

2.	The literature demonstrating this fact is already becoming abundant. For a good example, see Brym and Araj (2006).

3.	Incidentally, that transformation took place elsewhere in the Levant, and largely as a consequence of the Arab debacle in Palestine in 1948, for which the old leading oligarchies in other Arab countries (notably Egypt, Iraq, and Syria) were held responsible.

4.	The failed Camp David summit in 2000 between Ehud Barak and Yassir Arafat cannot be considered a good example of US engagement; its own failure can be easily traced to lack of seriousness in preparing for it. Palestinian negotiators then complained that the role of US mediators consisted simply of taking Israeli proposals back to the Palestinian delegation, after repackaging them as American "bridging proposals."

References

Arab American Institute. 2006. "Population Estimates of Americans of Palestinian Ancestry." October 17. http://archive.is/3NiRX.

Bamyeh, Mohammed. 2000. *The Ends of Globalization.* Minneapolis: University of Minnesota Press.

———. 2003. "Palestine: Listening to the Inaudible." *South Atlantic Quarterly* 102 (4): 825–49.

———. 2007. "The Palestinian Diaspora." In *Diasporas in Conflict*, edited by Hazel Smith and Paul Stares. New York: United Nations University Press.

Brym, Robert J., and Bader Araj. 2006. "Suicide Bombing as Strategy and Interaction: The Case of the Second Intifada." *Social Forces* 84 (4): 1969–86.

Cainkar, Louise, Ali Abunimah, and Lamia Raei. 2004. "Migration as a Method of Coping with Turbulence among Palestinians." *Journal of Comparative Family Studies* 35 (2): 229–40.

Farsoun, Samih, and Jean Landis. 1990. "The Sociology of an Uprising: The Roots of the Intifada." In *Intifada: Palestine at the Crossroads*, edited by Jamal Nassar and Roger Heacock. New York: Praeger.

Hanafi, Sari. 2000. "Palestinian Diaspora Contribution to Investment and Philanthropy in Palestine." October. www.palesta.gov.ps/academic/publication/diaspora.htm.

Hijab, Nadia. 2004. "The Role of Palestinian Diaspora Institutions in Mobilizing the International Community." Paper presented at the Economic and Social Commission for Western Asia (ESCWA) conference, "Arab-International Forum on Rehabilitation and Development in the Occupied Palestinian Territory: Towards an Independent Palestinian State," Beirut, October 11–14.

Hudson, Michael C. 1979. *Arab Politics: The Search for Legitimacy*. New Haven, CT: Yale University Press.

Mearsheimer, John J., and Stephen M. Walt. 2007. *The Israel Lobby and U.S. Foreign Policy*. New York: Farrar, Straus, and Giroux.

When Diaspora Interests
Shape Foreign Policy

CHAPTER FIVE

America's Role in the Northern Ireland Peace Process

Joseph E. Thompson

Ben Franklin is quoted as telling Americans, "You have a Republic, if you can keep it." Today he would modify his quote for Northern Ireland by saying, "You have peace, if you can keep it." Since Irish Americans and US government officials were an integral part of bringing about this peace process, this chapter will recount the historical stages in the formation of US policy toward Northern Ireland. These historical stages of the arenas and mechanisms through which Irish American and US government relations were enacted may also give insight for other diaspora–US government relations referenced in this book.

History is a bane for policy makers, especially those seeking to reconcile painful disputes between or within states. This was especially true with regard to the Irish conflict. Ironically, history is also the most useful tool to understand the differences that were at the heart of Northern Ireland's discord. The Northern Ireland conflict emanated from seeds of distrust, anger, triumphalism, and violence planted throughout the island's history.

These causes of Irish conflict were shaped by the three groups in control of the island's northern people during one or more historical periods: the Irish during the Gaelic-Ireland period (pre-1600s), the English during the Anglo-Ireland period (1600s to the present day), and the Scotch-Irish during the period of Northern Ireland's Stormont government (1921–72) that was established by Britain. On the basis of their interpretation of history, each community believed they had the absolute right to govern Northern Ireland. The two historical "golden eras"—Gaelic-Ireland and Anglo-Ireland—were ground into dust by Scotch-Irish misgovernment during the Stormont era. The winds of change stirred up this dust, and it became part of the stormy war clouds that rolled across the landscape of Northern Ireland in the 1960s. Slogans used by each Northern Ireland community during this violent period of "the Troubles" were "psychocultural dramas," based on symbols dredged up from the past—what Marc Ross has described as "conflicts between groups over competing, and apparently irresolvable, claims that engage the central elements of each group's historical experience and their identity and invoke suspicions and fears of the opponent" (2007, 25).

One important contributing symbol to the violence has been the notion that Northern Ireland is divided between the majority "Protestant" community and the minority "Catholic" community. Even though these two symbolic labels of religious identification (Protestant and Catholic) are no longer based on religious doctrine, they have been important components of the conflict. They evolved historically because every person living on the island was compelled to identify with one or the other religious label. Today, not all Protestants support the continued political "union" of Northern Ireland with Britain, and not all Catholics are infallibly for a "nationalist" united Ireland. Nonetheless, these one-dimensional terms have been handy conversational symbols for a much more complicated political, economic, and social situation in Northern Ireland. In the strict sense, therefore, the Northern Ireland conflict, to the extent that it persists in political polarization and sporadic acts of violence, is no longer a religious conflict. In fact, the religious divisional concept turns out to be very problematic to maintain because of the recent large increase of non-Christian immigrants to Northern Ireland (note the comic anecdote of the Northern Ireland immigration officer asking for the record whether the new immigrant is a "Catholic Buddhist" or a "Protestant Buddhist").

The labels *unionist* (or *loyalist*) and *nationalist* (or *republican*) are also applied in reference to Northern Ireland communities because these terms contain the stories and symbols that give deeper significance to the aspirations of Irish nationalist Catholics and unionist Scotch-Irish Protestants. The status quo group in Northern Ireland is usually depicted as Protestant unionists. The label *unionist* (with a lowercase *u*) refers to those who aspire to keep the six counties of Northern Ireland (Armagh, Antrim, Derry, Down, Fermanagh, and Tyrone) permanently united with Britain. *Unionist* (with a capital *U*) refers to political party members of the Ulster Unionist Party, the largest unionist party before the 1998 Belfast Good Friday Agreement. All too often this status quo community is labeled simply as "Protestant." Actually, unionists belong to Presbyterian, Baptist, Methodist, Episcopalian, Roman Catholic, and other Christian church denominations. Fanatical and extreme unionists are referred to as "loyalists." Loyalists are uncompromisingly against joining the southern Republic of Ireland to the point of verbally or physically supporting any means, even violence, to prevent a geographically united Ireland. Those who support this policy are committed to leaders of the now majority unionist/loyalist Democratic Unionist Party (DUP).

The term *Nationalist* (with a capital *N*) refers to members of the Social Democratic and Labour Party (SDLP), the largest nationalist party that worked to implement the peace process of the Good Friday Agreement. Lowercased, the term refers to those community members who aspire to the reunion of Northern Ireland's six counties with Ireland's twenty-six counties (thus you sometimes see green, white, and orange bumper stickers stating the mathematical oxymoron: $26 + 6 = 1$). The nationalists' geographically united Ireland would be governed by the Dublin government. Since religion is automatically associated with the Irish population, the accepted generalization about nationalists is that they are all Roman Catholics. Fanatical nationalists are referred to as "republicans." Republicans vehemently desire a united Ireland to the point of verbally or physically supporting activities that may use violence as a means to achieve this end, such as those employed by the Irish Republican Army (IRA). Too often IRA members, members of the republican Sinn Fein Party, are lumped together with Catholics, as though all three groups supported only violent aspirations.

Since ethnic identities, rather than religious identities, are the most politically significant social identities in the United States, Irish Americans (both Protestant and Catholic) developed their own uniquely diversified "Irish" culture that held onto links with Ireland and animosity toward Britain. US government officials had moved in the opposite direction after the period of the World Wars, showing disdain for Ireland and strengthening foreign policy ties with the British government. Thus the divergence between the foreign policy interests and goals of US government officials and Irish Americans was well established when Northern Ireland erupted in internal chaos.

Great ethnic diversity has distinguished the United States from most other nations, and more attention than ever before is now focused on hyphenated Americans and the meaning of their allegiance toward the United States and their country of origin. The first waves of European immigrants to the American colonies came overwhelmingly from the British Isles, which included Ireland. Thereafter, Irish Americans developed their own myths and stories from memories of first-, second-, and third-generation immigrants. These myths and symbols (such as St. Patrick's shamrock and the Great Famine of 1841–51) were assimilated into the culture by the constant arrival of Irish immigrants throughout US history. *Irish American Voluntary Organizations* offers an excellent description of the wave after wave of immigrants from Ireland, North and South, Protestant and Catholic, that built the complex culture of Irish Americans as they settled throughout the entire United States (Funchion 1983).

Few Americans realize that one-third of their presidents can claim direct Irish ancestry. John F. Kennedy is the president most fondly remembered as having an Irish Catholic heritage. Nixon, Reagan, and Obama join Kennedy as the four presidents with roots in the southern Republic of Ireland. The other twelve presidents, including Carter and Clinton, look to Northern Ireland as their Irish ancestral home. Presidents aside, the 1980 census reports that Irish Americans number well over forty million. For personal reasons, some choose to be indifferent regarding their Irish culture, while others aspire to be a vocal part of the vast number of Irish Americans. In either case, the arrival and integration of recent Irish immigrants into America's culture and their understanding of the northern conflict have affected the formation of US foreign policy toward Northern Ireland.

Four factors, when they merged, created the conditions for the violent conflict in Northern Ireland. First, the increasingly educated Catholic nationalist middle class in Northern Ireland demanded reform of the political and social system that had always discriminated against them. The British Education Act of 1947 had allowed Catholic children for the first time to attend higher education in Northern Ireland. Twenty years later these graduating students joined other recent graduates in the belief that, although they were Irish nationalists, they were also British citizens and were due the rights and respect ascribed to all British citizens.

Second, dissatisfaction grew among the Catholic nationalist community as they realized the degree to which they were being discriminated against by the Scotch-Irish unionist government controlling the Stormont parliament. Then, in 1968, the young students and recent graduates formed the Northern Ireland Civil Rights Association (NICRA), demanding equality for the nationalist population (replicated from the civil rights movement in America). Many from the Protestant unionist working class also joined NICRA to express their dissatisfaction with the poor conditions they were also subjected to by Stormont politicians. Initially both working communities were demanding a change in government management; they were not attempting to destroy or undermine Northern Ireland or to break the province's union with Britain. However, the more extreme ideological leaders among the Stormont unionist politicians, headed by the loyalist Ian Paisley and his DUP leaders, decided to rationalize to politicians in London that Northern Ireland's violence was essentially the work of the "traitor" Catholic community against the hardworking and loyal Protestant community.

Third, an economic downturn in traditional industries, such as Belfast shipbuilding, began to weaken the unionists' and loyalists' sense of security. Thus NICRA's public marches to promote civil rights for the nationalist cause prompted counterdemonstrations from the more extreme unionist groups—the loyalists. Loyalist counterdemonstrators quickly turned violent as their fear grew regarding the nationalists' motives. In January 1969 a student communist group (People's Democracy) defied Stormont's marching ban and organized a protest march from the eastern city of Belfast to the western city of Derry. The group was ambushed at Burntollet Bridge by loyalist demonstrators, while the police deliberately failed to protect the marchers. The whole bloody episode was caught on camera, and these violent images were flashed around the world.

Fourth, many in the Protestant loyalist and unionist communities were suspicious that the nationalist population was seeking to take over the government by promoting a geographically united Ireland, with subsequent domination by the Catholic religion. Loyalists took up arms together in the largest paramilitary organization in Northern Ireland, the Ulster Defense Association (UDA). The UDA started in September 1971 as a loyalist working-class group that initially excluded all politicians and clergy from its membership. Their goal was to violently root out all "traitors" in Northern Ireland. As a reaction to this violence, some members of the dormant official Irish Republican Army (IRA), who had earlier fought to expel the British from Ireland, split from the republican group and formed the more violent Provisional Irish Republican Army (Provo IRA) in 1972. This was an emergency effort to protect the Catholic nationalist communities in Belfast and Derry. As the rioting and acts of arson throughout Northern Ireland became more sectarian, the Stormont government completely lost control of the province. Unfortunately, Britain continued to ignore the political and economic problems of Northern Ireland.

Prior to the violent crisis in Northern Ireland, the United States had become closely tied to Britain so as to attain US foreign policy goals in Europe. The majority of Irish Americans had also become indifferent to the problems in Northern Ireland and focused instead on supporting US foreign policy that saw Soviet communism as the threat to their American way of life. The increase of Irish Americans who were unaware of things "Irish," aside from St. Patrick's Day parades and songs, encouraged a few academics to form the American Committee of Irish Studies (ACIS) in 1960. This group, however, never progressed beyond the initial ACIS interest in history and literature and thus missed the opportunity to educate Americans concerning Northern Ireland's contemporary political relationships with Britain, Ireland, and the United States. The safe, nonpolitical approach of the ACIS to things "Irish" in America did a tremendous disservice to the country because it left foreign policy formation to Anglophile bureaucrats in the US government or to the soon-to-appear Irish American Anglophobic republican leaders who envisioned violence as the way forward.

Relations between Irish Americans and the US Government

Jack Holland, a journalist who extensively covered Irish issues, wrote of US media coverage during the initial period of Northern Ireland violence that "there existed a general consensus on Northern Ireland among the major newspapers and magazines," that it "was basically the same as that of the British government," and that it "was remarkably consistent until about 1979" (1987, 196). The point Holland hoped to make concerned other less well-known reporters of Irish events who were deemed more accurate by Irish American republicans for not acquiescing to the British perspective. Being among the ignored minor reporters, he willingly provided information for the awakening Irish American public who sought to put right the perceived wrongs of the past.

Concern quickly grew among British and American officials that Irish Americans were seriously misunderstanding the Northern Ireland conflict. The pervasive consensus, among both Anglophilic and Anglophobic individuals, was the simplistic view, fostered by British government ignorance and American bureaucratic inattention, that the Northern Ireland violence was between Catholics and Protestants. Major newspaper reporters could have better described the violence as taking place between nationalists and unionists, or between republicans and loyalists, or between the haves and the have-nots, or between the Irish and the Scotch-Irish. Even more accurately, they could have read the Northern Ireland civil rights skirmishes as a struggle between an awakened angry socialist movement and a frightened unionist population.

A historical account is useful for understanding the evolving relationship between the Irish American public and US government officials regarding the Northern Ireland crisis. Although the full history from initial policies of strict US noninvolvement to subsequent wholesale involvement in Northern Ireland cannot be recounted here, incidents are described that best reflect the first diverging and then converging relationship between Irish American leaders and US government officials.

Some US policies were initiated at the lowest bureaucratic levels of America's Irish and British embassies or consulates, then rose to the State Department's Foreign Service officer (FSO) for Britain or Ireland/Northern Ireland, and eventually were passed on by the secretary of state to the National Security Council (NSC) for approval. The overwhelming majority of publicly announced American policy decisions were simple executive decisions requiring no legislation. Soon, however, other policies were to be driven by congressional demand. Nevertheless, from the time that violence erupted in Northern Ireland in the late 1960s until the 1990s there was an ongoing controversy in the relationship between Irish Americans and US government officials as to what constituted appropriate foreign policy goals.

This evolving relationship can be sketched out as having five stages: (1) initial US government opposition to passionate republican Irish American demands, (2) acknowledgment of Irish American demands by some US government officials, (3) eventual congressional acceptance of modified Irish American requests, (4) presidential involvement in the Irish American lobbying for Northern Ireland, and (5) the Irish American struggle to keep the US government focused on the Northern Ireland peace process despite sporadic setbacks. The Irish American influence in the formation of US foreign policy was not rigidly sequential. Rather, it required a constant holistic effort to move each stage forward at its own pace.

Stage 1: Time-Honored Relationships (pre-1970)

At the outset, US government officials and the Irish American population accepted their status quo relationship regarding Northern Ireland. On one side of the relationship, US government officials, especially those in the State Department, acted as though there were no option for American involvement in the Irish province, since it was a fundamental part of the United Kingdom of Great Britain and Northern Ireland. Though US government officials might attend St. Patrick's Day parades and other "Irish" events, they had no interest in establishing an official relationship with Irish American leaders regarding foreign policy toward Northern Ireland. On the other side, Irish Americans assumed they could not have any influence on US foreign policy. Instead, the few Irish American leaders interested in Northern Ireland acted as though a change could be made only from within the island itself. Thus the only way to make this change was to have Britain leave Northern Ireland, even if this required the use of violent paramilitary force.

The time-honored relationship between Irish American leaders and US government officials was based on a personal and professional understanding that the ethnic immigrant group should not infringe on the government's policy of strict noninvolvement in Northern Ireland. This was best exemplified when President Richard Milhous Nixon went to visit Ireland and made no statements on the violence taking place in the North.

Nixon's first personal visit to Ireland was in 1970, just after Northern Ireland's violent upheaval. When he arrived at Shannon Airport, the Irish *taoiseach* (prime minister) John Lynch greeted Nixon and his wife and immediately reminded him of his Milhous "forefather" who had emigrated from Limerick City to settle in Philadelphia in 1753. The NSC adviser, Henry Kissinger, had expressed a personal opposition to Nixon's visit to Ireland as a possible distraction from the major foreign policy issues facing US-UK relations. The president, however, had ignored Kissinger's concerns and had insisted that NATO and American support of British policy would remain the focus of his trip. His personal Irish American attitude toward the northern violence would not infringe on his professional political leadership of the United States. Thus, during his entire sojourn in Ireland, Nixon made no reference to the crisis in Northern Ireland.

However, 1969 had been a watershed year for all groups involved in Northern Ireland: British prime minister Harold Wilson's Labour government sent an increasing number of British troops to assist the province's bungling Royal Ulster Constabulary (RUC) police force; the Stormont government of Northern Ireland's prime minister Terence O'Neill was unable to quell the rising violence in both communities; the UDA and its paramilitary commando groups countered all and any changes suggested by the government; the IRA would soon split into several groups (one group more militant than the others); Northern Ireland civil rights leaders visited the United States for the first time; and a few members of the US Congress began to realize the political leadership possibilities that millions of Irish Americans might represent.

At the time, foreign policy making was viewed principally as the result of decisions and actions by the president, his closest advisers, and other relevant officials in the executive branch of government. However, Nixon and Kissinger had a deep distrust of the very State Department organization responsible for foreign policy formation. Their mutual disdain for Secretary of State William Rogers and his bureaucracy meant that decision making regarding major issues, such as the Soviet Union, NATO, and Vietnam, was centralized in the White House. The White House and the NSC extended a policy of least resistance toward State Department decisions on such minor issues as the Northern Ireland conflict. Nixon's and Kissinger's preoccupation with creating a new approach to foreign policy issues permitted the State Department to remain in control of Irish policy, as long as it remained within "realpolitik" parameters. The State Department bureaucrats decided to delay allying themselves with either Rogers or Kissinger until they saw who would be the real foreign policy decision maker in the new administration, that is, their actual boss.

Unlike Congress and Irish Americans, who relied principally on media reporting and visits overseas to develop an informed opinion, the State Department also relied on its field reports and diplomatic contacts as an important element in the formation of US policy. Northern Ireland reports, therefore, came originally from Neil McManus, who had been assigned to be the US consul general in Belfast in 1967. For personal health reasons, McManus allowed his vice-consul Michael Steruber (who was on his first assignment after a brief stint in the Vietnam conflict) to be responsible for all day-to-day reports. Steruber's reports were tailored to support the unionist position, as based upon past correspondence with his superiors in the US Embassy in London. As was the custom, Belfast's memorandums were sanitized and summarized by the US Embassy in London to support UK policy before being passed on to Washington as part of the total embassy report. The student unrest and demonstrations on "Bloody Sunday" in 1972, for example, were mentioned only briefly in the embassy reports to Washington, and the nationalists' sense of injustice and grievance regarding the treatment of Irish Catholics was ignored completely.

Grover Penberthy, US consul general during the worst of the initial violence (1971–74), continued his predecessor's practice of gathering information only from British officials and Northern Ireland unionist leaders. Even though US officials did not reach out to nationalist community leaders in Northern Ireland, the State Department believed its source of information was better than Irish American claims of British and loyalist violence. Washington bureaucrats were fed what they wanted to hear, and the misinformation was then confirmed by the UK Embassy in Washington. These US Consulate/Embassy reports would soon be in stark contrast with the testimonies of better-informed Irish American leaders.

While the Nixon administration was developing a realist balance-of-power role for the United States in the world, Congress was undergoing its own transition of power. Although Congress had achieved moderate success in limiting presidential foreign policy making, the Democratic Party reforms in the 1970s left congressional leaders less effective and more susceptible to influence by special interest groups. It was not surprising, then, when turf battles ensued in Congress between its leaders and others who chose to support the initial viewpoints of Irish American republicans. The question soon surfaced as to which congressional group or individual would eventually lead the crusade for Northern Ireland. Ironically, more energy was spent trying to pose as the ethnic group's leader than was spent deliberating over foreign policy. Grassroots Irish American leaders quickly came to view Congress as privileged elites concerned only with their own prerogatives rather than with the needs of the suffering Northern Irish people.

Meanwhile, squabbles among active Irish American groups in the United States matched the confusion on the streets of Northern Ireland. Irish American leaders were desperate to hear and to have their members hear about the events in Northern Ireland. In a brief show of solidarity, therefore, the New York Ancient Order of Hibernians in America (AOH) joined with other Irish American leaders to invite Bernadette Devlin, a student leader for the communist civil rights marches and later elected as the youngest member of the

British Westminster Parliament, to tour the United States during the summer of 1969. Irish American leaders believed that she would give a true version of events to all interested Americans. Devlin, naturally, gave her contemporary socialist version of the conflict during her whirlwind tour of American cities. This presentation caught all Irish Americans off guard. Irish American leaders were angry at her communist interpretation and confused by the absence of the simplistic "us Irish versus those Brits" approach that had served Irish American immigrants over many generations. Younger Irish American radicals were glad that Devlin spoke about contemporary events but were also confused by her European socialism. Devlin's visit quickly became a total embarrassment to the Irish Americans who had sponsored it.

Devlin's visit should have jolted Irish Americans out of their traditional misunderstanding of Northern Ireland, but her complex message was quickly overshadowed by a more familiar (and more simplistic) interpretation of events when more British troops were sent to suppress the growing loyalist violence in Derry and Belfast. Since no member of Congress had specialization in Northern Ireland affairs or had officially visited Northern Ireland, House Speaker John McCormack (D-MA) recklessly used the media reports of discrimination against Northern Ireland citizens to defend civil rights protesters and to mistakenly characterize the British military action as one targeting Catholic nationalists without adequately investigating the situation. Since congressional leaders subscribed to Irish American legends that the British had always unjustly treated the Irish, they immediately believed the worst of the media reports. Anyone having an Irish-sounding name or having membership in an Irish American group assumed that this was sufficient grounds for seeking an Irish American leadership position in Congress.

Irish American events in the United States rapidly mirrored the direction of the republican movement on the ground in Northern Ireland. Michael Flannery, John McGowen, and Matthew Higgins launched the Irish Northern Aid Committee (Noraid) at a press conference held at the Irish Institute in New York City in June 1970. Strident advocacy for a united Ireland, achieved through violence and gunrunning, was soon the hallmark of Noraid. Noraid leaders quickly established organizations in New York, Philadelphia, Boston, Chicago, Savanna, Houston, San Francisco, and other Irish American AOH centers throughout America. Noraid became the only published voice of Irish American groups, and news from Northern Ireland was slanted to fit its particular republican viewpoint. Only when Noraid activity began to infringe on British interests did the US State Department and Justice Department become interested in curtailing activities perceived as hostile to the continuation of the US-UK status quo policy.

Noraid and Irish American leaders quickly came to believe that Congress was too satisfied with quiet diplomacy regarding Northern Ireland. After personal meetings between Noraid leaders and some members of Congress, the congressional leadership of Irish Americans began to settle on a few individuals during and after the Nixon impeachment. Congressman Mario Biaggi (D-NY) took the lead by having his legislative assistant Bob Blancato assigned to the congressional subcommittee on Northern Ireland. Biaggi then flew to Dublin to investigate the claim that members of the republican movement in the Republic of Ireland were being denied visas to the United States. Frederick Burns O'Brien of the US Customs Service and Sean Walsh accompanied Biaggi and his staff on the trip. Biaggi, smarting under the brush-off he received from US officials in the Dublin Embassy, which had always followed the lead of the American Embassy in London, went public with his support for the IRA republican cause.

When Biaggi returned to America, he convinced Congressman Joshua Eilber (D-PA), the Immigration Subcommittee Chairman of the House Judiciary Committee, to plan hearings on the Irish visa issue. Congressman Leo Zeferetti (D-NY) went a step further and called on the US government to speak out publicly against the abusive British rule in Northern Ireland. The growing dissent in Congress concerning Britain's policy in Northern Ireland was beginning to seriously concern the State Department and the British government. As yet, State Department officials were not interested in forming any meaningful relationship with the leaders of Irish America.

The Irish and British ambassadors to the United States, John Molloy and Sir Peter Ramsbotham, made a joint request to House Speaker Carl Albert (D-OK) not to hold another committee meeting, as had been done one month after the Bloody Sunday incident. That committee meeting and its report of British violence had added fuel to the growing Irish American anger. Speaker Albert decided not to hold any official committee hearing on the visa issue, but he followed the advice of Congressman Tip O'Neill (D-MA) and Senator Ted Kennedy (D-MA) and requested that the Library of Congress's Congressional Research Service (CRS) produce a report entitled *Developments in Northern Ireland, 1968–1976*. The report spread the blame for Northern Ireland's increased violence among several parties, including the US administration. Noraid also used this report to challenge the United Nations to investigate British torture of Irish prisoners. Officials in the US State Department, who believed they knew what was best for American foreign policy on this issue, reached a point of utter bitterness toward the public activity of Irish American republican leaders.

More than ever before, Senator Kennedy and Congressman O'Neill began to seek out Northern Ireland nationalist leaders to better clarify the issues and US policy alternatives. On the one hand, no meeting with an Irish American leader or government official in Washington, D.C., could give as much up-to-date information and insight as a phone call to John Hume and other leaders of his Northern Ireland Social Democratic and Labour Party. Therefore, O'Neill began to invite Hume to Washington every St. Patrick's Day for a special luncheon. Seated on both sides of Hume at these luncheons were important Washington politicians and government officials. Thus O'Neill guaranteed that US foreign policy decision makers heard the nationalist antiviolence voice. On the other hand, Irish American republican leaders were in contact with and supported the actions of Biaggi, Zeferetti, and Noraid, and all too often they publicly supported the Provo IRA's acts of violence. Apart from the US government's attempts to contain the gun-running and money laundering by Noraid, no coherent policy was proffered to the Irish American public as to what positive cause they might rally around. The question also remained whether internationally decried human rights violations were a valid issue for the US government to take up, given its policy of realpolitik.

In this first stage of the peace process, therefore, the profound divergence between the interests and goals of Irish American leaders and those of US government officials was centered on the question of what was actually happening in Northern Ireland. At the root of these political and bureaucratic brawls stood different conceptions concerning the requisites for peace and security and the requisites for justice. The issue of Northern Ireland challenged Americans to perceive justice and peace either in stark opposition or in complementary tension. All the cases in this book have experienced this time-honored relationship stage. Unfortunately, some have gotten caught in this phenomenon and been unable to move on to the next stage.

Stage 2: Adjusting Relationship Patterns (1970–80)

The quiescent Irish American constituency began to awaken during the 1970s. As described for stage 1 of the process, the first Irish American groups in the United States to respond to the violence in Northern Ireland were the AOH and Noraid republicans. Frustrated and angered by White House and State Department apathy toward reported atrocities in Northern Ireland and unable to motivate any congressional action other then personal posturing, leaders of the AOH and Noraid invited thirty delegation leaders from different Irish American organizations throughout the United States to attend a meeting in New York City on September 28, 1974. John "Jack" Keane, the recently elected national president of the AOH, who had strong sympathetic ties with Noraid, chaired the discussion. The major topic discussed among the Irish American members was how they could influence the US government to support a policy advocating a united Ireland.

As was typical of many ethnic meetings, there was great discussion of the issue, ending with a soft challenge. The AOH and Noraid leaders were asked to think about creating an independent Irish American lobbying group in the United States that would work in unison with the AOH and Noraid. Despite initial promises of support from those in attendance, the creation of an umbrella Irish American lobby to influence foreign policy failed to stir any immediate definite supporters. Thus the lobby idea lay dormant for several months. This hesitancy is not unusual for small-group leaders, for it is often difficult to relinquish the power to control decisions.

The imagination, courage, and energy of an immigrant Northern Ireland Catholic priest made the dream of an Irish American lobby a reality. Because of his outspoken support for the violent actions of the IRA, Sean McManus was discreetly requested by his Catholic Church superiors to choose between the vocation of a silent Redemptorist priest and that of a political rabble-rouser priest outside Ireland. By deciding to go to America, McManus attempted to have his cake and eat it too.

Arriving in New York, McManus promptly made contact with AOH and Noraid leaders regarding when and how to bring the Northern Ireland crisis to the attention of Congress and Irish American groups throughout the United States. With Charles McCafferty of the Minnesota AOH and Fred O'Brien, McManus organized a successful boycott of a highly publicized Northern Ireland soccer match that was played at Gaelic Park in New

York. McManus, O'Brien, and McCafferty used this success to resurrect the concept of an Irish American lobby. The group became known as the Irish National Caucus (INC), with McManus as its head. Few, if any, Irish Americans would dare question the motives of a militant Catholic Irish republican priest. Cynical pundits would refer to the influence of the "priesthood" on US foreign policy toward Northern Ireland.

The INC was formed as an umbrella organization having voluntary overlapping membership with all Irish American organizations. McManus set three objectives for the lobbying group: to be the only Irish American lobby dealing directly with US government officials, to be the centralized source of information for the media, and to present Northern Ireland news from the perspective of Irish republicanism. These decisions and INC activity propelled McManus to become Britain's nemesis in America, the driving force that would eventually erode Britain's influence on US foreign policy. Irish American outrage, orchestrated by the INC, quickly built up against Britain's and America's policy of noninvolvement toward Northern Ireland. British imperatives and mistakes in enforcing a policy of "criminalizing" the IRA and the republican movement in Northern Ireland (but not the UDA loyalists) became the fuel for the republican Irish American success. The US government, by omission, allowed Irish American republicans to fan the traditional anger against the British into effective results.

Because of the connections between the INC, Noraid, and the Provo IRA, the US government singled out the INC for special surveillance. Jack Holland (1987) and Tim Pat Coogan (2000) describe in great detail the persons, places, and dates of Irish republican gun-running and money laundering in America. Records show, however, that INC activities in support of Noraid stopped around 1975 when McManus began to concentrate primarily on the issue of human rights violations in Northern Ireland. The overlapping membership between Noraid and the INC, due mostly to the ongoing scarcity of active Irish American interest in northern issues, swelled the ranks of both groups with sufficient numbers to look impressive to American politicians.

Britain's antiterrorist crackdown on all IRA activity but not loyalist paramilitary violence, the illegal apprehension in Birmingham of six Northern Ireland republicans, a ban on all Irish republican travel—these issues and others played into the hands of the INC. The publicity of these events and the desperate condition of northern nationalists convinced additional Irish American leaders and congressmen to take up the Irish cause by adding their names to the INC membership list. Members of Congress now believed that a humanitarian foreign policy was preferable to the government's policy of realpolitik, so they began to develop a relationship with Irish American nationalist and republican leaders as well as with leaders in Northern Ireland.

On October 27, 1976, six days before the presidential election, Democratic Party candidate Jimmy Carter met formally with over fifty representatives of the INC in Pittsburgh. Carter voiced a few platitudes about civil rights in Northern Ireland, the need for a reunification of Ireland, and the promise of American economic assistance if peace were to come to the Irish province. For what it was worth in limited ethnic votes, the INC gave Carter its endorsement. Carter's speech is remembered not for its impact on winning the presidency but for the hope that it inspired in many Irish Americans regarding Northern Ireland's crisis. Britain and the State Department viewed this action as nothing more than another in a long series of ignorant political decisions by candidates seeking to win an election. Not surprisingly, Carter and his administration soon attempted to distance themselves from these remarks.

The question of Northern Ireland, however, would not disappear from the focus of America's foreign policy. Mairead (Corrigan) Maguire, Nobel Peace Prize laureate and cofounder of the Peace People in Northern Ireland, made a special visit to Washington with the support of Irish American leaders to plead with Carter and congressional leaders for a more enlightened approach to Northern Ireland. John Hume used the empathy Americans felt for the goals of the Peace People to convince the four most important Irish American congressional leaders—Kennedy, Moynihan, O'Neill, and Carey (eventually known as the "Four Horsemen")—to issue a joint St. Patrick's Day message in 1977. Their message, and every succeeding yearly statement, repeated two assertions: Ireland should be united, and Americans should not in any way support the violence in Northern Ireland. Irish Americans had always emphasized the need for Britain to withdraw from the North, but with congressional leaders' unequivocal condemnation of the paramilitary violence of the IRA and its affiliated groups, such as Noraid, was a radical break with traditional Irish American platitudes.

It was at this stage that House Speaker O'Neill, who was crucially important to an already beleaguered president, came quietly to the fore. O'Neill asked for a meeting between the now recognized Four Horsemen and Secretary of State Vance to discuss Northern Ireland. The proposed successful deal was that the congressional leadership would link the creation of an assistant secretary position for a Human Rights Division in the State Department, something President Carter wanted, with substantial US aid to Northern Ireland and a public condemnation of paramilitary violence, which nationalist Irish Americans had sought as a change in US policy. Irish American lobbying and government reverse-lobbying had emboldened the congressional Democratic Party leaders to propose this foreign policy option to the president.

The majority of Irish Americans were content with Carter's proposed economic support, and congressional leaders were pleased that the president had supported them. Irish American republican groups, however, were very dissatisfied with the moderate tone of the presidential and congressional messages. McManus was frustrated as he went about Washington dropping in on government staffers to dispense INC information. All his lobbying was to no immediate and direct avail, though indirectly it did eventually force the congressional leadership to support his efforts to change the American policy toward Northern Ireland. It soon became apparent to McManus and the INC that personal visits did not impress government officials, for there are always visitors thronging the halls of the US government and demanding to be heard on every conceivable issue. A more organized approach was needed to attract attention within the government labyrinth if the INC was to be an effective lobby.

McManus, O'Brien, and Bernadette McAuliffe from the office of Congressman Silvio Conte (R-MA) decided to form a special congressional committee for the Irish American republican movement. The only congressman at the time willing to speak so openly for the republican movement was Biaggi, whose constituency was only 6 percent Irish American. He voluntarily and courageously stood up against the silence of Irish American leaders in Congress by publicly forming the Ad Hoc Congressional Committee for Irish Affairs. Like many other government committees in Washington, this committee soon acquired a permanency that made the "ad hoc" title into an oxymoron. Despite being ignored by the congressional leadership and prevented from legislating on Irish issues, the Ad Hoc Congressional Committee joined with the INC to successfully make the Northern Ireland question a public issue of American foreign policy.

Irish Americans were slow to realize that foreign policy was about launching specific tactics, not issuing statements. Once they recognized the need for specific tactics, they began to travel to Northern Ireland in greater numbers just to be in touch with republican leaders and the families of those in prison. The US government official who had to deal with these emotional visitors to Northern Ireland was Michael Michaud. Appointed the US consul general to Belfast in 1980, Michaud brought a deeper personal insight to events because of his ever-widening contacts within Northern Ireland society. The State Department was just beginning to be receptive to the perceptions and opinions of Irish Americans and prominent Northern Ireland nationalists.

In this second stage, therefore, the relationship patterns between Irish Americans and US government officials were adjusting to the changing source of information. The British Embassy's first permanent secretary, Stephen Wall, also noticed a shift in the State Department's attitude toward Northern Ireland and Irish American leaders. This change in US government perception was reported back to London, where it resulted in a change in Northern Ireland's priority on Margaret Thatcher's list of political items of importance. The Irish American relationship with the US government was beginning to make once-divergent foreign policy interests and goals convergent in ways that would result in more dramatic changes during the third stage.

Stage 3: Crossroads for Change (1980–90)

The Northern Ireland issue had moved from Irish American demonstrations and street protests to congressional involvement and was about to storm the White House. Any in-depth analysis by the White House and the NSC had faced the tremendous hurdle of their lack of familiarity with Northern Ireland politics. The White House staff and State Department bureaucrats had persisted in their perception of Northern Ireland as a foreign policy "tar baby." US government officials involved in policy formation were only now gradually accepting the involvement of Irish Americans.

The easiest way the State Department initially used to avoid contact with Irish Americans was to assign to its Washington political desk one FSO who handled both Ireland and Northern Ireland issues. Within such a contrived organizational structure, any public query about the US government's policy concerning Northern Ireland or Ireland was answered by a junior FSO assigned to the political "Irish Desk." Meanwhile, a senior FSO assigned to the State Department's political "UK Desk" decided all Northern Ireland policy issues. More important for US policy formation, information gathered and reported from Northern Ireland emanated primarily from a British perspective, secondarily from the unionist community through the US Consulate in Belfast, and finally from the southern Irish perspective of the US Embassy in Dublin. This process totally ignored northern Catholic nationalist and Irish American perceptions about Northern Ireland's future.

Despite US government efforts to ignore the Northern Ireland issue, several domestic and international events forced Northern Ireland onto the front burner of American policy formation. First, American politicians found that more than forty million Irish Americans had registered in the 1980 census. Prior to this census count, the accepted wisdom was that twenty million Irish Americans existed in the United States. With the number doubling overnight, politicians and their statistical bean counters suddenly discovered Irish Americans to be an important ethnic group. Up to this point politicians and government bureaucrats had believed that Irish American lobbying emanated from only one source, the republican-based Noraid and INC, bolstered by the Ad Hoc Congressional Committee for Irish Affairs.

With the huge jump in Irish American population estimates, American politicians were anxious to appease this "newfound" constituency. However, there were four different Irish American groups with different interests and goals. First, the most vocal, yet small group of Irish American republicans looked to Noraid and the AOH for leadership. The US government continued to steer clear of any relationship with these groups espousing paramilitary violence to drive Britain from the island. Second, although US congressmen continued to join Biaggi's Ad Hoc Congressional Committee to placate strident demands by republican constituents, mainstream Irish American nationalists had no interest in a special liaison with politicians regarding the Northern Ireland issue. Moreover, mainstream Irish Americans were not interested in taking sides in the turf struggles for power between congressmen. Third, Irish Americans in the corporate world were neither beguiled by republican leaders nor impressed by the shallow speeches and actions of nationalist congressmen. Finally, the majority of Irish Americans were unfocused and confused by republican versus nationalist versus State Department perceptions of Northern Ireland.

Then, on March 1, 1981, Northern Ireland republican inmates in the Maze Prison announced the beginning of their second hunger strike. Irish Americans listened and read the day-after-day news of Provo IRA prisoner Bobby Sands's refusal of food. In essence, the hunger strike represented a power struggle between republican paramilitary prisoners and the British government. The prolonged and single focus of the ten republicans who chose death over personal dishonor revived the interest of Irish Americans in the Northern Ireland conflict. Irish American sympathy began to shift from the nationalist groups to the republican groups. Along with the Irish Embassy in Washington, D.C., Irish American moderate nationalists and congressional leadership were now portrayed by Irish American republicans as inept and unable to influence US foreign policy. To the British government, which was constantly seeking to undermine the IRA's influence in the United States, the sudden American outburst of support for republican prisoners and their hunger strike was both frightening and appalling.

Meanwhile, a new congressional organization consisting of seventy members of Congress was announced on St. Patrick's Day in 1981. The Friends of Ireland, led by Speaker O'Neill and Senator Kennedy, was not just venom in the IRA veins but also a challenge to the organization's influence in America. It had more potential political clout than any existing Irish American group, including the INC and the Ad Hoc Congressional Committee. Despite initial setbacks, the influence of the Friends of Ireland began to grow incrementally. This rise in influence can be traced back to the private and confidential meeting between Kirk O'Donnell from the Speaker's office, Werner Brant from the House majority whip's office, and Jim Sharkey of the Irish Embassy in Washington. One of the five strategic decisions they implemented was to expand the range of positive activities accessible to all Irish Americans, including moderate nationalist Northern Ireland visitors invited to attend "Irish" events in America.

Irish American republican groups and the Friends of Ireland, however, did join to strongly urge President Reagan to intervene, or at least to engage Thatcher in a dialogue on the hunger-strike issue. George Shultz, who replaced Haig as secretary of state in 1982, signaled to the British government a quiet diplomatic change in US foreign policy emphasis toward Northern Ireland. Thatcher responded by asking that the US government send three American citizens to Britain's Ditchley Conference to begin the Northern Ireland peace process, and the US government agreed.

Sir Charles Carter, a British specialist on the Northern Ireland crisis, brought together government policy makers from Britain, Ireland, and Northern Ireland and three Americans: one representing the White House, one representing Congress, and one being myself, the only American academic who had lived and conducted research in Northern Ireland during the Troubles. Dennis Blair, a staff member in Reagan's NSC, was assigned to contribute to the conference's cultural discussions. Britain and Ireland knew that the entire White House staff supported UK policies, but the White House staff needed to discover the complexities of Northern Ireland's unionist/loyalist and nationalist/republican communities. Werner Brant, representing the Speaker's office, was assigned to the conference's economic discussions. Britain and Ireland knew that members of Congress supported the nationalist community, but congressmen needed to know the extent of Northern Ireland's financial needs. As an academic just ending a sabbatical at the Queen's University of Belfast Institute of Irish Studies and an ACIS member, I was assigned to the conference's political discussions so the British and Irish politicians could measure the likely future role of America and Irish Americans regarding Northern Ireland. Upon returning to America, the challenge, as expressed in *American Policy and Northern Ireland: A Saga of Peacebuilding* (Thompson 2001), was to bring some reality to leaders of the Irish American community through radio and television interviews across the United States, as well as delivering research papers on Northern Ireland to ACIS conference members. The United States, with its quiet diplomacy, had finally become thoroughly involved in the Northern Ireland issue.

The American role in Northern Ireland also continued to grow stronger with each British mistake. Stephen Wall accurately predicted in his reports to London that O'Donnell from the Speaker's office and Gary Parker from Kennedy's office would be successful in creating a formal legislative link between Dublin and Washington: the Ireland–United States Parliamentary Group. The Friends of Ireland also believed that it would be to their advantage to be seen as influencing foreign policy formation, since this would attract additional support from Irish American leaders. Speaker O'Neill assigned O'Donnell and Brant to immediately develop an approach to convince members of Congress to support American efforts for increased Northern Ireland economic development. Irish sympathizers in Congress then began to actively influence US policy toward Northern Ireland rather than simply to speak about it. To this end, the first American "green" State Department FSO, Samuel Bartlett from Boston, was appointed consul general to Belfast. Bartlett was the behind-the-scenes internal force of change in the State Department's understanding of nationalist and republican groups in Northern Ireland. His first controversial decisions were issuing visas to republican

Northern Ireland politicians to visit the United States and denying visas for the first time to extreme loyalist politicians such as Ian Paisley.

In a demonstration of goodwill, the United States offered Ireland and Britain individual Extradition Treaties with regard to accused IRA members so as "to deter the spread of terrorism." This suggested a US policy change at the end of Reagan's first administration that would find fulfillment in his second administration with the Anglo-Irish Agreement of 1985. The agreement confirmed three permanent relationships. First was both Ireland's and Britain's recognition of the permanent status of the Irish province within the United Kingdom unless the majority of the people of Northern Ireland voted for a change in the future. Second was the formation of an annual intergovernmental conference jointly chaired by the UK secretary of state for Northern Ireland and the permanent Irish ministerial representative to Northern Ireland. Third was Britain's initiation of the process for a devolved government for Northern Ireland. Irish American leaders and Congress did not believe that the agreement was the final answer to the crisis but considered it an important first step toward reconciliation on the island. The thin edge of the interventionist wedge was inserted when the Extradition Treaty and the International Fund for Northern Ireland were submitted to the US Congress. The United States no longer regarded Northern Ireland as completely a British domestic matter.

The International Fund for Northern Ireland was intended to be the economic "bricks and mortar" of the Anglo-Irish Agreement. The title of this economic package in America was quickly altered by O'Donnell and Parker to read "the International Fund for Ireland," inasmuch as Irish Americans would more readily accept the title of "Ireland" than the official title of "Northern Ireland." The White House and the State Department agreed with this congressional title change in light of everyone's wish not to unnecessarily agitate Irish American leaders.

Prominent Irish American corporate leaders, who until this time had stayed quietly outside any public involvement, now decided to play devil's advocate. They decided to inform the White House and the State Department that, since moderate nationalists seemed to be slipping in their influence in foreign policy formation (as evidenced by the inability of the Friends of Ireland to produce a successful pro-Irish policy), the only alternative for Irish American business leaders would be for the Irish American economic and social elite to switch their support to Noraid. If the moderate Irish American leaders were unable to provide visible and demonstrable success with the Supplementary Extradition Treaty and the International Fund for Ireland, then the sole existing representative of the Irish American voice would be Noraid. The White House, State Department, Britain, and Ireland viewed this shocking possibility with alarm.

If things were not difficult enough for the US government officials attempting to pass the Extradition and International Fund Treaties in the US Senate, the creation of the Irish American Unity Conference and the launching of the MacBride Principles were flash-in-the-pan efforts by Noraid to attract Irish American support for republican ideology. A tall Texas millionaire, James Delaney, believed in the republican movement and agreed to fund many local chapter activities of the Irish American Unity Conference. McManus quickly allowed this new Irish American group to establish its lobbying office in Washington, and soon the cross-membership and funds were working for the INC agenda.

In 1984 the New York City Irish American republicans created a campaign that would make Catholic nationalist unemployment in Northern Ireland another important political issue. The INC introduced the MacBride Principles, which were based on the Sullivan Principles scheme for apartheid in South Africa. The success of the MacBride Principles was measured by the five states and five cities that immediately approved these measures for their local Irish American groups.

After several closed-door sessions with government officials from America, Britain, and Ireland, the Friends of Ireland finally convinced these policy makers to formulate serious policy changes toward Northern Ireland. The State Department appointed a new US consul general to Belfast, Douglas Archard. He was married to a Northern Ireland citizen, so his reports on the political nuances of unionist and loyalist groups were a marked improvement from those of previous "British apologists." The British government in turn implemented the Fair Employment Act of 1989, which addressed the discrimination laws against Catholic nationalist workers. Ireland began to address the cross-border activity of the IRA groups, and the US government ratified the Supplementary Extradition Treaties and approved the Irish funding request.

Several important personnel changes in Irish American leadership occurred by the end of 1988. Speaker O'Neill had retired from Congress, and his retired general counsel O'Donnell took with him a wealth of information and institutional memory accumulated from his deep interest in Northern Ireland. Brant had moved on to be the House sergeant-at-arms before retirement, and Biaggi had resigned after his conviction on corruption charges. The Reagan administration was pleased by the presidential electoral success of Vice President George Bush, but Irish American leaders were concerned that the new administration would ignore the Northern Ireland issue that they had worked so hard to bring before the government.

During this third stage, therefore, all interested parties had attempted to openly lobby Irish American leaders and US government officials regarding the Northern Ireland conflict. All parties desired the goal of peace, but it continued to elude their best attempts.

Stage 4: Commitment to the Peace Process (1990–2000)

While nothing dramatic occurred in America regarding Northern Ireland during the Bush Senior administration, some significant developments on both sides of the Atlantic escaped general notice. These quiet developments would lay a solid foundation for the rapid progress of the peace process during the Clinton administration. For example, one was improved routine contact between the US consul general in Belfast and all political entities of Northern Ireland. More accurate reports from Belfast made the State Department better able to communicate this information to government decision makers and Irish American leaders.

Realizing the growing importance of knowledgeable Irish Americans who were now involved in the formation of US foreign policy, Sir Brian Mawhinney, the Belfast-born spokesman for the British Conservative government, decided in 1989 to establish a Northern Ireland Bureau in Washington, D.C. The bureau was opened by Derrick Wheeler and initially housed in the British Embassy. Although the stated purpose of the bureau was to facilitate economic and cultural information requests from Americans, its political contacts with the Washington elite and those beyond the Beltway became immeasurably effective, especially during the month of March—America's "Irish" season.

Straight away Irish American leaders publicly expressed their disappointment that they had to use the British Embassy for contact with the Northern Ireland Bureau. Not until the Northern Ireland government was reestablished in 1999 did the bureau move outside the embassy with consulate status to facilitate Irish American and government official requests for information. Meanwhile, Secretary of State James Baker decided to use an upcoming scheduled Woodrow Wilson Center's conference on Northern Ireland as the occasion to announce a change in the role of the United States in Northern Ireland affairs. Attending the conference meetings held in the US State Department were government policy makers from the United States, Ireland, Britain, and Northern Ireland, as well as Irish American leaders.

Kenneth Longmeyer, the political desk FSO for Ireland/Northern Ireland, wrote the Woodrow Wilson Center's conference speech for Ralph Johnson (Deputy Secretary of State Lawrence Eagleburger's deputy assistant for Europe). The statement acknowledged that congressional and Irish American leaders were demanding a clear, explicit explanation of "what US policy is and what their government is doing about Northern Ireland." Johnson ended his speech by affirming: "We believe that our excellent relations with both Ireland and the United Kingdom enhance our ability to play a constructive role." This constructive role was soon realized in the Clinton administration.

Clinton's campaign team believed that Irish Americans voted as an ethnic bloc. Chris Hyland, Clinton's campaign officer, therefore, asked Niall O'Dowd, editor of the New York City republican newspaper *Irish Voice*, for assistance to reach the Irish American electorate. O'Dowd agreed to assist the campaign and suggested that Hyland contact former congressman Bruce Morrison (D-CT) for suggestions. Morrison had been Clinton's classmate at Yale and had previously worked for Hillary Clinton.

Hyland, Morrison, and O'Dowd quickly arranged "an Irish evening" for New York Irish Americans to meet presidential candidate Clinton. Several notable Irish Americans were also in attendance, including Mayor Raymond Flynn of Boston, Ray O'Hanlon and Patrick Farrelly (both from Irish American republican newspapers), and Martin Gavin of Noraid. At the April 6, 1992, meeting Clinton made a campaign promise to the audience that if he were elected he would appoint a special envoy to Northern Ireland and, despite the Bush administration's denial of a visa, would grant a visa to the republican Gerry Adams of the Sinn Fein Party. Clinton gave the audience the impression that he understood and empathized with Irish American attitudes toward Northern Ireland. Moreover, his campaign team spread the word that Clinton, Irish American via his maternal ancestors, had had a personal interest in the Irish issue since his studies at Oxford in the late 1960s, when the Troubles in Northern Ireland erupted. The Irish American evening in New York triggered the formation of the Irish Americans for Clinton/Gore Association, which later became known as Americans for a New Ireland Agenda. The Irish American leaders of this organization had one overriding objective—to involve the Clinton administration in a Northern Ireland peace process. By avoiding the usual Irish American republican demand for a definitive yes/no on a "united Ireland" or "Brits Out" decision, the new association accepted a psychological strategy that was moderate and not an in-your-face approach. Several Irish American leaders then arranged a meeting with Nancy Soderberg, who had transferred from Senator Kennedy's office to be the primary adviser on Northern Ireland in the NSC. Rather than employ the confrontational approach used by the Ad Hoc Congressional Committee and the INC, the Irish American leaders worked in tandem with the White House staff. This was a bottom-up commitment to US foreign policy formation rather than the traditional top-down manipulation of the interests and goals of Irish Americans.

Developing connections with members of the White House staff is different from having personal friends in important government positions. Presidential appointments can take on a special significance when the individual chosen for a very public position holds symbolic meaning for the ethnic diaspora group. This symbolic appointment occurred when Clinton nominated a Kennedy to be his ambassador to Ireland. Clinton believed that his choice of Jean Kennedy Smith as ambassador demonstrated his personal commitment to the Irish American community. Upon assuming her duties in Dublin, Ambassador Smith immediately sought and received permission from the State Department to visit Northern Ireland. The US consul general Valentino Martinez arranged for Smith to meet as many politicians as possible in Belfast and Derry. These actions pleased all Irish Americans and Northern Ireland leaders.

House Speaker Thomas Foley, Secretary of State Warren Christopher, Janet Reno of the Justice Department, Director Louis Freech of the FBI, and the CIA—these government leaders joined forces in opposition to recognizing the growing strength of the Irish American movement in America. It would take the personal involvement of an Irish American business leader, William Flynn, and an Irish immigrant, Niall O'Dowd, to finally tip the balance in the US government toward the moderate Irish American cause. Flynn had multiple connections with Washington politicians and a special connection to the Kennedy family through his bodyguard, Bill Barry, who had worked for Robert Kennedy. Flynn was an integral part of the Irish American movement (his father having immigrated from Loughinisland, County Down, Northern Ireland). He also personally rejected any form of violence and had been involved in several international conflict-resolution issues through his position as chairman of the National Committee on American Foreign Policy. After a lengthy discussion in 1993 with two Noraid members in his New York City office (they challenged him to act in a non-violent manner for Ireland as he was acting for other international issues) and a visit to Northern Ireland to talk with Gerry Adams and Father Alex Reid (a Redemptorist priest who had initiated the dialogue between Adams and Hume), Flynn committed himself to search for a nonviolent resolution of the conflict.

With the blessings of President Clinton, O'Dowd led an Irish American peace delegation to Northern Ireland and acted as an intermediary between Northern Ireland republicans and the White House. Kennedy, Hume, and O'Dowd played key roles in eventually securing an American visa for Gerry Adams when the peace process would come under attack by the unionist politicians and the British government.

In America's "search for peace and reconciliation in Northern Ireland," Clinton announced new economic and political initiatives to assist reconciliation. To this end, Clinton appointed Jim Lyons to be the US observer to the International Fund for Ireland in 1993. He had been a personal friend of the president for many years, having been the attorney general of Arkansas during Clinton's gubernatorial years. To counter this American move, the British government hastily arranged for an economic conference in Belfast that would exclude the Northern Ireland republican leaders from attending. The White House, however, successfully demanded that Adams and his republican Sinn Fein politicians be allowed to attend the Belfast conference. This was a clear indication that the Clinton administration's interests and goals had completely converged with those of Irish American leaders in setting the political and economic agenda for Northern Ireland.

The spotlight quickly shifted to the Irish American Democratic senator from Maine, George Mitchell. He was appointed by Clinton not (yet) as a peace envoy but as something more practical—an economic envoy. Mitchell immediately reached out to British, Irish, and Irish American leaders of all points of view, that is, nationalist/republican and unionist/loyalist, economic and political, domestic and foreign. Once Mitchell became a major player, the "American component" created a momentum and a venue for moving the process through other initiatives, such as visas, economic conferences, and political discussions.

With this positive movement in the United States, the White House decided to expand the involvement of Irish American leaders. Rosemary O'Neill, as an outstanding State Department FSO and eldest daughter of the former House Speaker, was asked by Clinton to arrange a special luncheon between State Department policy makers and two academics (Paul Arthur of the SDLP and me) to discuss other facets of a Northern Ireland peace process. One important step was the appointment of Kathleen Stephens as US consul general to Belfast. Stephens was transferred to Belfast from her NSC position so as to closely monitor events that would soon involve the first presidential visit to Northern Ireland. The US government had moved beyond Bartlett's analysis of nationalist and republican groups and beyond Archard's analysis of unionist and loyalist groups. Now the White House required intelligence reports.

Riding the momentum of his administration's policy toward Northern Ireland, Clinton visited the island in December 1995. Thousands of people crammed the streets of Derry and Belfast to see and hear Clinton during his well-planned visit. Irish Americans were enamored with his commitment to bring Northern Ireland to the forefront of US foreign policy. In essence, the president told the American people and the entire world that the United States was deeply involved in an effort to bring about a peaceful resolution to the violence in Northern Ireland. Thus it was a great relief to Irish American leaders that Clinton was reelected for a second term as president. His image as a peacemaker for Northern Ireland had endeared the president to all Irish Americans.

Important personnel changes made during the transition to a second-term administration meant the loss of NSC advisers Lake and Soderberg, who left the White House for other governmental positions. The new NSC adviser, Samuel "Sandy" Berger, was unaccustomed to the slow, painful peace process of Northern Ireland and requested that his new staff discover why it was stalled. Flynn, in a speech before the National Committee on American Foreign Policy, believed there was only one reason for the serious delay in Northern Ireland. He avowed it was "not from a lack of integrity, but rather the reactions of a Tory government straining to hold every possible vote in order to stay in power [in the United Kingdom]." To stay in power, British prime minister John Major depended on the support of the nine Unionist Westminster members from Northern Ireland.

Bolstered by this image of their importance in London, Unionist leaders decided to share their vision of Northern Ireland's future with their supporters in America. What better time to have a lecture tour in the United States than the celebrations surrounding St. Patrick's Day, suggested Jeffrey Donaldson, director of the Unionist Party's North American bureau, and Ann Smith of the newly established Unionist Party Information Office in Washington. Donaldson and two members of the Westminster Parliament, David Trimble and Ken Maginnis, were the major speakers on the tour. At these gatherings, Irish American leaders and members of the Orange Order in America were shocked at the shallow and defensive thinking by Unionist politicians regarding the political future of Northern Ireland. These meetings produced neither media coverage nor acceptance among either Irish Americans or Washington officials.

Lacking the support of Irish Americans and US government officials, and out of power when Tony Blair and his Labour Party won a landslide victory in Britain, the Unionist politicians agreed to participate in Britain's proposed All-Party political talks with Adams and his republican Sinn Fein Party. When George Mitchell was appointed to this purely political position as chairman of the All-Party Talks, Jim Lyons assumed the position of special adviser to the president and secretary of state for economic initiatives in Ireland and Northern Ireland.

Mitchell grabbed this opportunity to reconvene the lagging political negotiations. After twenty-two months of on-again/off-again negotiations, the Belfast Agreement (better known as the Good Friday Agreement) was signed by all political parties on April 10, 1998. No one was more elated than Mitchell and his closest associate, Martha Pope, at the successful conclusion of the complicated and bitter meetings, as he so tellingly relates in his book *Making Peace* (Mitchell 1999). Every Irish American group in the United States celebrated the news of the peace agreement. There was a very positive feeling at every level of relationship between US government officials and Irish American leaders.

The fourth stage of the relationship between US government officials and Irish American leaders had demanded a real converging commitment to the peace process. Now that Northern Ireland was on the path to greater tranquillity and the paramilitary violence had subsided, a generation of peace was possible.

Stage 5: Maintaining Policy Convergence (post–2000)

The Irish American strategy after the Good Friday Agreement was to persist in keeping government officials focused on the Northern Ireland issue. To this extent, Rosemary O'Neill convinced the State Department to assemble a group of Irish American leaders for meetings with the president's special envoy for Northern Ireland. One of the obligations of taking on this honorific assignment was for the special envoy, after every visit to Northern Ireland, to meet with Irish American leaders in Washington and let everybody in on the latest developments in Northern Ireland affairs. The special envoy meetings were chaired by Richard Haas, who eventually moved from the State Department to be president of the Council on Foreign Relations in New York City; then for three years by Mitchell Reiss, who in due course returned to the College of William and Mary in Virginia as the vice-provost of International Affairs; and then by Paula Dobriansky, who went on to accept a position in a Washington law firm.

At this writing, the Obama administration has suggested splitting the position in two—a special economic envoy and a special political envoy. Irish American leaders were initially very sensitive about whoever assumed these positions, since the US government's selection of anyone less than acceptable would be considered a snub of Irish Americans. US government officials and Irish Americans were relieved when Hillary Clinton, as secretary of state, accepted both the economic and political envoy positions. Government officials will need to continue to encourage positive relations with Irish American leaders during this fifth stage as the Northern Ireland communities continue in their struggle to remain within the peace process.

There is no better example of the convoluted relationships of convergence and divergence between the interests and goals of any ethnic group and US government officials than America's experience in the Northern Ireland peace process. This chapter intended, not to produce a laundry list of "dos and don'ts" as gleaned from Irish American activity during the US involvement in Northern Ireland, but to summarize the peacemakers' attempts to implement goals within each stage of the peace process. Ethnic group concerns are the physical and ideological glue that will bind people to the ideals of the peace process when they are confronted by future difficulties. These basic conditions will offer a glimmer of hope for the future of every diaspora group seeking a resolution to the violence in their home country. Although a formula to end violence worldwide is not guaranteed, a consensus exists among policy analysts regarding the basic prerequisites for any peace process.

The mitigation of Northern Ireland violence was realized after successful attainment of five conditions. Four of the five needed to evolve within the domestic realm of those confronted by violence, and the fifth one within the international realm (in this case the United States). The four domestic conditions for Northern Ireland and its political leaders were (1) people living in the Northern Ireland conflict reaching the point at which changing the status quo of violence became less painful than being locked in a stalemate; (2) the nurturing of community/political leaders in Northern Ireland, who were then given legitimate authority to bring an end to the violence; (3) the design of homegrown institutional structures in Northern Ireland to deal competently with the crisis; and (4) an adequate period of haggling in which indigenous leaders were permitted to discuss various alternatives, which could then be sold to their respective peoples. The final, international condition was (5) US support for the nonviolent positions of Northern Ireland's political leaders.

Before the first condition was met, when violence was rampant throughout Northern Ireland, Irish American leaders presumed that the republican paramilitary leaders had correctly perceived the conflict as a result of a single rational cause. The Northern Ireland conflict, US government officials and Irish American diaspora leaders were led to believe, stemmed directly from either IRA violence or the British military presence. US government officials presumed that America had no possible role to play in the Irish situation, and the diaspora leaders presumed that only by supporting the paramilitary IRA could Ireland be free of British rule. Thus there was no reason for government officials to be in touch with Irish American diaspora leaders, and vice versa.

However, violence and murder do not bring peace to any community. They foster fear, not peace. Nearly thirty years of British "direct rule" elapsed before the violent struggle between Northern Ireland's communities eventually brought citizens and paramilitary leaders alike to address this common realization.

The second condition for the development of the peace process was the creation of new representative positions that would legally strengthen the political culture of Northern Ireland. Many Irish American leaders and US government officials doubted that London's gerrymandering schemes were the most promising means of undoing the discrimination of the Stormont government and fostering nonviolence in Northern Ireland. Unfortunately, republican leaders went along with the British proposed plan, reasoning that the Stormont government needed to be dragged kicking and screaming by pressure from London to do the perceived moral thing for their citizens. But if it was wrong for the opposition to use illegal methods to stay in power, why was it acceptable for the republican group to use the same methods to redress grievances? Peace is never attained by illegal decisions. Accountability needs to be linked with representation.

Irish American republican leaders believed that British gerrymandering within the Belfast districts was acceptable because it allowed Gerry Adams (Sinn Fein Party) to win the Westminster seat from the moderate nationalist Joe Hendron (SDLP). However, such a political change made it more difficult for the moderate nationalist leaders to work with US government officials. This second condition for peace was achieved not from the bottom up, as the first condition had been, but from the top down.

The third condition for peace was the creation of acceptable political governance structures in Northern Ireland. The establishment of a legitimate governing body with the authority to legislate the province's future continues to hinge on cross-community trust. The many cross-community projects supported by US government officials and Irish American groups helped expand the nonviolent culture in Northern Ireland. These voices for peace that were nurtured over the years by cross-community work and reconciliation projects have always been supported by Irish Americans. The Ulster Project Delaware, which continues to bring youth members of both Northern Ireland communities to Delaware for the summer, the project of America's Habitat for Humanity to build houses for all those burned out of their homes during the violence, and the work of the Irish Lobby for Immigration Reform in the United States are but three of many attempts to engender trust within Northern Ireland communities. In addition, US government officials have made many other such contributions through contacts with officials from Britain, Northern Ireland, and Ireland. Irish American leaders and American officials continue to encourage Northern Ireland's path toward community trust, which facilitates the coming together of Northern Ireland politicians in homegrown government structures.

The fourth condition required a period of negotiation during which the elected political leaders were permitted to discuss alternative resolutions to their conflict. More important, these resolutions then needed to be sold to the people, including diaspora Irish Americans. In a sense, Northern Ireland people needed to integrate the three previous domestic conditions into their political culture. Irish Americans also needed time to absorb the changes, inasmuch as these diverged dramatically from the traditional Irish American culture.

Irish Americans and US government officials can be separated into three groups, each holding a particular viewpoint regarding this fourth domestic condition for peace in Northern Ireland. Each viewpoint hinges on the group's perception and interpretation of the authority crisis. According to the first viewpoint, all Northern Ireland events are opportunities to measure the degree of animosity between the unionist and nationalist communities, or, as they would bellow, between Catholics and Protestants. Some Irish Americans and government officials characterize Northern Ireland as a deeply divided society where violence will always exist. Pointing to the recent criminal activity and killings by the extreme branches of the IRA and loyalist groups in Northern Ireland (Associated Press 2013; McDonald 2012), they claim that political leaders will never be able to sell any serious concept of peace in the region.

The second viewpoint offers a slightly more detailed and less pessimistic picture: that the expanding leadership base throughout the province permits for more elected representatives from the new popular political parties. Those who hold this viewpoint envision that support for defeatist politicians will eventually decline, or that fanatical politicians will become more moderate so as to remain in power. Their best example is the change in Ian Paisley's loyalist politics to support the new Northern Ireland government. However, these leaders believe that political dialogue is possible in Northern Ireland only if the US government continues to pressure Northern Ireland politicians and the British government to stay the course toward peace.

According to the third viewpoint, peace in Northern Ireland must be the combined result of implementing all five conditions, which together have a synergistic effect. These supporters (aptly labeled "peace builders") are convinced that the moment to resolve Northern Ireland's future has arrived and that all parties must continue down this path toward lasting peace.

In the case of Northern Ireland, not all of the four domestic conditions have been fully achieved yet, as evidenced by the slow implementation among extreme loyalists and republican paramilitary groups of agreements to put all their weapons "beyond use." Their decommissioning is a necessary element in the peace process. The challenge is to continue to strengthen the Irish peace process despite possible attempts to subvert it.

The final, fifth condition is an international context that supports the nonviolent positions of political leaders. This became the primary role for moderate Irish American leaders dealing with the US government during all of Northern Ireland's peace process. From 1969 on, every decision by the US government built layer upon layer of involvement in the Northern Ireland conflict, eventually allowing President Clinton to be a full participant in the peace process. These decisions were the direct result of Irish Americans' consistent demands upon their government officials.

At the outset, Northern Ireland received no special consideration from the White House or State Department in terms of foreign policy. They viewed the conflict as an internal issue for Britain to handle, and any potential American political involvement as intrusive. In reality, however, the United States was already involved in the Northern Ireland conflict. The US government supported British decisions regarding Northern Ireland, and the republican Irish American diaspora was a major network source of IRA money, guns, and moral support. Active in the margins of the IRA and Sinn Fein Party networks in America were the INC and the Ad Hoc Congressional Committee. As the republican INC and Ad Hoc Congressional Committee grew stronger, so did Dublin's commitment to lobby in support of Irish constitutional nationalism and the Irish American leaders in Congress.

The Irish American politician who did the most to persuade Congress to support constitutional nationalism in Northern Ireland was Speaker O'Neill. He loudly castigated the IRA, Noraid, the INC, and the Ad Hoc Congressional Committee for their culpable ignorance of the republican violence that had harmed so many innocent victims. O'Neill and other nationalist Irish Americans believed that these republican diaspora groups were deliberately misleading the American public.

With the constant Irish American push for change, the US government eventually worked to produce political agreements and economic funding for Northern Ireland. President Clinton took credit for what many committed individuals had achieved over twenty years. However, once Clinton was committed "to the cause," he threw the power of the presidency behind the peace process. Consequently, now that the United States is integral to Northern Ireland's peace process, it behooves Irish American leaders and US government officials to continue to be involved in Northern Ireland. This will be especially difficult in a struggling world economy, but the relationship between Irish American leaders and US government officials needs to be more than symbolic.

Initially, the US government considered Northern Ireland to be of little strategic worth and had no set objectives with respect to the Northern Ireland conflict. A surge of American interest in "Irishness," as exemplified by the popularity of *Riverdance* and a bull market of US investment in Northern Ireland, came about after relationships between the US government officials and Irish American leaders improved. The foreign policy that eventually prevailed was due to personal connections, group lobbying, and committed individuals with legitimate authority who wielded their influence at critical moments in Northern Ireland's history. An international context that supported change in Northern Ireland was created by Irish American leaders who believed in their role as peace builders. It is important to note that the success of all of the conditions for peace depends on an honest and strong relationship between Irish American leaders, US government officials, and British, Irish, and Northern Irish politicians. The US government and Irish American leaders have judged that peace is possible for the people of Northern Ireland, but only if their political leaders persist in nurturing its conditions.

References

Associated Press. 2013. "Ireland: 8 Face Charges of I.R.A. Ties." *New York Times*, July 5. www.nytimes.com/2013/07/06/world/europe/ireland-8-face-charges-of-ira-ties.html.

Coogan, Tim Pat. 2000. *Wherever Green Is Worn: The Story of the Irish Diaspora*. New York: Palgrave.

Funchion, Michael, ed. 1983. *Irish American Voluntary Organizations*. Westport, CT: Greenwood Press.

Holland, Jack. 1987. *The American Connection: U.S. Guns, Money, and Influence in Northern Ireland*. New York: Viking.

McDonald, Henry. 2012. "Northern Ireland Prison Officer Ambush Prompts Fears of Sectarian Shooting War." *Guardian*, November 1. www.theguardian.com/uk/2012/nov/01/northern-ireland-prison-officer-ambush-analysis.

Mitchell, George. 1999. *Making Peace*. New York: Alfred A. Knopf.

Ross, Marc Howard. 2007. *Cultural Contestation in Ethnic Conflict*. Cambridge: Cambridge University Press.

Thompson, Joseph E. 2001. *American Policy and Northern Ireland: A Saga of Peacebuilding*. Westport, CT: Praeger.

CHAPTER SIX

Cuban Americans and US Cuba Policy

Lisandro Pérez

When people ask me about Cuba, it makes me think of three things: Florida, Florida, and Florida.
—Karl Rove

The words attributed to President George W. Bush's chief political strategist are not a revelation to even a casual observer of US Cuba policy. It has been quite evident since the 1980s that the Cuban diaspora in the United States, a majority of it residing in Florida, has exerted a determining influence on maintaining and even tightening a US policy that seeks to isolate and change the regime in Havana. That policy is now more than half a century old, raising questions about the ability of the more powerful sectors of the Cuban community to successfully sustain their opposition to any changes that would soften what has been a hostile US policy toward the Cuban government, a policy that has estranged the United States, and its citizens, from one of its closest neighbors.

Origins and Evolution of the Conflict

Almost no one in Cuba or in the United States could have anticipated the far-reaching consequences of the overthrow of the government of Fulgencio Batista on January 1, 1959. Batista's unconstitutional and unpopular government abruptly ended with his departure from the island on that day, creating a power vacuum that was immediately filled by the army of rebels headed by Fidel Castro. A thirty-two-year-old lawyer and former university activist who had managed to put together from his guerrilla hideout in the eastern mountains a national movement to topple the Batista government, Castro was viewed somewhat warily by Washington when he swept into power. He promptly assumed the role of trustee of the long-postponed Cuban revolution that José Martí, the venerated nineteenth-century nationalist, had envisioned for the Cuban nation, a revolution characterized by social justice, equality, and sovereignty. It was a discourse of change, of popular nationalism, and of revolution, all coming from the immensely popular leader of a nation only ninety miles from the United States where US corporations had invested hundreds of millions of dollars in virtually every economic sector.

Evidence of Washington's guarded reaction to the new revolutionary government in Cuba was the refusal of President Eisenhower to meet personally with Fidel Castro when the new leader traveled to Washington in April of 1959 on an unofficial visit, invited by the National Press Club. Subsequent actions by both governments would place the two nations on a collision course. Between 1959 and 1962 a complete turnaround took place in the relations between the United States and Cuba, changing from the "ties of singular intimacy" that had characterized the relations between the two countries since the nineteenth century to one of the most contentious relationships of US foreign affairs that took Washington to the brink of nuclear war in October of 1962. During that period the United States eliminated the sugar quota (a long-standing trade provision favorable to the island), Cuba nationalized all US companies, the United States severed diplomatic relations with Havana and imposed a trade embargo while Cuba became a trading partner and an ally of the Soviet Union, central economic planning replaced capitalism, the United States attempted a military invasion of the island to topple the regime, and the Soviet Union introduced offensive nuclear missiles into the island, leading to an epic confrontation with the United States.

After decades of a Cuba economically and politically dependent on the United States, a total transformation took place in just a few short years, one that perhaps not even Fidel Castro fully anticipated. The result was the establishment of hostile relations between the two countries that have lasted for half a century. Neither country has gained by this development, and the Cuban family has been the greatest loser. Separated by migration and a long-standing feud with the United States, Cuba is a divided nation.

It would be a mistake to explain the protracted conflict between the United States and Cuba solely in political and economic terms. The confiscation of American properties, the ostensible justification for the embargo, does not go far enough as an explanation for why the conflict between the two nations has spanned five decades. Nearly sixty thousand American lives were lost in the war in Vietnam, yet the United States has normalized relations with that country. In the Cuban case, several factors have contributed to keeping the two nations distant from each other. One may have been a sense of betrayal in Washington that a nation that had historically been so close to the United States would align itself with the other side, the Soviet bloc, at the height of the Cold War. In the years prior to the Revolution, no country exceeded Cuba in the volume of its exchange of passengers with the United States. Politically, economically, and even culturally, the United States had shaped twentieth-century Cuba. If indeed emotion has played a role, then it has been heightened by the fact that it is personal: the individual who engineered that "betrayal" has survived into the new millennium.

Whether such intangible factors as emotion and personality have played a role in sustaining the conflict between the two countries may be questionable. But what is far clearer is the role of the Cuban diaspora in the United States in maintaining a policy of hostility and isolation toward the island.

The Cuban Diaspora in the United States

The 2010 US Census counted 1,785,547 persons who identified themselves as being of Cuban "origin or descent." While those of Cuban origin represent less than 4 percent of the Hispanic or Spanish-origin population of the United States, their tendency to concentrate in southern Florida gives them a majority in one of the metropolitan areas of the United States in which Hispanics constitute a majority of the population: Greater Miami. The nearly 940,000 Cuban-origin persons residing in the Florida counties of Miami-Dade and Broward represent 53 percent of all Cubans in the United States (US Census Bureau 2010).

The Cuban presence in the United States has been shaped by the emigration from the island since the Revolution of 1959. Of the nearly 1.8 million Cuban-origin persons in the United States in 2010, slightly more than 1.1 million were actually born in the island. In contrast, the 1950 US Census found fewer than 35,000 Cuban-born persons in the United States. The present-day Cuban diaspora, therefore, is composed almost entirely of immigrants whose presence in the United States is linked to the process of revolutionary change in Cuba.

The fact that the contemporary Cuban presence in the United States is largely a product of the Cuban Revolution should not, however, lead us to underestimate the historical importance of Cuban migration to the United States dating back to the early nineteenth century. Migration to the United States, permanently or temporarily, has long been a recurrent response to political processes and upheaval in the island and a barometer of the increasingly intimate relations between the two countries.

As early as the mid-nineteenth century a pattern was established for Cuban American communities that was followed well into the twentieth century: a migration initiated by the alienated or persecuted upper sectors of Cuban society, eventually followed by other social classes, creating communities marked by an active interest and participation in movements to change the political status of the homeland. That pattern would be repeated by the post-1959 migrants from Cuba. In the next section we will examine the important parallels between the historical and contemporary Cuban presence in the United States in the very dimension of the diaspora we are examining here: its influence on US policy toward the island. Here we will look at how the migration waves from Cuba to the United States have been determined by political events and processes, making the US Cuban diaspora, now and before, essentially a political product and therefore, not surprisingly, a diaspora vitally interested in US policy toward the island.

The most important Cuban American communities in the nineteenth century all owed their origins and development to two related factors: (1) the burgeoning commerce between the United States and Spain's island colony, and (2) the long struggle to extricate Cuba from Spanish control. Key West, New Orleans, and New York housed the earliest and most numerous communities of Cubans in the United States. Although their numbers were modest (none probably exceeded three thousand in population), they were communities that played a prominent role in the economic and political history of Cuba and its relations with the United States. New York became, after the Civil War, the most important Cuban community for most of the remainder of the century. In fact, during the 1870s and 1880s Cuban New Yorkers constituted the largest community of Latin Americans east of the Mississippi (Pérez 2009, 136).

The outbreak of the first war for Cuban independence in 1868 was a watershed event in the history of Cuban migration to the United States. Many landowners, businessmen, and intellectuals who supported the Cuban cause found themselves persecuted by the Spanish authorities and their properties confiscated or embargoed. They flocked to New York, where they had previous business contacts and even financial accounts. The 1870 US Census showed that many of the prominent Cuban landholding families were living in Manhattan that year, creating for the first time a Cuban community of exiled elites. They were eventually joined by cigar makers, craftsmen, and professionals as the conflict in Cuba dragged on for years. The war finally ended in 1878 without achieving independence, and many families chose to return to the island. Most, however, elected to stay in Greater New York, where the 1880 US Census counted 2,220 Cuban-born persons that year (Pérez 2010, 104–5).

Starting in 1886 another Cuban American community rapidly rose to prominence with the opening of cigar factories in Ybor City, just east of Tampa. Ybor City was the creation of Vicente Martínez Ybor, a Spanish-born cigar manufacturer who had to flee Cuba during the 1868 conflict. On a large tract of land that he had purchased outside Tampa he built not only his factory but also an entire community, with public buildings and housing for the workers. Ybor City was, in effect, an immigrant "company town," as Martínez Ybor succeeding in attracting other cigar manufacturers to open factories in his new development. Ybor City became a major center for the manufacture of cigars, importing from Cuba not only the tobacco leaves but also the workers. The Cuban population of the area boomed, and by the 1900 Census it was the largest Cuban American community in the United States, with more than 3,500 Cuban-born persons.

After World War II and during the early 1950s, Cuban migration increased substantially. This was largely a labor migration spurred by employment opportunities in New York, a phenomenon with origins and characteristics similar to those of the Puerto Rican migration to the city during the same period. But by the mid-1950s the political climate in Cuba had worsened under the dictatorship of Fulgencio Batista, and many left for political reasons. By 1957 more than twelve thousand persons were leaving the island every year, mostly for New York but also for the fairly new winter resort city near Cuba: Miami.

By the time of the Cuban Revolution in 1959, there was already a well-established century-old migration path from Cuba to the United States in response to political events in the island. During the next five decades, however, that revolution would propel an exodus from Cuba that would dwarf any previous human flows from the island to the United States.

There have been four major migration waves from Cuba to the United States since the rise of the present Cuban government in 1959. Although those waves have differed greatly in their characteristics, they have all been the result of a protracted international conflict that has utilized migration as a political tool. A climate of hostility and an absence of normal relations between the two countries, combined with the geographic fact that Cuba is an island, have made migration difficult and generally unavailable except when the two governments, unilaterally or bilaterally, made politically based decisions that allowed migration to take place.

The first wave occurred from 1959 to October 1962. The approximately two hundred thousand persons that composed this wave were automatically granted refugee status by the US government, exempting them from the restrictions imposed on most other nationality groups. A federal program was established in 1961 to assist in the resettlement and economic adjustment of the new arrivals.

In this wave Cuba's displaced elite was disproportionately represented. The contentious transition to socialism affected first and foremost, although not exclusively, the upper sectors of Cuban society. This initial wave has been singularly important in shaping the character of the Cuban presence in the United States. Those arriving at this time had skills and an educational level that facilitated their adjustment to life in the United States and gave them a lasting political and economic hegemony within Miami's Cuban American community. They regarded themselves as reluctant migrants, compelled into exile as they lost the internal class conflict that led to the entrenchment of the socialist order, and they consequently became the principal standard-bearers in the sustained struggle against the Cuban government. They are frequently referred to as the "historical exile."

The second wave started in the fall of 1965, when the Cuban government allowed persons from the United States to go to Cuba in boats to pick up their relatives. Some five thousand persons left from the designated port, Camarioca, before the US government halted the boatlift and agreed to an orderly airlift. Also known as the "freedom flights" or "the aerial bridge," the airlift brought 260,500 persons in twice-daily flights from Varadero, Cuba, to Miami until both governments agreed to end it in 1973. It was the largest of all the waves, but more orderly than the others and much less intense, taking place over eight years. As with the earlier wave, the airlift arrivals were automatically granted refugee visas, facilitating their entry into the United States.

Looking to once again defuse tensions in the island, the Cuban government in 1980 opened another port, Mariel, to allow unrestricted emigration.

What became known as the Mariel boatlift lasted for six months and brought to the United States more than 125,000 Cubans. It was a disorganized exodus on private vessels that went to Cuba from Florida to pick up relatives of persons already living in the United States. More than just relatives boarded the boats, however, resulting in a wave with a profile that was closest to the Cuban population itself, with significant representation from Cuba's lower socioeconomic and nonwhite sectors, as well as writers, artists, professionals, and even government officials. Also arriving in the boatlift were convicted felons and inmates of mental institutions, placed on the boats by the Cuban government. Public attention in the United States, especially in the press, focused on the presence of those felons and inmates among the arrivals. Despite the negative press that the Mariel arrivals received, the bulk of the *marielitos* made successful and productive adjustments to life in this country. But it was clear, after the boatlift was finally halted, that the welcome mat that the United States had always extended to Cubans had worn thin.

On August 11, 1994, responding to an alarming rise in unauthorized, and even violent, departures from the island, the Cuban government announced that it would not detain anyone trying to leave the island in a raft or other vessel, thus initiating the fourth wave. Remembering the Mariel experience, however, the Clinton administration was unwilling to hold the door open for Cubans. Rescued rafters were sent to camps in the US Naval Base at Guantánamo, Cuba, with the expectation that they would never be admitted into the United States. Nearly thirty-seven thousand Cubans were rescued by the US Coast Guard, and most were interned in Guantánamo.

What became known as the Rafter Crisis of 1994 was halted after only a month when the two governments negotiated an agreement whereby the United States committed itself to admit at least twenty thousand Cubans a year through the normal visa process, as well as the rafters held in Guantánamo. The Cuban government, in turn, agreed to accept the return of any future unauthorized migrants interdicted by the US Coast Guard before reaching US shores. This has become known as the "wet-foot, dry-foot policy." Because of the 1966 Cuban Refugee Adjustment Act, which grants any Cuban already in the United States the right to apply for permanent residence in the United States, those Cubans arriving and stepping on US soil (dry-foot) are allowed to remain, even if they entered in an unauthorized manner. But if the Coast Guard interdicts them at sea, even a few feet from shore (wet-foot), they are placed on a Coast Guard vessel and returned to the island under the terms of the 1995 agreement with the Cuban government.

As a result of the 1995 agreement, some twenty thousand Cubans arrive each year through the normal visa process. In addition, unauthorized migrants continue to enter, usually doing so with the help of smugglers with powerboats who bring them either across the Strait of Florida or to Mexico, where they eventually make their way to the United States. Figures from the Immigration and Naturalization Service show that the 2000s was the decade in which the most Cubans entered the United States, a surprising fact given the perception that Cuban migration was largely a phenomenon of the early 1960s and 1970s.

The fact that postrevolutionary Cuban migration to the United States has taken place over a span of half century, arriving in distinct waves, each under different conditions and with different characteristics, is of paramount importance in understanding the contemporary Cuban presence in the United States. It means that it has become increasingly difficult to generalize about Cuban Americans, and, more germane to our topic here, that there is a growing heterogeneity within the diaspora on the issue of US policy toward the island, a point explored more fully later in this chapter.

Patterns of Diaspora Involvement in the Conflict: A Historical Perspective

The involvement of the postrevolutionary Cuban diaspora in the conflict between the US and Cuban governments follows the patterns of political activism established by the historical Cuban communities in the United States. Those patterns can be summarized as follows: (1) the leading role of elites in shaping diaspora influence on US Cuba policy; (2) regime change in the island as the overriding goal; (3) attempts to involve the United States in accomplishing the goal; (4) the exertion of influence over members of the US Congress, as well as access to the highest levels of the executive branch; and (5) despite some success in securing the implementation of US policies consistent with the goal, a failure, generally, to achieve a change in the political situation in the island.

Elite Leadership
As noted previously, the "historical exiles," those who arrived in the early 1960s alienated by the transition to socialism and who were disproportionately

drawn from Cuba's upper socioeconomic levels, have largely determined, until recently, the political agenda of the Cuban diaspora and have tended to dominate its political discourse. That agenda reflects the elites' interest in recovering the homeland through a policy of hostility and isolation toward the island. Almost without exception the leadership and organizations of the diaspora have been dominated by those from this wave of arrival, Cubans who embrace the term *exile* to represent the primacy they place on the status of the homeland. Their leadership of the exiles' agenda is reinforced by their higher socioeconomic position within the diaspora.

Almost without exception, elites have figured prominently in the history of Cuban migration to the United States, and especially in the diaspora's efforts to influence US policy toward Cuba. The annexationist movement of the 1840s was headed by the landed aristocracy, men who attempted, through various means, to separate Cuba from Spain and annex it to the United States. Reflecting the interest of plantation owners in preserving slavery by adding Cuba to the Union as a slave state, the annexationist movement not only sponsored expeditions of mercenaries to the island but also tried peaceful means, such as attempting to persuade the US government to purchase Cuba.

The war of 1868 to 1878 was actually started by the eastern planter elites. They were represented in New York and Washington by many of the Havana sugar planters who were forced to leave the island by Spanish persecution during the war. In Washington, those elites carried out an intensive campaign in Congress and in the executive branch to have Washington recognize the rights of belligerency of the Cuban rebels and support their cause.

The independence movement started by José Martí in 1892 was a purposeful departure from the pattern of elite-led diaspora political movements. One of the most salient features of the Partido Revolucionario Cubano (PRC), which Martí founded in the United States, was that it started as a grassroots movement among cigar makers. Aware of how elite interests had frustrated previous separatist movements, Martí was intent on building his party from the ground up.

The Goal: Regime Change

The uncompromising struggles of the postrevolutionary "historical exiles" against the government led by Fidel and Raúl Castro are consistent with the history of Cuban political activism in the United States. Unlike other diasporas in the United States that have mobilized themselves to support the government of their homeland, the Cubans in the United States have always sought to change the political system of their place of origin, whether in the contemporary efforts to oust Castro and socialism or in nineteenth-century struggles to eradicate Spanish colonialism. Cuban American activism has always centered on changing the political order in Havana.

Advocating a Role for the United States

Although Cuban elites have at times participated directly in purely nationalist efforts to change the island's political system, their political activities have historically included advocating for a US role in the efforts to change the government in Cuba. The postrevolutionary exiles have certainly made US involvement central to their agenda. Those efforts have a strong precedent in the history of the Cuban presence in the United States. As noted previously, the annexationist movement and the 1868–78 war for independence both involved concerted attempts by the elites in the diaspora to persuade the United States to become involved in the effort to oust the Spanish from the island.

In this regard, Martí's activities are once again the exception. His grassroots campaign very pointedly excluded any initiative to involve the United States. He painstakingly built in the Cuban diaspora throughout the world a civilian-based movement that eventually would culminate in the launching of a Cuban-led military uprising on the island in 1895. A man gifted with foresight, Martí had lived in New York since 1880 and had seen the stirrings of American expansionist sentiment. Since his vision went beyond the ousting of the Spanish to the creation of a sovereign Cuban nation, he saw no benefit at all, and only danger, in calling the attention of the United States to his diaspora-based independence movement. His premature death on a Cuban battlefield in 1895 left the Cuban Revolutionary Party in New York in the hands of men whose instincts lay with lobbying the press and the US government to take action on behalf of the Cuban insurgency. Modern historiography has given a great deal of credit to the leadership of the Cuban diaspora in helping to create a climate in the United States that led to the entry of the United States into the war against Spain in 1898 (Offner 1992, 226–27).

Access and Influence at the Highest Levels of the US Government

In the past three decades, Cuban Americans have exerted enormous influence on the formulation of US policy. They have done so, as we shall see, by fund-raising for members of Congress and by accessing the highest levels of the executive branch. That is also a well-established pattern in the Cuban diaspora. The annexationists were able to persuade President James Polk to make an offer to the Spanish for the purchase of Cuba. The members of the landed aristocracy who represented the rebels in the 1868–1878 war cultivated relations with members of Congress, had unqualified support from Secretary of War John Rawlins, were invited to audiences with President Ulysses Grant, and were virtually fixtures in the office of Secretary of State Hamilton Fish (Nevins 1957, 182–93). Martí's successors in the Cuban Revolutionary Party in New York exerted influence in Washington primarily through their relations with the New York press, which overwhelmingly supported US entry into the war against Spain (Wisan 1934, 182–86).

Failure to Achieve the Goal

President Polk's offer to buy Cuba was flatly turned down by Madrid. The intense lobbying in Washington by the planter aristocracy in support of the rebels during 1869 and 1870 was eventually quashed by Secretary of State Hamilton Fish as he single-handedly steered the Grant administration away from involvement in Cuba and in the opposite direction, aggressively enforcing the neutrality laws by prosecuting those who organized expeditions to Cuba from US soil. Martí's successors did get what they wanted, but it was a Pyrrhic victory. With the US entry into the war, the subsequent occupation of Cuba by US military forces, and the promulgation of the Platt Amendment, the quest for Cuban sovereignty was compromised well into the twentieth century. They had succeeded in bringing about Martí's worst nightmare.

The postrevolutionary exiles have been successful in maintaining and reinforcing a hostile US policy toward Cuba, but the goal of such a policy has eluded them: sweeping the Castro brothers from power. Many Cubans in the United States see themselves as exiles, not immigrants. If the mission of exiles is to recover the homeland and the goal of immigrants is to make a successful economic adjustment to the new country, then we can echo here the words of one Cuban American social scientist: "Cubans in the United States have been a failure at what they say they are, and a success at what they say they are not" (Grenier and Pérez 2003, 99).

Diaspora–US Government Relations

In the half century of activism intended to overthrow the socialist government in Havana, the Cuban diaspora has gone through several stages in its relationship with the US government. Not only have strategies and actors shifted over time, but the very nature of the relationship with Washington has changed, as Cuban Americans have gone from being mere agents of US Cuba policy to being key actors and shapers of that policy.

The 1960s and 1970s: Cuban Americans as Agents of US Policy

The rapid deterioration of US-Cuba relations between 1960 and 1962 led to the formulation of plans in Washington for the forcible overthrow of the Castro government. The exodus of Cuban exiles provided the manpower for the elaboration of a strategy that would use the arriving Cubans as an invasion force organized and directed by the Central Intelligence Agency, but without the direct involvement of US military personnel in the actual operations in the island. A large CIA recruitment center was established in Miami, and Cubans leaving the island, many of them young men from elite families, were signed up to go to Central America and train for an invasion of Cuba. Washington's plans toward Cuba largely explain the favorable treatment given to Cubans leaving the island during this period. They were automatically granted refugee status and welcomed into the country despite arriving without appropriate authorization. The exodus from the island not only increased the number of recruits for the planned invasion but also seemed to provide the evidence that the Cuban government was unpopular, thereby creating a favorable context for Washington's plans to overthrow it. The migration was therefore encouraged as consistent with US policy toward the island.

The Bay of Pigs invasion launched in April of 1961 was a total disaster, a black eye for the new American president, John Kennedy. But the efforts to use Cuban exiles as agents to destabilize the Cuban government did not stop there. The CIA continued to support and train Cubans for covert expeditions to the island. The Bay of Pigs and the covert operations were emblematic of an era when Cuban Americans acted as soldiers in a policy conceived in Washington, in effect taking orders from officials of the US government. By the late 1960s the program of destabilizing the Castro government using Cuban exiles was largely abandoned, but the United States had trained a cadre of individuals in covert operations and the handling of weapons and explosives. Even if the United States might no longer employ them against the Cuban government, many of those individuals had not abandoned their goal as exiles to overthrow the Havana government, and they continued to apply their training whenever they believed they were acting in a way consistent with the struggle against Fidel Castro's rule. That these CIA-trained individuals even existed was famously brought to light in 1971 when most of the Watergate burglars were Cubans acting under orders from their former CIA boss.

The Carter Administration: The Politics of Desperation

To date, Jimmy Carter has been the only US president to initiate a concerted effort to normalize relations with Cuba (Kornbluh and LeoGrande 2009, 93). From the beginning of his term, his administration took steps intended to establish closer ties with the island. It was in many ways an unprecedented attempt to redefine US-Cuba policy in a way that challenged the former Cold War basis of that policy. The US national interest with respect to Cuba was temporarily steered in a direction opposite to the traditional interests of the Cuban diaspora in keeping the island isolated.

Carter opened the US Interests Section in Havana and authorized the establishment of the Cuban Interests Section in Washington. The prospect of a rapprochement between Havana and Washington raised the specter for many exiles that the struggle to overthrow the Havana regime was doomed. Their feelings of powerlessness turned up the temperature in the diaspora and the discourse against the Cuban government, and its perceived supporters became shriller. Especially targeted by the exiles were those within their own ranks who in 1978 had accepted an invitation from the Cuban government to go to Havana and sit down with top governmental leaders to discuss matters of mutual interest. The outcome of what became known as the Diálogo of 1978 was that for the first time Cubans in the United States were allowed to return to visit family members.

During the Carter administration it first became evident how emotionally many Cuban Americans were attached to the struggle for the recovery of the homeland, and the violent extremes to which some of them were willing to go to further it. Facing the prospect of a lost battle for keeping Cuba isolated, and perceiving treason from within the diaspora, some of those individuals who had been trained by the CIA swung into action. The years of the Carter administration, when all seemed lost to the "historical exiles," were the years when terrorism within the Cuban diaspora in the United States reached its peak. Among the prominent acts of violence were the assassination of a Cuban government official in New York City, the murder of two of the participants in the Diálogo, the killing of an alleged sympathizer of the Cuban government in a hospital parking lot in Miami, and the bombing shortly after takeoff of a civilian Cubana Airlines airplane bound for Havana from Barbados, with the loss of all seventy-three persons on board.

In the end, Cuban military adventurism in Africa made it difficult for President Carter to continue on the road to normalizing relations with Havana. By 1980, his administration was preoccupied with two events that dimmed the prospects for his reelection that year: a hostage crisis in Teheran and a boatlift from Cuba.

The Election of 1980: A Watershed Event

Until 1980, it was Washington, waging a Cold War and intent on destabilizing the government in Havana, that carried the ball in pursuing a policy of hostility and isolation toward the island. Starting that year, however, a new set of forces and actors came into play to maintain, and even reinforce, that long-standing policy. That year marked the beginning of a shift in the role of Cuban exiles from mere agents or implementers of US policy to protagonists in the formulation of Washington's policy toward the island.

The catalyst for the entry of Cuban exiles as principal players in US Cuba policy was the presidential election of 1980. The candidacy and election of Ronald Reagan in that year had two consequences: they dramatically increased the participation of Cuban Americans in the US electoral system, and they prompted the formation of a lobby group in Washington.

Up until the 1980 election, many Cubans in the United States, especially the elderly, had been slow to apply for US citizenship and thus become eligible to vote, despite having long met the requirements to do so. The 1966 Cuban Adjustment Act had made it possible for Cubans living in the United States to easily obtain their permanent resident visa. Their reluctance to take the next step to naturalization was based on the persistence of an "exile" ethos that caused them to focus on the affairs of the homeland in the hope of a possible return in the future. Many Cubans who had arrived in the 1960s continued to cling to a self-image of "reluctant" migrants, rejecting US citizenship.

The Reagan candidacy, however, made participation in the US electoral system consistent with the exile agenda of recovering the homeland. The

Republican candidate was viewed as an ideologically committed anticommunist who gave every indication he would be tough on Fidel Castro. Further, it was important to vote against the incumbent, whose administration was perceived as disastrous for the exiles' anti-Castro cause. Becoming US citizens and voting in the presidential election, far from being a sign of assimilation into the United States, was actually a strategy within the traditional exile agenda.

Lobbying: The Cuban American National Foundation

By 1980, a successful entrepreneurial class with accumulated surplus capital had emerged within the Cuban diaspora. This new prosperity could be tapped to create a presence in Washington that would further the anti-Castro agenda, and the election of a president perceived as friendly to that agenda seemed a propitious moment for such a step. This convergence of economic and political conditions made possible the creation of the Cuban American National Foundation (CANF). In fact, according to some reports, the founding of CANF is directly linked to the Reagan presidency. Richard Allen, Reagan's national security adviser, is said to have met with Jorge Mas Canosa, an exile leader, to urge him to establish CANF along the lines of the American Israel Public Affairs Committee, which lobbied for Israel (Erikson 2008, 112).

Up until the founding of CANF, the principal Cuban exile organizations were engaged in strategies that can best be described as marginal or even shadowy: covert activities, paramilitary actions, terrorism, street demonstrations, boycotts. CANF, however, followed the traditional formula of legitimate US interest groups, especially the pro-Israel organizations: campaign contributions, political fund-raisers, lobbying, information dissemination, and media relations. It was anti-Castroism "the American way." Their ultimate goal was the overthrow of the Castro government through a US policy of hostility and isolation.

CANF members were typically successful businesspeople who had made their wealth in the United States and who gave thousands of dollars annually to further the organization's work. In addition to annual dues that reached the thousands of dollars, CANF members were expected to contribute to its periodic fund-raisers in Miami. One of the keys to CANF's success was the leadership of Jorge Mas Canosa. Originally only one of several prominent Cuban Americans who founded CANF in 1981, Mas Canosa eventually became the undisputed leader of the organization, largely through personal attributes that were well suited for the role of CANF chairman. In Washington, where CANF opened offices and established a very visible presence, Mas Canosa gained access to the highest levels of the executive branch. In May of 1983, for example, Mas Canosa hosted a visit by President Reagan to Little Havana, where the president, dressed in a *guayabera* and seated next to a similarly attired Mas Canosa, lunched at a Cuban restaurant.

Mas Canosa was especially effective in lobbying members of Congress. Part of his success was due to the fact that in the 1980s and early 1990s there was little stimulus to change the direction of US Cuba policy. CANF operated nearly in a vacuum in Washington. There was little organized opposition to their efforts to place greater pressure on the Castro government, and most members of Congress, reflecting their constituencies, had no particular stake in Cuba policy one way or another. This left the field open for CANF to exert considerable influence through even modest campaign contributions. Typically, Mas Canosa would invite a senator or representative who was on a committee of special interest to CANF to go down to Miami, where he would hold a large fund-raising dinner, summoning CANF members to attend and contribute to the honoree's campaign chest. The member of Congress could expect to return to Washington with tens of thousands of dollars in campaign contributions and ready to do CANF's bidding on Cuba. After all, it was not likely that the congressperson's constituency back home, say in the Midwest, would take any notice of how their representative voted on Cuban matters. One estimate is that between 1982 and 2000 CANF, through its Free Cuba PAC, invested more than $1.6 million in congressional and presidential races (Erikson 2008, 111).

Mas Canosa and CANF worked both sides of the aisle. Despite the Cuban diaspora's traditional preference for the Republican Party, some of CANF's greatest lobbying successes came in persuading Democrats to support the CANF stance on Cuba. The two congressmen from southern Florida, Claude Pepper and Dante Fascell, both Democrats, were staunch CANF allies largely because of the influence Mas Canosa had on their constituencies. CANF would also support the candidacies of challengers to incumbents who had not been receptive to the influence of the organization. The best example, and one that crossed party lines, was Mas Canosa's strong financial backing for the successful campaign of Joseph Lieberman to unseat moderate Republican Lowell Weicker in Connecticut.

The successes on the Hill and in the White House gave CANF considerable weight when dealing with officials at lower, but critical, levels of the executive branch. Mas Canosa and CANF were practically fixtures at the Cuban Desk at State. In 1991, when I asked an official at the Cuba Desk why they paid so much attention to CANF lobbyists, his answer was "Because they are always in our face."

The list of CANF accomplishments during the heyday of Mas Canosa's influence in Washington is impressive. CANF can take credit, for example, for the establishment in the 1980s of Radio and TV Martí, stations under the auspices of the US government that broadcast to the island as an alternative to Cuba's state-run radio and television stations. Despite the inability of TV Martí to overcome the jamming of its signal by Cuba, and despite the criticisms of Radio Martí's slanted coverage, both programs survive to this day.

CANF also played a critical role in the passage of both the 1992 Cuban Democracy (Torricelli) Act and the 1996 Cuban Liberty and Democratic Solidarity (Helms-Burton) Act. Both served to tighten and codify the embargo. One consequence of those laws, therefore, is that the embargo is no longer simply an executive order but the law. It would now take an act of Congress to lift it.

Jorge Mas Canosa's success as leader of CANF was based not only on his work in Washington but on the popularity he enjoyed among many in Miami. He had the ability to play in Washington the role of the Cuban American businessman who was serving as lobbyist for a patriotic cause dear to the hearts of Cubans. But in Miami he appealed to the grassroots in the community by playing the role of the traditional Cuban politician, denouncing his opponents with strident rhetoric and appealing to the emotions of the older exiles. This enabled him to legitimately claim the role of the most influential Cuban exile leader, not only because he had the ear of members of Congress, cabinet secretaries, and even the president of the United States, but also because he fought the battles, real or imagined, against alleged supporters of the Cuban regime in the streets of Miami, denouncing any softening of the hard stance against the Cuban regime. When he died in 1997 at the age of fifty-eight he was irreplaceable as the leader of CANF. No one person in CANF was able to effectively succeed him in both worlds: the corridors of Washington and the sidewalks and airwaves of Miami. The CANF leadership fell to his US-born son, Jorge Mas Santos, whose instincts led him to moderate somewhat CANF's position and to emphasize almost exclusively the lobbying efforts in Washington. CANF's hard-line base in Miami felt neglected, and, after some acrimony, a splinter group was formed, the Miami-based Cuban Liberty Council, composed of older and more strident anti-Castro former members of CANF.

The death of Mas Canosa and the subsequent fracturing of CANF no doubt contributed to a waning of the organization's influence. But even before Mas Canosa's death, forces were in place that were to transform the nature of Cuban American influence on US Cuba policy. It was a shift from a lobbying strategy to one in which Cuban Americans themselves became part of the US government.

A Line Is Blurred: The US Government Is "Us"

By the late 1980s the surge in electoral participation in the diaspora had created a noticeable Cuban American voting bloc in Florida and, to a lesser extent, in New Jersey, both key electoral states. Politicians learned that those blocs could be easily swayed by supporting a hard line, even if in rhetoric only, against the Cuban government. It is a tactic that has been used by both Republican and Democratic candidates for Congress and the presidency, and it has given prominence to the "Cuban American vote," especially in Florida.

One result of the growing importance of the Cuban American vote has been the election of Cubans to Congress. It started in 1989 when Republican Ileana Ros-Lehtinen was sworn in as the first Cuban American in Congress, replacing the deceased Claude Pepper in Florida's eighteenth congressional district. She was followed in 1993 by Lincoln Díaz-Balart of Florida, also a Republican, and Robert Menéndez of New Jersey, a Democrat. All three were committed to maintaining a hard line toward the Cuban government, and by the late 1990s they represented a force from within the legislative branch that started to replace the waning influence of CANF on US Cuba policy.

The 2000 presidential election served to highlight even more the importance of the Cuban American vote, given the deciding and controversial role played by Florida in the outcome of the election. Since a large majority of Cuban Americans voted for George W. Bush, many in the diaspora claimed that the Cuban vote had been responsible for electing the next president. George W. Bush must have thought so as well, for during his administration members of the Cuban diaspora gained an unprecedented presence in the US government. Mel Martínez, a Republican from Orlando, was named secretary of housing and urban development, and Otto Reich, also Cuban, was initially named in a temporary recess appointment as assistant secretary of state for Western Hemisphere affairs (Senate Democrats objected to a permanent appointment) and was later moved to the National Security Council as special envoy to Latin America. Meanwhile, in 2002, Mario Díaz-Balart, from Florida, joined his brother Lincoln in the House of Representatives. Two years later, Mel Martínez, the cabinet secretary, was elected to the US Senate, but another Cuban, Carlos Gutiérrez, was appointed to the cabinet in 2005 as commerce secretary. Congressman Bob Menéndez was appointed to the Senate when the incumbent senator from New Jersey, Jon Corzine, was elected governor of that state. Menéndez subsequently won a full term as senator. Replacing him in the House of Representatives in 2006 was Albio Sires, a Cuban and a Democrat and former Speaker of the New Jersey General Assembly.

In summary: during the Bush administration two Cubans served in the cabinet, another Cuban occupied the highest position in Latin American matters in both the State Department and the National Security Council, and six Cuban Americans were in Congress: four House members and two senators. Some were Republicans, and others Democrats, but all (except Mario) were Cuban born, and all were strong supporters of continuing the current US policy toward the island. In many ways, this level of representation in the US government, especially in the US Congress, blurred the lines between the diaspora and the US government. By the decade of the 2000s, Cubans were in the government in key positions to influence from within the formulation of US policy toward the island. The influence of these diaspora insiders during the Bush administration can be examined by looking at the drafting and adoption of a document that is emblematic of the manner in which Cuban exiles shaped US Cuba policy, at least until 2008: the *Report to the President by the Commission for Assistance to a Free Cuba*, or Powell Report.

The Powell Report and a Diaspora Divided

As the 2004 presidential election neared, hard-liners in the diaspora were becoming restless. The decisive support that Cuban Americans in Florida had given to George Bush in 2000 and the growth in the numbers of their own in positions in the US government had not resulted in any tangible progress toward a tougher policy on Cuba. In 2003 a group of Cuban American state legislators in Florida even sent a letter to the president essentially threatening to withdraw their support for the reelection campaign if the White House did not take steps to tighten even further US sanctions on the island.

Given what was at stake in Florida, the Bush administration responded with the appointment of a commission chaired by Secretary of State Powell and Mel Martínez. The Commission for Assistance to a Free Cuba (CAFC) counted on the cooperation of virtually every agency of the US government. The entire project was reputedly under the supervision of Otto Reich at the National Security Council, and the commission's final report was put together by José Cárdenas, a former staffer at CANF who by this time was employed at the State Department. The commission's origins and its results were therefore a product almost entirely of the influence and presence of Cuban Americans in the US government.

The commission was given a twofold charge: (1) identifying additional measures by which the United States could help the Cuban people expeditiously end the Castro dictatorship; and (2) identifying US government programs that could assist the Cuban people during a transition (Commission for Assistance to a Free Cuba 2004).

The commission's 423-page report (dubbed the Powell Report) was delivered to the White House in May of 2004 and was officially adopted by the president on May 20. By June 16 of that year the Office of Foreign Assets Control of the Treasury Department had issued a new set of regulations implementing the provisions of the report that addressed the commission's charge of "hastening the arrival of a transition in Cuba."

As a reflection of the traditional diasporic agenda for US Cuba policy, the Powell Report is an extraordinary document. Also extraordinary were its consequences for the Cuban family and the creation of divisions within the diaspora.

The lengthy portion of the report that sets out how the US government could "assist the Cuban people during a transition" is essentially a detailed blueprint for a comprehensive US involvement in administering a new Cuba, a Cuba with a clean slate that would make possible an intimate US role in virtually all aspects of national life, from health and education, to governance, justice, and the economy, even to the administration of a national park service (complete with the training of rangers), the establishment of safe and drug-free schools, ESL programs in the schools, and the distribution of toolkits for parents' involvement in their children's education. It is not a stretch to say that it is a plan for a protectorate. Such US involvement was predicated on the implicit assumption that there would be a "rupture" scenario, on the scale of 1933 or 1959, that would transform Cuba virtually overnight and immediately set the conditions for pervasive foreign involvement. For example, plans are outlined for "responding rapidly to changes on the island" including mobilizing humanitarian emergency relief efforts, such as the distribution of non-fat dry milk, initiating immediate immunization programs for childhood illnesses, making sure schools stay open, providing public security and law enforcement during the "initial stages" of a transition, and immediately providing temporary building materials for housing rehabilitation.

That portion of the report is emblematic of the historical tendency, discussed earlier, of the Cuban elites in the diaspora to assign a primary role to the United States in the process of regime change in Cuba. In fact, the entry of the United States into Afghanistan only a few years before may have inspired those responsible for the report to see a comparable role for the United States in Cuba, including the ascendancy, on the coattails of a US intervention, of a government led by former exiles. The report also reflects a common diaspora theme with respect to regime change in Cuba: the belief in the inevitability of a rupture scenario. It is a testament to how well the leaders of the diaspora have sold that scenario to Washington. No other scenario of change is contemplated in the report, not even the one we seem to be embarked on: the gradual disappearance of Fidel Castro's personal authority, replaced by that of his brother and supported by the country's political and legal institutions. Consequently, the United States has no plan for dealing with the transition scenario that is developing in Cuba.

But the far more consequential aspects of the Powell Report were those measures it prescribed for "hastening the transition." Up to $36 million over two years was set aside for funding "democracy-building activities" in the island, including support to groups so that "they can take their rightful share in the pro-democracy movement." An additional $18 million was allocated to pump up the Radio and TV Martí broadcasts to Cuba. The provisions that caught the most attention, however, were those seeking to limit the flow of dollars to the island by severely curtailing family visits and remittances, provisions that were quickly translated into regulations by the US Treasury Department. Henceforth, Cubans in the United States could visit family members only every three years (with no provision for emergency humanitarian visits), and those visits were limited to immediate family members:

grandparents, grandchildren, parents, siblings, spouses, and children. The report in effect redefined who was a family member. Those with only uncles, aunts, nephews, or nieces in Cuba, for example, no longer had family in Cuba, according to those new provisions. They could no longer visit those relatives or send them any money. The allowed per diem for travel expenses to the island was dropped from $164 to $50.

The new travel regulations served to widen a rift that had long been developing within the Cuban diaspora. As presented earlier, the diaspora's agenda has long been dominated by the "historical exiles" who arrived in the 1960s and who were disproportionately drawn from Cuba's upper socioeconomic levels. Those exiles have maintained a political and economic hegemony in the community, largely controlling the political discourse and exerting the greatest influence over US Cuba policy. All of the Cuban Americans mentioned earlier as occupying positions in the executive branch and in Congress are from that cohort of "historical exiles," whose priority has always been the recovery of the island through a policy of hostility and isolation.

But, as was also established earlier, postrevolutionary Cuban migration has now spanned a half a century, and the current decade will have seen the largest number of arrivals from the island in that fifty-year history. Many of those more recent arrivals do not arrive with the recovery of the homeland as their priority and instead are much more similar to traditional immigrants in that they wish to succeed in their new country and send help to the family members they left behind. The migration of the "historical exiles" was a class-influenced phenomenon in which entire families migrated. The more recent waves, however, were more likely to involve individual decisions to leave, which had the effect of separating families. In other words, the earlier exiles tend not to have family members in the island, while almost all of those who have arrived more recently left family behind, and their priority is visiting and helping them.

Seen in that context, the regulations regarding travel and remittances proposed by the influential members of the diaspora and incorporated into the Powell Report represent an imposition of the agenda of the earlier exiles on, and to the detriment of, the priorities of the more recent arrivals. The report therefore highlighted for the first time that there were differences within the diaspora on priorities regarding US policy toward the island and that the traditional agenda had prevailed largely because of the greater influence exerted by the "historical exiles," who were of higher socioeconomic status and were more likely to be citizens and to vote than those who had arrived from Cuba from 1980 onward.

The Policy in Crisis

By 2008 the decades-old policy that had culminated in the Powell Report was in crisis. Several developments served to erode support for a policy of hostility and isolation that had long been the priority of the Cuban diaspora.

Lack of Support for the Restrictions on Family Travel and Remittances
Even many of those who had long supported hard-line measures felt that the restrictions on family travel and remittances had gone too far and were hurting the Cuban family. There was also a sense that an injustice had been committed against the less powerful in the community. The Florida International University Cuba Poll conducted in 2007 among Cuban Americans in Miami found that 64 percent of those interviewed favored a return to the travel and remittances regulations that had existed prior to the implementation of the Powell Report's stricter recommendations (Institute for Public Opinion Research and Cuban Research Institute 2007).

Castro's Illness
The incapacitation of Fidel Castro in July of 2006 brought into question one of the tenets of the diaspora's traditional hard-line policy that was highlighted in the Powell Report: the inevitability of the rupture scenario. The events since Castro's illness have supported the view that the forces of continuity may prove more powerful than the forces of radical change. The fact that Cuba has remained stable since the incapacitation of Castro has been an unexpected and sobering result that has left most exiles, and Washington along with them, feeling powerless, hemmed in by their own expectations and by a strategy that made them unable to influence any changes when the house of cards did not fall. True, the man has not died, and that may well be a critical difference. But he was incapacitated and he turned over power without a whimper of dissent, without loss of political control, without a single crack in the unity of the ruling elite.

"The Exhaustion of the Model"
In the early 1990s, Cuban economists coined the phrase "the exhaustion of the model" to cryptically refer to the failure of the centrally planned model to resolve the country's economic crisis. The phrase can also be applied to the decades-old US policy of isolating Cuba. The unpopular overreach of

the family-related restrictions, the absence of any consequences from Castro's illness, and the likelihood that the Cuban government will survive him are specific factors that can be added to a general sense in the diaspora that the policy has run its course, that after five decades it has clearly failed to achieve a change in Cuba. The 2007 FIU Cuba Poll recorded the lowest level of support for the US embargo in the sixteen years that the poll has been taken: down to 57 percent from 66 percent only three years before. At the same time, a majority of respondents (55 percent) voiced support for allowing unrestricted travel to the island (Institute for Public Opinion Research and Cuban Research Institute 2007).

Certain aspects of the policy, especially those measures that received large allocations of funds as a result of the Powell Report, have come under critical scrutiny in recent years. In November of 2006 a report of the General Accounting Office noted that the funds provided through USAID for "democracy-building assistance" to groups in Cuba were in many cases mismanaged, required greater oversight, and were largely ineffective in supporting prodemocracy groups in the island (US Government Accountability Office 2006, 3–5). The operations of the Office of Cuba Broadcasting, responsible for Radio and TV Martí, have also come under GAO scrutiny and criticism, particularly for shortcomings in adhering to sound journalistic practices (US Government Accountability Office 2009, 2).

The hard-line model for US-Cuba policy has no doubt also suffered from the increasing pluralism of voices from within the diaspora. As noted earlier, the various waves of migrants from Cuba have different interests and priorities in that policy. Newer generations of Cuban Americans have also contributed to the greater heterogeneity of views that is now evident in the community.

An Opportunity for Change

On November 4, 2008, Barack Obama not only carried the state of Florida and Miami-Dade County but also received the highest percentage of the vote that a Democratic presidential candidate has ever received among Cuban Americans, nearly 37 percent—even though Obama had not engaged in the usual anti-Castro rhetoric when he addressed CANF during a campaign stop in Miami. In fact, on that occasion he pledged to eliminate all restrictions on family travel. By the 2012 election, the support for the Democratic candidate had risen dramatically, according to one exit poll in South Florida, which gave Obama a 53–47 margin over Mitt Romney among Cuban Americans (Caputo 2012).

The increase in support among Cuban Americans for the Democratic candidate has at least two related explanations, both of them bad news for the traditional hard-liners. One is that the greater pluralism within the diaspora has eroded the usually strong support for the Republican Party, increasing the number of Cuban Americans willing to vote for a Democrat. One exit poll on election day 2008 showed that while some 85 percent of Cubans in Miami-Dade sixty-five years of age and above voted for John McCain, 55 percent of Cuban Americans twenty-nine and under voted for Obama (Woods 2008, 1B). The other, related, explanation is that many Cuban voters may have voted with other issues in mind than Cuba—the economy, for example.

Neither of those developments bodes well for the possibility of maintaining a monolithic position on Cuba within the diaspora. The 2008 and 2012 election results mean that the current US president has no debts to the hard-liners in the Cuban American community when it comes to Cuba policy. That has thus far not necessarily translated into a dramatic change in that policy in this administration. The only change that has thus far taken place since President Obama took office is one that candidate Obama promised he would implement: the repeal of the 2004 restrictions on family travel and remittances. Restrictions on academic and cultural travel have also been relaxed (76 Fed. Reg. 5072–78 [January 28, 2011]). The basic outlines of the policy, however, remain in place.

But the White House has recently demonstrated that even if it is not willing to change the basic outlines of US Cuba policy, it is firmly committed to allowing family travel and remittances. In December 2011, as the 2012 election season drew closer, the White House vigorously opposed an attempt by House Republicans, led by Representative Mario Díaz-Balart, to reinstate the Bush-era restrictions on Cuban American travel and remittances by inserting those restrictions into the year's end massive spending bill. The Cuba travel provision was finally struck from the bill, a casualty not only of White House opposition but also of the outcry that was heard from Miami against the measure (Steinhauer and Pear 2011, A20). For the first time it became evident that the Cuban American hard-liners in the US Congress were becoming increasingly isolated from their own community, at least on the issue of family travel and remittances.

Despite the success in overturning the attempt to reinstate the Bush-era restrictions, limitations on family travel and remittances, albeit more liberal ones than the 2004 regulations, are still in place, as are the embargo and the travel ban on Americans. Most of those provisions cannot be lifted by executive order but require an act of Congress, and the Cuban Americans are still there, pledging to oppose at least some of the changes to the current policy. Whether the president and Congress have the political inclination and will to follow the recommendations of many of who seek to change the Cuba policy through various approaches remains to be seen.[1] Some of the political actors who in principle favor changes may nevertheless not be willing to spend political capital to make them happen.

The analysis in this chapter suggests that the Cuban diaspora is no longer the overriding force it once was in maintaining a policy of isolation toward Cuba. Whereas that policy has thus far involved a perceived or alleged convergence of US national interests and diasporic interests, both the US government and the Cuban diaspora now do not seem as intent as they were in the past in maintaining it indefinitely. In that sense, a new convergence between Washington and Miami may be emerging to explore ways to change US Cuba policy. More than anything else, that new convergence for change may be based on the desire to turn the page on what has been a long chapter in US-Cuba relations that has not benefited the interests of either country. It remains to be seen if President Obama, before he leaves office in 2016, will apply to Cuba the principle he enunciated before the UN General Assembly on September 23, 2009, that is, to choose not to "drag the arguments of the twentieth century into the twenty-first" (White House 2009).

Note

1. For leading examples of recommendations from scholars or organizations on how to best change US-Cuba policy, see Sweig (2009); and Emergency Network of Cuban American Scholars and Artists for Change in U.S.-Cuba Policy (ENCASA/US-CUBA) (2008).

References

Brookings Institution. 2009. "U.S. Policy toward a Cuba in Transition: Roadmap for Critical and Constructive Engagement." February. www.brookings.edu/reports/2009/02_cuba_roadmap.aspx.

Caputo, Marc. 2012. "Poll: Obama Got Big Share of Cuban American Vote, Won among Other Hispanics in Florida." *Miami Herald*, November 8. www.miamiherald.com/2012/11/08/3087889/poll-obama-got-big-share-of-cuban.html#storylink=cpy.

Commission for Assistance to a Free Cuba. 2004. *Report to the President by the Commission for Assistance to a Free Cuba.* May 6. http://2001-2009.state.gov/p/wha/rls/rm/32272.htm.

ENCASA/US-CUBA. 2008. "Charting a New Course on U.S.-Cuba Policy: Seizing a Historic Opportunity." www.lawg.org/storage/documents/encasa.pdf.

Erikson, Daniel P. 2008. *The Cuba Wars: Fidel Castro, the United States, and the Next Revolution.* New York: Bloomsbury Press.

Grenier, Guillermo J., and Lisandro Pérez. 2003. *The Legacy of Exile: Cubans in the United States.* Boston: Allyn and Bacon.

Institute for Public Opinion Research and Cuban Research Institute. 2007. *2007 FIU Cuba Poll.* www2.fiu.edu/~ipor/cuba8/.

Kornbluh, Peter, and William M. LeoGrande. 2009. "Talking with Castro." *Cigar Aficionado*, January/February.

Nevins, Allan. 1957. *Hamilton Fish: The Inner History of the Grant Administration.* Vol. 1. Rev. ed. New York: Frederick Ungar.

Offner, John L. 1992. *An Unwanted War: The Diplomacy of the United States and Spain over Cuba, 1895–1898.* Chapel Hill: University of North Carolina Press.

Pérez, Lisandro. 2009. "Sugar, Slaves, and the Rise of Cuban New York." In *New York 400: A Visual History of America's Greatest City with Images from the Museum of the City of New York*, edited by John Thorn, 135–38. New York: Museum of the City of New York; Philadelphia: Running Press.

———. 2010. "Cubans in Nineteenth-Century New York: A Story of Sugar, War, and Revolution." In *Nueva York: 1613–1945*, edited by Edward J. Sullivan, 97–107. New York: New York Historical Society.

Steinhauer, Jennifer, and Robert Pear. 2011. "Lawmakers' Temporary Deal Averts Government Shutdown." *New York Times*, December 16.

Sweig, Julia. 2009. "Memo to President Obama." *Cigar Aficionado*, January/February, 76–84.

US Census Bureau. 2010. "Table PCT-11: Hispanic or Latino by Specific Origin." *2010 Summary Census File 1.* http://factfinder2.census.gov/faces/tableservices/jsf/pages/productview.xhtml?fpt=table.

US Government Accountability Office. 2006. *Foreign Assistance: U.S. Democracy Assistance for Cuba Needs Better Management and Oversight.* Washington, DC: US Government Accountability Office. November.

———. 2009. *Broadcasting to Cuba: Actions Are Needed to Improve Strategy and Operations.* Washington, DC: US Government Accountability Office. January.

White House. Office of the Press Secretary. 2009. "Remarks by the President to the United Nations General Assembly." September 23. www.whitehouse.gov/the_press_office/Remarks-by-the-President-to-the-United-Nations-General-Assembly.

Wisan, Joseph E. 1934. *The Cuban Crisis as Reflected in the New York Press, 1895–1898.* New York: Columbia University Press.

Woods, Casey. 2008. "Analysis of Cuban American Vote." *Miami Herald*, November 6.

When Government Interests Shape Foreign Policy

CHAPTER SEVEN

Diaspora Lobbying and Ethiopian Politics

Terrence Lyons

The Ethiopian diaspora has influenced politics in Ethiopia, despite its quite limited success lobbying the US government. The diaspora, which tends to be dominated by a highly partisan opposition, has lobbied Washington to reduce its support of the authoritarian ruling party and to prioritize democracy and human rights, but this aim has been frustrated because Washington's more pressing concerns relating to counterterrorism in the Horn of Africa have led it to maintain an important security partnership with Addis Ababa. Many in the diaspora perceived that there were more promising opportunities to influence Ethiopian politics through other entry points and strategies than ethnic lobbying. In the context of the 2005 Ethiopian elections, the diaspora became more directly engaged in politics. Activists raised money, framed political debates, brokered party alliances, and in some cases returned home to run for office. The diaspora's influence therefore has been significant despite its lack of success in changing US foreign policy priorities. Engagement in homeland politics need not be mediated through the host country government, and lobbying is only one choice from a broader repertoire of potential transnational political strategies.

Political dynamics in Ethiopia and around the world have been transformed by globalization and the development of innovative transnational social networks. These new political processes are rooted in communities and networks that are increasingly less restricted by geographic location. As a result, the relevant constituencies participating in a particular political campaign may live in different countries or move between locations. Networks of activists and supporters are less bound by the need to work in close proximity to their homeland or to accept notions that actors outside a state or territory are not members of communities rooted within a specific jurisdiction. While politics has been delinked from territory with regard to processes and actors, this does not mean that transnational politics generally focuses on universal issues such as global social justice or cosmopolitan democracy. Rather, transnational politics is intensely focused on specific locations, identities, and issues. Politics remains fundamentally about local, parochial issues even while political processes are increasingly transnational (Al-Ali and Koser 2002; Lyons and Mandaville 2010; Lyons and Mandaville 2012).

The Ethiopian diaspora is a "conflict-generated diaspora" (Lyons 2007): that is, a network of those forced across borders by violence or repression. Such diasporas are characterized by traumatic memories and important symbolic ties to the homeland. Often they also have preexisting links to extensive social and political networks that are instrumental in their flight from war. Recent economic research has argued that diaspora remittances may sustain parties engaged in civil war (Collier and Hoeffler 2000); others have noted that remittances are often critical to basic survival of the most vulnerable in conflict and postconflict contexts (Fagen and Bump 2006; Newland and Patrick 2004). Beyond supplying resources, however, conflict-generated diasporas frequently play prominent roles in political debates and in the validation of party strategies and leadership. These forms of cross-border participation in the politics of countries of origin are increasingly important as "political entrepreneurs" recognize the value of mobilizing in this way and establish new networks and creative transnational practices (Adamson 2002; Lyons and Mandaville 2012).

Conflict-generated diasporas, being sustained in part by traumatic memories, tend to compromise less and thus to reinforce and exacerbate the protracted nature of conflicts. In Ethiopia and in cases such as the Tamil, Armenian, and Irish, these diasporas often frame homeland conflict in categorical, hard-line terms, thereby strengthening confrontational leaders and organizations and undermining others seeking compromise. In other cases, diaspora groups have transformed themselves from supporters of militant elements to key partners with peacemakers, as seen in the Irish American diaspora and the Good Friday Agreement (Cochrane 2007). Conflict-generated diasporas therefore have the resources and the ability to frame conflicts in ways that fundamentally alter local conflict dynamics (Zunzer 2004; Mohamoud 2005).

The Ethiopian diaspora in North America has its origins in Ethiopia's violent political transitions and protracted conflicts, and many remained engaged in networks that have sought to influence political outcomes in the homeland. As illustrated below, the diaspora played a crucial role in the political opening of 2005 and the subsequent crisis and crackdown. Their strategy included direct support for political change in Ethiopia through fund-raising, debating, political party building, and some prominent individuals' return to Ethiopia to run for office. Members of the Ethiopian diaspora lobbied Congress, made direct appeals to the State Department, and in general sought to shape the debate on US policy toward Ethiopia through press releases, demonstrations, and participation in policy roundtables at various think tanks.

Diaspora lobbying efforts, however, are best understood as one component of a larger set of transnational political relations. At various times leading members of the opposition in Ethiopia and in the diaspora perceived opportunities to influence events on Capitol Hill or in the State Department. At other times demonstrations at the United Nations, World Bank, or Carter Center seemed more promising. Some members of the diaspora engaged in transnational politics by lobbying Washington, while others participated by fund-raising for homeland political parties, and still others wrote online blogs to influence political debates. Each of these specific domains of engagement should be understood in relation to the others. Diaspora lobbying is one of a larger set of transnational political activities and often not the most important.

With regard to their lobbying efforts, the Ethiopian diaspora soon became frustrated at their inability to change US policy. Washington's interests in counterterrorism and stability in the Horn of Africa diverged from the diaspora's interest in replacing the incumbent regime. Members of the diaspora continually emphasized that democratization and respect for human rights were consistent with both US values and long-term stability, but in the more immediate framework of policy decisions security concerns and interests in regional counterterrorism cooperation dominated.

The State Department tended to view the Ethiopian diaspora as a legitimate domestic constituency group and met with representatives on a periodic basis but also saw them as out of date, "extremist" in their refusal to work with the incumbent regime and accept incremental change, and not particularly useful for US foreign policy. The diaspora had little to offer to advance Washington's strategic interests in counterterrorism. They had more success in lobbying Congress and in particular encouraging key members of the House of Representatives to take actions to which both the State Department and the Ethiopian government objected. In 2007 this initiative culminated in the passage by the House of Representatives of the Ethiopian Democracy and Accountability Act (HR 2003). They targeted members of both parties that had interests or responsibilities for Africa and human rights, as well as members from districts that had particularly large concentrations of Ethiopians.

While the State Department, the White House, and the Pentagon listened politely but otherwise did not encourage the diaspora, the Ethiopian government and embassy pressed Washington to take steps to marginalize diaspora opposition. The ruling party in Ethiopia recognized that its opposition gained considerable advantages through transnational mobilization and that delinking political parties within Ethiopia from their diaspora support networks would undermine the opposition. In particular, Addis Ababa wanted several opposition groups active in the United States to be placed on the list of terrorist groups so that fund-raising would be made illegal. Ethiopian authorities classified the Ogaden National Liberation Front (ONLF), the Oromo Liberation Front (OLF), and Ginbot 7 as terrorist organizations and expressed their displeasure that leaders of these groups could engage in political activities in the United States. While the diaspora failed to shift US policy priorities, the Ethiopian government also failed to get a US ban on key diaspora political organizations.

The Ethiopian Diaspora

It has been estimated that the United States contains 73,000 Ethiopian-born residents. If second and subsequent generations are included, the total rises to 460,000, with particular concentrations in Washington, D.C., Los Angeles, and New York (Terrazas 2007; Solomon 2007, 116–17). Precise numbers are hard to gather, but most Ethiopians insist that the community in the Washington area alone has a population between 100,000 and 250,000. The Adams Morgan neighborhood around Eighteenth Street served as the cultural and political home of the Ethiopian diaspora until real estate prices in the 2000s drove many businesses toward U and Ninth Streets (Chacko 2003; Abrams 2008).

The diaspora has created a wide range of organizations and newspapers, maintains dozens of websites, e-mail lists, and influential blogs, and broadcasts a number of regular radio and television shows on cable networks and the Internet. A number of Ethiopian Orthodox churches have been established across North America, and publications like the *Ethiopian Yellow Pages* help Ethiopian-owned businesses and professionals support one another (Kaplan 2006). The Ethiopian Sports Federation of North America (ESFNA) has a soccer league with twenty-five teams and an annual tournament that draws tens of thousands and is an opportunity to renew old friendships, build solidarity, and listen to prominent keynote speakers and major diaspora musicians. Professional associations such as the Ethiopian North American Health Professionals Association (www.enahpa.org) supply distance education, specialized training for Ethiopian medical professionals, visiting surgical teams, collections of medical books and equipment, and financial support in response to the health care crisis in Ethiopia.

Most diaspora organizations and media focus on cultural, professional, and economic self-help initiatives rather than partisan politics. Many of the social and professional organizations, however, contribute to the web of transnational relationships and social capital that in turn is used by more political organizations to mobilize the community to support various movements engaged in political struggles in the homeland. Ethiopian grocery stores stock not only *injera* and Ethiopian spices but CDs from Ethiopia, inexpensive phone cards to facilitate keeping in touch, discount travel offers, and money transfer services. Political leaders in the North American diaspora are able to mobilize large and relatively wealthy constituencies and to play prominent roles in the transnational politics of Ethiopia in part because the diaspora community is organized and institutionalized.

Migrants and refugees have come in waves in response to violence or political repression in the homeland or new opportunities in the United States, with clear political and social differences among the "generations" of migrants. The first wave of those associated with Emperor Haile Selassie's regime fled the Marxist military government known as the Derg in the early 1970s. These were followed by leftist opponents such as supporters of the Ethiopian People's Revolutionary Party (EPRP) who fled the period of "Red Terror" in the mid- to late 1970s. Others have left following the coming to power of the Ethiopian People's Revolutionary Democratic Front (EPRDF) in 1991. Increasingly members of the diaspora move back and forth between North America and Ethiopia, sometimes managing investments and maintaining residences in both. Finally, the US government's Diversity Visa program, which distributes visas by lottery to underrepresented countries, has brought in a broad range of Ethiopians who are not particularly political in their orientations.

A significant portion of the Ethiopian community in North America arrived following the political violence of the mid-1970s, and many of these now have children who have grown up in North America. As is inevitably the case, the American-born generation has different attachments to the homeland. In some cases, notably the Armenians and the Irish, diasporas have retained highly salient symbolic ties to the homeland, but in many cases the second generation's attachment becomes weaker and more generalized (Levitt and Waters 2002). Some of these young Ethiopian Americans have moved toward a "Habesha" identity that emphasizes the historical glories of Ethiopia's imperial past, the Orthodox highland cultures, and transnational cultural figures such as Bob Marley and Teddy Afro (Hafkin 2006). This framing has the advantage to some in the diaspora of blurring the lines between polarized political positions of many Amhara (associated with the opposition) and Tigreans (linked to the ruling party in Ethiopia) as well as the sovereign (if not cultural) lines between Ethiopians and Eritreans. There is a disjuncture between this emerging identity and politics in Ethiopia, since it distances many Oromos, Muslims, and others from the periphery and includes some Eritrean Americans.

While relatively small in numbers, some very vocal political leaders, organizations, and media are based in the diaspora. These partisan groups run the full gamut of political points of view, and squabbles among them are characteristic of diaspora politics. Given the official embassy's active engagement and profile, those who support the government have less need to establish independent diaspora organizations or media, leaving these organizations and publications more often in the hands of opposition leaders. Organizations close to the government such as the Tigray Development Association, however, do hold regular and quite successful fund-raising events in North America, and an important pro-EPRDF website operates out of California (aigaforum.com).[1] The Ethiopian Embassy in Washington has an active office dealing with diaspora relations, and the Ethiopian Ministry of Foreign Affairs has a General Directorate in charge of Ethiopian Expatriate Affairs. The EPRDF government regards the diaspora both as a threat and as a community to woo.

The Ethiopian Diaspora and the Political Crisis of 2005

The importance of transnational political links and the engagement of the Ethiopian diaspora in homeland politics were made dramatically clear in 2005. While the diaspora's involvement in Ethiopian politics was critical, its ability to shape US foreign policy was minimal. The transnational opposition movement emphasized direct political action through fund-raising, party building, and political debates rather than lobbying of the State Department or the White House. In 2005 opportunities to reach their desired outcome of political change seemed greater from engagement in electoral politics in Ethiopia than from attempts to change US policy toward Ethiopia, with its emphasis on security and counterterrorism.

The transnational links that were prominent in 2005 are not new. When the opposition Southern Coalition entertained the idea of engaging with the EPRDF regime and competing in the 1995 elections, the diaspora was sharply critical and labeled Beyene Petros, the coalition's leader, as a traitor. Unable to ignore this pressure, the Southern Coalition ultimately boycotted the 1995 elections (*Indian Ocean Newsletter* 1995). The ruling coalition also relies upon support in the diaspora. When splits within the Tigray People's Liberation Front (the core of the EPRDF coalition) erupted in March 2001, both factions immediately sent high-level delegations to the United States to shape how the diaspora understood the intraparty conflict and to build support for their respective factions (*Indian Ocean Newsletter* 2001). Many of the most vigorous and dedicated supporters of Oromo self-determination and the OLF are in the diaspora. These supporters have insisted on uncompromising and unqualified demands—liberation of all Oromia by military means—and have supported OLF military leaders who pursue this agenda.

Opposition political leaders active in Ethiopia find it imperative to travel to key centers of the diaspora in North America and Europe in order to campaign and build valuable transnational political links. Bulcha Demeksa, leader of the Oromo Federal Democratic Movement, which won a bloc of seats in the 2005 elections, explained the importance of the diaspora to his political goals in Ethiopia: "Our educated people are concentrated here [in Minnesota]. If these people do not help us, who else will help us? First, by providing leadership, and secondly, with financial help. I come, and other politicians come, to allow people here to see problems developing in their country; to see if they accept our proposals; and to listen to their suggestions and proposals"

(McGill 2008). Hailu Araya, a spokesperson for the opposition Coalition for Unity and Democracy, traveled to North America with a delegation in 2007 to thank the party's supporters. He explained: "The Ethiopians in the diaspora have been helpful, so supportive in many ways such as diplomatically, financially, and so on. So we wanted to come to this country to meet them face-to-face and say thank you to them. The other thing is there is a struggle going on in Ethiopia to establish democracy there, and this democracy needs the support of the people not only in Ethiopia but also outside Ethiopia. And we are here to discuss with them how best we can work together to promote the struggle for democracy in Ethiopia" (Araya 2007). Bulcha, Hailu, and other opposition leaders recognize that their political campaigns in Ethiopia are embedded within transnational political processes. Some tasks (fund-raising, development and validation of political proposals, designation of leaders) are done in North America, while other tasks (selecting candidates, mobilizing voters, sitting in or boycotting the parliament) are done in Ethiopia. The specific geographic focus of these activities varies, with different locations having comparative advantages in one or another set of political activities. These activities are more meaningful and effective, however, when they are linked and coordinated with each other.

The 2005 elections demonstrate the influence of diaspora on Ethiopian politics because a shift in strategy by key leaders in the diaspora to endorse and support participation in the elections was critical to the decision by Ethiopian opposition parties to compete. In significant measure as a result of this change of strategy, the 2005 elections presented the Ethiopian people with a remarkable opportunity to express their political views. In contrast to national elections in 1995 and 2000, opposition parties did not boycott the polls but instead competed vigorously across the most populous regions (Aalen and Tronvoll 2009).

The two main opposition coalitions in 2005 had deep roots in the diaspora. The United Ethiopian Democratic Forces (UEDF) was created in 2003 at a convention held in the United States and included diaspora-based parties such as the Ethiopian People's Revolutionary Party as well as parties based in the homeland such as Merera Gudina's Oromo National Congress and Beyene Petros's Southern Coalition. The Coalition for Unity and Democracy (CUD) also had links to powerful diaspora fund-raisers and media outlets. The CUD included several key leaders who had been prominent members of the diaspora, notably Berhanu Nega and Yacob Haile Mariam, both of whom had been university professors in the United States.

The period immediately before the election was marked by debates on public policy, large and peaceful political rallies, and a sense of excitement. According to official results, the EPRDF and allied parties won 367 seats (67 percent) while the opposition took 172 seats (31 percent), with 109 going to the Coalition for Unity and Democracy (CUD). This outcome represented a major setback for the incumbent party and an important opening for the opposition, which previously had held only a handful of seats. Many in the opposition and particularly some prominent leaders in the diaspora, however, pressed further and insisted that the EPRDF had lost the election and that massive fraud had taken place. Violence erupted following electoral protests in June 2005, and the summer and early fall of 2005 saw a series of investigations of complaints, revoting in some constituencies, donor-sponsored talks between the government and opposition, and escalating controversy and tension.

In this heated context the two opposition coalitions engaged in a lengthy and sometimes public series of consultations to set their postelection strategies. Some favored a strategy of taking up their seats in parliament and in the Addis Ababa municipal government and using these positions to build a stronger opposition in preparation for local elections and the next round of national elections in 2010. Others, however, argued that accepting results that they and their supporters believed were fraudulent would make a mockery of democracy and that the opposition should stick to its principles and boycott the parliament. Some of the most vocal elements in the diaspora supported this position and accused those willing to participate in the parliament of betraying the cause. These debates took place in Ethiopia, within the diaspora, and through media that linked multiple locations of this networked political discourse. Internet sites were particularly powerful, as debates within and between what were often stridently partisan sites served as a major platform for political debate and as a means to assess the positions of key constituencies (Wonqette 2005). During the heady days of summer 2005, pro-EPRDF websites such as Aiga Forum and opposition sites such as the *Ethiopian Review* would exchange barbs and allegations on a daily basis; *Weichegud! Ethiopian Politics* and *Ethiopundit* provided regular, sometimes satirical and often highly partisan analysis; and *AddisFerengi* and *Seminawork* provided field reports from Ethiopia. While some blogs were based in Ethiopia, the slow speed, high cost, and lack of access to the Internet in Ethiopia meant that most of the debate originated in the diaspora. The government blocked access to many of these influential Internet sites and blogs, suggesting that it recognized the importance of transnational political debate and the threat it posed.

Given the critical role of transnational networks, key opposition leaders traveled to Europe and North America at the same time that public meetings were being organized within core opposition constituencies such as the ones in Addis Ababa. In September 2005 some CUD leaders, such as Berhanu Nega and Lidetu Ayalew, were urging participation, while others, notably Hailu Shawel, promised cheering diaspora audiences that he would boycott.[2] This transnational debate within the opposition was extensive and included vigorous participation from actors based in Ethiopia, actors based in the diaspora, political leaders traveling between Ethiopia and North America, and some who had recently returned to Ethiopia from abroad.

When parliament convened on October 11, most UEDF members took their seats, while all but a handful of the CUD initially boycotted. On November 2 and 3 violence exploded across Addis Ababa. The government arrested most of the leadership of the CUD along with private newspaper editors and leaders of key civil society organizations. By bringing charges against its leading critics, the EPRDF effectively criminalized dissent and sent an unmistakable message that effective opposition would not be tolerated. Ethiopian prosecutors charged some 131 opposition politicians, journalists, and civil society leaders with crimes ranging from genocide to treason. In another indication of the influence of the diaspora, seventeen of those indicted were based abroad and included diaspora leaders in North America and Europe.

The EPRDF regime vigorously criticized the diaspora's response to the postelection crisis and labeled its opponents "extremists." The June 2005 "Diaspora Forum" column published by the Ministry of Foreign Affairs characterized those in the diaspora campaigning to discredit the elections as "remnants of the Dergue" and "former Red Terror perpetrators" who were "fanning violence through demonstrations from Atlanta to Amsterdam from Canada to Brussels."[3] Another ministry attack suggested that the diaspora-based opposition consisted of "fringe groups" and "small-minded hooligans" who used "intimidation and force" and "hatred and violence."[4] The regime portrayed the diaspora as illegitimate participants with no rightful role in Ethiopian politics rather than as part of a broader set of political networks that formed a transnational body politic.

US-Ethiopian Relations

While the Ethiopian diaspora has played a significant role in shaping political dynamics within Ethiopia in recent years, it has had far less influence on US policy toward Ethiopia. Washington's perceptions of key US interests in Ethiopia and the political goals of the main diaspora leaders differ. US relations with Ethiopia have rarely received high-level attention and have generally been seen through the lens of other, more pressing interests such as Cold War competition, Middle Eastern resources, or most recently global terrorism. The divergence between the agenda pressed by leaders in the Ethiopian diaspora and the priorities of officials in the Department of State has limited prospects for successful diaspora lobbying.

The United States had close relations with Ethiopia prior to 1974, but the relationship became very distant and tense in the aftermath of the 1974–77 revolution that brought a brutal Marxist-military regime to power. It is notable that although the pro-Soviet regime of Mengistu Haile Mariam faced multiple insurgencies, Washington did not apply the Reagan Doctrine to Ethiopia and fund anticommunist insurgent groups. It did, however, create the Voice of America's Amharic service to provide a platform for diaspora-based opposition politicians (Henze 1985). Contacts between the US government and the Washington-based representatives of the insurgent groups existed, but the diaspora had minimal influence on policy toward Ethiopia. In 1991 Washington helped facilitate the transition that brought the Ethiopian People's Revolutionary Democratic Front to power, and relations have been close ever since. The Clinton administration regarded Prime Minister Meles Zenawi as part of an impressive new generation of African leaders and worked with Addis Ababa on issues such as the containment of the National Islamic Front regime in Sudan. The 1998–2000 border war between Ethiopia and Eritrea cooled relations, but the search for allies in the global war on terrorism after 2001 created a new basis for cooperation. The Bush administration viewed Ethiopia as a strategic partner in the war against terrorism. Both Washington and Addis Ababa had concerns about Islamist groups operating in Somalia and allegations of links between some of these groups and such global terrorist networks as al-Qaeda (Menkhaus 2009).

Washington perceived that it needed a close relationship with Ethiopia in order to pursue its strategic interests in the Horn of Africa, with particular emphasis on counterterrorism. This relationship, however, came with a cost.

Ethiopia, like other pivotal states in difficult regions such as Pakistan and Mubarak's Egypt, is a sometimes awkward bedfellow that receives US support for security reasons but then pursues its own, sometimes brutal, agenda regardless of pressure from Washington. While policies that emphasize human rights and democratization need not conflict with a long-term agenda to promote stability and counterterrorism, in the short term policy makers perceive a trade-off, and in the case of US-Ethiopian relations counterterrorism has trumped democratization.

Many in the diaspora exaggerate the degree of Washington's influence in Addis Ababa. Some argue that Meles Zenawi remained in power as a result of US support and that he could not survive a shift in Washington's policy. Washington, however, has limited leverage in Ethiopia. Most assistance is tied to specific humanitarian programs or initiatives such as the President's Emergency Plan for AIDS Relief (PEPFAR), and it is difficult to attach political conditionality on such programs. In 2007, for example, about 50 percent of US assistance to Ethiopia went to HIV/AIDS prevention, 38 percent to emergency food relief, and 7 percent to child survival, family planning, and malaria prevention and treatment. Only 1 percent went to governance programs (Atwood, McPherson, and Natsios 2008).

The 2005 election demonstrates both the potential and the limits of using external pressure to promote political reform in Ethiopia. The major donors responded to the crisis with clear statements criticizing the government and with the suspension of significant levels of assistance. Following the violent demonstrations and arrests of November 2005, the Development Assistance Group (DAG) for Ethiopia, which includes the United States and other major bilateral and multilateral donors, adopted a tough posture and stated, "These disturbances weaken the environment for aid effectiveness and poverty reduction. . . . As a result of the situation, the DAG is collectively reviewing development cooperation modalities to Ethiopia."[5] In December 2005, international donors put $375 million in budget support on hold, sending another message suggesting that business as usual would not be possible in the context of this political crisis. In January 2006, a US Department of State press release stated, "Steps that appear to criminalize dissent impede progress on democratization" in Ethiopia.[6]

The Ethiopian government, however, remained unmoved. Addis Ababa repeatedly stated that the elections were free and fair, that the response of security forces to demonstrations was appropriate, and that charges against opposition politicians, journalists, and civil society leaders were based on solid evidence and long-standing Ethiopian law. By June 2006, in the context of the escalating internal conflict in Somalia, Assistant Secretary of State for African Affairs Jendayi Frazer met with Meles and other Ethiopian officials and stated that relations between the two countries were good. Ethiopian intransigence and US concerns about terrorism in the region led diplomats to accept a status quo that they concluded would not change and to get on with other business. Washington's diverse interests and priorities did not allow for a single-minded focus on democratization and human rights.

Officials at the State Department, the White House, and the Pentagon generally regard the diaspora as unhelpful with regard to key US national interests in Ethiopia. The diaspora has little ability to support US counterterrorism, Washington's principal concern, and the opposition's tendency to boycott elections and the parliament generates considerable frustration. Organizations and leaders within the diaspora were little known outside the Ethiopian community before 2005, leaving many policy makers unclear on how best to engage them. The Ethiopian diaspora, in turn, does not understand why Washington pursues what it regards as shortsighted policies that compromise fundamental US values and risk instability in the longer run. Many suggest that if only Washington officials understood that the current regime was authoritarian and supported by a small minority of the Ethiopian population, then US support would end and a more democratic and stable alternative would emerge.

The Ethiopian government and embassy, in turn, resented Washington's attitude toward activities of the opposition based in the diaspora. Ethiopian officials referred to opposition groups such as the Ogaden National Liberation Front, the Oromo Liberation Front, and Ginbot 7 (a fraction of the CUD) as terrorist organizations that targeted civilians with bombs and government officials with assassination. Washington, however, did not place these groups on the list of terrorist groups, so their political activities and most importantly fund-raising remained legal in the United States. The Ministry of Foreign Affairs saw this as a double standard on terrorism, where terrorists who targeted Africans were not treated as seriously as terrorists who targeted Americans.[7] A pro-EPRDF website asked why "Ethiopia's most wanted terrorists roam America freely!" (Dange 2009).

Diaspora Lobbying

Both the enthusiasm of the 2005 election and the disillusionment and frustration of the aftermath inspired some within the Ethiopian diaspora to become more active in Ethiopian politics. Along with their transnational involvement through their political networks, many in the diaspora organized to participate in lobbying campaigns in Washington and elsewhere. The diaspora effectively mobilized an advocacy network that staged marches and other demonstrations, lobbied members of the US Congress, the State Department, and the World Bank, and sought to generate interest in the media. Diaspora leaders testified before Congress, circulated petitions in support of specific legislation, and encouraged Ethiopian Americans to write to their members of Congress.

One specific focus of the campaign in the United States was for passage of the Ethiopia Democracy and Accountability Act of 2007 (HR 2003). This legislation placed limits on security assistance, called for visa restrictions against anyone involved in killing demonstrators, and authorized $20 million over two years to assist political prisoners, human rights organizations, and other programs to strengthen the rule of law. The president could waive all of these provisions on national security grounds, making the legislation largely symbolic.

Organizations such as the Ethiopian American Council maintained pressure on Congress and mobilized members of the diaspora to lobby their local representatives as well as the leadership in both the House of Representatives and the Senate. Critics of the regime in Addis Ababa found effective entry points into the policy-making process by reaching out to members of Congress with large diaspora communities and by forming alliances with human rights advocacy groups (Snyder 2007). Major leaders and organizations in the diaspora made passage of this legislation their top priority in 2007. Advocacy packets were developed and distributed. Along with extensive talking points, the packets provided contact information for congressional offices and advocated direct visits to district offices with follow-up phone calls (Coalition for H.R. 2003 2007).

Both groups within the diaspora and the Ethiopian embassy in Washington hired professional lobbying firms to promote their agendas. DLA Piper and former House majority leader Dick Armey (R-TX) lobbied on behalf of the Ethiopian government and in particular against the congressionally sponsored sanctions included in HR 2003. The firm stated that it was "crucial for the United States to have friends and allies in the strategically important Horn of Africa region who are committed to democracy, stability, and moderation" (Silverstein 2007). At other times McGuireWoods Consulting and Hunton and Williams registered as lobbyists for the Ethiopian government (*Indian Ocean Newsletter* 2005). Diaspora supporters of the Coalition for Unity and Democracy hired New York governor Rudolph Giuliani's firm, Bracewell and Giuliani, to lobby on their behalf. The firm reportedly helped set up meetings between opposition figures and the White House. A member of Bracewell and Giuliani suggested that its primary mission had been to secure American support for the release of jailed Ethiopian opposition leaders (Lipton 2007). Lobbyists on behalf of the Ethiopian government often emphasized the partnership between Addis Ababa and Washington with regard to counterterrorism policies. Those working to promote the perspectives of the opposition tended to frame their campaigns around democracy and human rights. These two different ways of framing the issues tended to favor the Ethiopian government's agenda in the eyes of many US policy makers.

On October 2, 2007, HR 2003 passed the House of Representatives, a major victory for the diaspora's lobbying initiative. The Ethiopian government responded with great umbrage. The minister of foreign affairs attacked what he called "neocolonial" meddling in Ethiopia's internal affairs, some argued that cutting assistance to Ethiopia would only hurt the most vulnerable, and others suggested that US-Ethiopian cooperation on counterterrorism might suffer if the bill became law. The Ethiopian Embassy in Washington issued a statement saying that the House of Representatives had "approved irresponsible legislation that, if it becomes law, would create fresh obstacles to Ethiopia's bold efforts towards comprehensive democratic reforms. The legislation would undermine regional stability in the Horn of Africa by jeopardizing vital security cooperation between the United States and Ethiopia."[8] While the diaspora saw passage of HR 2003 as a significant accomplishment, the success did not change US policy toward Ethiopia. In the end, the bill was not brought up for a vote in the Senate and it lost momentum in subsequent Congresses.

In addition to well-established forms of lobbying, the opposition within the Ethiopian diaspora challenged the regime on multiple fronts. Lobbying NGOs, universities, and church organizations often appeared to be more promising as means of applying pressure on the EPRDF than lobbying Congress or the White House. For example:

- Influential nongovernmental organizations were targeted, including the Carter Center in Atlanta for its failure to condemn the 2005 elections and the Clinton Foundation for taking funds from Sheik Mohammed al Amoudi, a major financial supporter of the ERPDF (Ethio-American Civic Associations Alliance 2009).

- Ethiopians organized demonstrations in front of Senator Inhofe's office in Oklahoma City after Inhofe made remarks that the diaspora regarded as pro-EPRDF.

- The Oromo Youth Association (2009) wrote a letter of protest to the president of Cornell University asking him to suspend its partnership with Bahir Dar University in Ethiopia "until the regime stops its practice of ethnic segregation and discrimination against Oromo students."

- Supporters of the Oromo Liberation Front and the Ogaden National Liberation Front demonstrated in London to protest Meles Zenawi's participation in the G-20 meeting in March 2009.

- In Germany in 2009, members of the diaspora protested when the city of Tubingen proposed a sister-city relationship with Mekelle, the capital of Tigray Province. These demonstrations were followed by pro-EPRDF demonstrations, and both sides posted rival YouTube videos to dispute the other's account of the size of the rival demonstrations.

Mobilization by members of the diaspora from the Ogaden region provides another illustration of conflicts between the Ethiopian government and elements of its opposition playing out through contentious forms of transnational politics. Violent conflict in the Somali-inhabited Ogaden region of eastern Ethiopia escalated sharply in 2007 and 2008. Sympathizers and supporters of the insurgent Ogaden National Liberation Front (ONLF) and authorities in Addis Ababa competed to influence how the conflict was framed and understood by the international community. The Ethiopian government claimed that the ONLF was a terrorist organization and a proxy for its regional rival Eritrea and therefore a legitimate target for security forces. Sympathizers and supporters of the ONLF, in contrast, alleged that the ruling party was guilty of "war crimes" and "acts tantamount to Genocide against the Ogaden people" (ONLF 2009). The more immediate goal of both the diaspora and the Ethiopian government was not to press for a specific policy change but to influence how the international community regarded the conflict in the Ogaden.

Some in the diaspora compared the Ogaden to Darfur, thereby tapping into a popular narrative and set of symbols around "genocide," the use of local militias (with comparisons to the *janjaweed*), and the use of violence to seize energy resources (recalling Khartoum's policies toward oil-rich areas of southern Sudan). The Ethiopian government responded with a contrasting narrative of "terrorism" and the need to use force against violent Islamist groups with links to al-Qaeda. Both parties understood that whether the conflict was framed as "crimes against humanity" and "genocide" or as a response to "terrorism" would shape international policy responses.

While common interests in counterterrorism dominated US-Ethiopian relations, Washington refused to place the ONLF on its list of terrorist groups. When asked about the Ethiopian government's request for this, US assistant secretary of state Jendayi Frazer replied, "We really looked at the ONLF differently after the killing of the Chinese workers in the Oagaden [an ONLF attack that left many civilians dead], but we have not declared it a terrorist organization" (Kennedy 2007). ONLF political activities and most importantly fund-raising therefore remained legal in the United States.

In the aftermath of the 2005 election, some in the diaspora have continued to try to influence policy in Washington but with very limited success. Many in the diaspora supported "Ethiopians for Obama" and engaged in US domestic politics with the expectation that America's first "Kenyan American" president would support the struggle for democracy in Ethiopia (Fears 2008). Some individual members of the diaspora received appointments in the administration, notably Daniel Yohannes, who was named chief of the Millennium Challenge Corporation. Addis Ababa's support for Washington's counterterrorism policies, however, remains central to US foreign policy. The State Department announced that it was "recalibrating" policy toward Ethiopia to balance security interests with interests in democracy and human rights, and Washington criticized the 2010 election, in which the ruling party won 99.6 percent of the seats. To date, however, policy has remained largely the same and security issues receive more attention than democracy and human rights. Opportunities for the diaspora to influence politics in Ethiopia by lobbying the US government or by directly engaging in politics as it did in 2005 have closed.

The Ethiopian diaspora played a number of critical roles in recent political events in Ethiopia but not primarily because of its ability effectively to lobby Washington to change its policies. More important than ethnic lobbying has been the diaspora's ability to raise funds, frame political debates, and act as gatekeeper for opposition strategies and thereby shape whether opposition parties participate or boycott elections and the parliament. In the dramatic 2005 elections, both major opposition coalitions had links to the diaspora and relied upon supporters abroad for funds, publicity, and advice. Key strategies and positions were the outcome of transnational political processes in which leaders in multiple locations in both the diaspora and the homeland participated. Lobbying the US government was part of these campaigns but was only one aspect of a larger strategy and a larger process of transnational politics. The divergence between Washington's interest in building a security partnership on counterterrorism with the incumbent regime and the diaspora's interest in political change, democratization, and human rights made it difficult for diaspora lobbying to alter US policy. The diaspora had greater success in Congress, as evidenced by the passage of HR 2003, but even this victory remained largely symbolic and did not lead to a change in Washington's policies regarding Ethiopia.

Notes

Support for this research has been provided by the MacArthur Foundation through its funding of the Global Migration and Transnational Politics project at the Center for Global Studies, George Mason University. The author would also like to thank David Shinn, Ted Dagne, and the participants of the Social Science Research Council–US Institute of Peace workshops for helpful comments.

1. See Ethiopian News Agency (2006). Note that the state-run media in Ethiopia cover fund-raising events in the North American diaspora, further suggesting the influential links between homeland and diaspora communities.

2. See Shawel (2005). The *Ethiopian Review* (2005), an opposition website, attacked Berhanu and asked why he "wants to work with the murderous regime of Meles Zenawi."

3. Ministry of Foreign Affairs, "Diaspora Forum: Election and the Diaspora," June 2005, www.mfa.gov.et/Press_Section/Newsletter.php?Page=Newsletter6/Newsletter6.htm (no longer available).

4. Ethiopian Ministry of Foreign Affairs, "A Week in the Horn," March 27, 2009, www.mfa.gov.et/Press_Section/Week_Horn_Africa_March_27_2009.htm (no longer available).

5. Statement by the Development Assistance Group, Addis Ababa, November 11, 2005.

6. US Department of State, press statement, "Political Dissent and Due Process in Ethiopia," January 6, 2006, http://2001-2009.state.gov/r/pa/prs/ps/2006/58773.htm.

7. Ethiopian Ministry of Foreign Affairs, "Terrorism, Double Standards, and the International Community," *Week in Review*, November 21, 2008, www.mfa.gov.et/Press_Section/Week_Horn_Africa_November_21_2008.htm (no longer available).

8. See *AllAfrica.com* (2007) for full text. See also Jopson and Dombey (2007).

References

Aalen, Lovise, and Kjetil Tronvoll. 2009. "The 2008 Ethiopian Local Elections: The Return of Electoral Authoritarianism." *African Affairs* 108 (430): 111–20.

Abrams, Amanda. 2008. "Will Ninth Street's Ethiopian Pioneers Survive?" *DC North*, July. www.capitalcommunitynews.com/publications/dcnorth/2008_July/html/WillNinthStreetEthiopianPioneers.cfm.

Adamson, Fiona B. 2002. "Mobilizing for the Transformation of Home: Politicized Identities and Transnational Practices." In *New Approaches to Migration? Transnational Communities and the Transformation of Home*, edited by Nadje Al-Ali and Khalid Koser, 155–68. London: Routledge.

Al-Ali, Nadje Sadig, and Khalid Koser, eds. 2002. *New Approaches to Migration? Transnational Communities and the Transformation of Home*. London: Routledge.

AllAfrica.com. 2007. "Statement by the Embassy of Ethiopia on House Passage of H.R. 2003, October 2, 2007." October 6. http://allafrica.com/stories/200710060053.html.

Araya, Hailu. 2007. Interview by Voice of America, September 19. Audio at http://abbaymedia.com/audio-archive/.

Atwood, J. Brian, M. Peter McPherson, and Andrew Natsios. 2008. "Arrested Development: Making Foreign Aid a More Effective Tool." *Foreign Affairs* 87 (November/December): 123–32.

Chacko, Elizabeth. 2003. "Ethiopian Ethos and the Making of Ethnic Places in the Washington Metropolitan Area." *Journal of Cultural Geography* 20:21–42.

Coalition for H.R. 2003. 2007. "H.R. 2003, Ethiopia Democracy and Accountability Act of 2007: U.S. Senate Advocacy Packet." October 18. www.ethiopolitics.com/pdfiles/SENATEADVOCACYPACKET_HR2003.pdf.

Cochrane, Feargal. 2007. "Irish-America, the End of the IRA's Armed Struggle, and the Utility of 'Soft Power.'" *Journal of Peace Research* 44 (2): 215–31.

Collier, Paul, and Anke Hoeffler. 2000. "Greed and Grievance in Civil War." World Bank Policy Research Working Paper 2355. http://elibrary.worldbank.org/doi/book/10.1596/1813-9450-2355.

Dange, Dag. 2009. "Would the US Immigration Grant Asylum for Al Qaeda or Ginbot 7?" *Aiga Forum*, April 28. http://aigaforum.com/articles/Dag_on_Ginbot7.htm.

Ethio-American Civic Associations Alliance. 2009. "Letter to President Clinton." *Washera Ethiopian Politics* (blog), March 12. http://washerastyleethiopianpolitics.blogspot.com/2009/03/letter-to-president-clinton.html.

Ethiopian News Agency. 2006. "TDA Organizes Fund-Raising Night in Seattle." *Ethiopian Herald,* August 22.

Ethiopian Review. 2005. "Berhanu Nega Is Going against the People's Desire." Editorial. September 21. www.ethiopianreview.us/12546.

Fagen, Patricia Weiss, and Micah N. Bump. 2006. *Remittances in Conflict and Crises: How Remittances Sustain Livelihoods in War, Crises, and Transitions to Peace.* New York: International Peace Academy.

Fears, Darryl. 2008. "African Immigrants among Obama's Enthusiastic Backers." *Washington Post,* July 6.

Hafkin, Nancy. 2006. "'Whatsupoch' on the Net: The Role of Information and Communication Technology in the Shaping of Transnational Ethiopian Identity." *Diaspora: A Journal of Transnational Studies* 15 (2/3): 221–45.

Henze, Paul. 1985. *Rebels and Separatists in Ethiopia: Regional Resistance to a Marxist Regime.* Santa Monica, CA: RAND Corporation.

Indian Ocean Newsletter. 1995. "Ethiopia: Negotiations in Washington." February 11.

———. 2001. "Ethiopia: Diaspora Unconvinced and Angry." June 9.

———. 2005. "A Lobbyist in Washington." November 5.

Jopson, Barney, and Daniel Dombey. 2007. "Ethiopia Bill Faces Bush Backlash." *Financial Times,* October 3.

Kaplan, Steve. 2006. "Vital Information at Your Fingertips: *The Ethiopian Yellow Pages* as a Cultural Document." *Diaspora: A Journal of Transnational Studies* 15 (2/3): 247–63.

Kennedy, Brian. "Ethiopia: Advocate Says Ogaden Crisis Strikingly Similar to Darfur." *AllAfrica.com,* October 3, 2007. http://allafrica.com/stories/200710031116.html.

Levitt, Peggy, and Mary Waters, eds. 2002. *The Changing Face of Home: The Transnational Lives of the Second Generation.* New York: Russell Sage Foundation.

Lipton, Eric. 2007. "Giuliani's Firm Lobbied for Bill Considered Threat." *New York Times,* December 4. www.nytimes.com/2007/12/04/us/politics/04giuliani.html?_r=1&emc=eeta1.

Lyons, Terrence. 2007. "Conflict-Generated Diasporas and Transnational Politics in Ethiopia." *Conflict, Security, and Development* 7 (4): 529–49.

Lyons, Terrence, and Peter Mandaville. 2010. "Think Locally, Act Globally: Toward a Transnational Comparative Politics." *International Political Sociology* 4:124–42.

———. 2012. *Politics from Afar: Transnational Diasporas and Networks.* New York: Oxford University Press.

McGill, Douglas. 2008. "An Ethiopian Politician on the Stump in Minnesota." *Twin Cities Daily Planet,* August 5. www.tcdailyplanet.net/article/2008/08/05/ethiopian-politican-stump-minnesota.html#.

Menkhaus, Ken. 2009. "Somalia: They Created a Desert and Called It Peace(Building)." *Review of African Political Economy* 36 (120): 223–33.

Mohamoud, A. A. 2005. *Mobilising African Diaspora for the Promotion of Peace in Africa.* Amsterdam: African Diaspora Policy Center.

Newland, Kathleen, and Erin Patrick. 2004. *Beyond Remittances: The Role of Diaspora in Poverty Reduction in Their Countries of Origin.* Washington, DC: Migration Policy Institute.

Ogaden National Liberation Front. 2009. Statement. *OgadenToday.com,* September 15. www.ogadentoday.com/news.php?readmore=60.

Oromo Youth Association. 2009. "Protest Letter to Cornell University," *Gadaa.com,* March 24. http://gadaa.com/oduu/?p=590.

Shawel, Hailu. 2005. "Development and Democracy in Ethiopia: A Private Discussion with Hailu Shawel." American Enterprise Institute,

Washington, DC, September 16. http://ethiopianewsforum.com/view-topic.php?f=2&p=22714.

Silverstein, Ken. 2007. "Bipartisan Duo of Ex-Congressional Heavyweights Blocking Action against Ethiopia." *Harper's*, July 25. www.harpers.org/archive/2007/07/hbc-90000631.

Snyder, Jim. 2007. "Ethiopian Diaspora Keeps Pressure on US Congress." *Hill*, July 25.

Solomon, Addis Getahun. 2007. *The History of Ethiopian Immigrants and Refugees in America, 1900–2000: Patterns of Migration, Survival, and Adjustment.* New York: LFB Scholarly Publishing.

Terrazas, Aaron Matteo. 2007. "Beyond Regional Circularity: The Emergence of an Ethiopian Diaspora." Migration Policy Institute, www.migrationinformation.org/Profiles/display.cfm?ID=604.

Wonqette. "Once upon a Letter." *Weichegud! Ethiopian Politics* (blog), October 25, 2005. http://weichegud.blogspot.com/2005_10_01_archive.html.

Zunzer, Wolfram. 2004. *Diaspora Communities and Civil Conflict Transformation.* Berghof Occasional Paper No. 26. Berlin: Berghof Research Center for Constructive Conflict Management. http://edoc.vifapol.de/opus/volltexte/2011/2543/pdf/boc26e.pdf.

The Haitian Diaspora: Building Bridges after Catastrophe

Daniel P. Erikson

In January 2010, Haiti was struck by a 7.0 magnitude earthquake that devastated the capital city of Port-au-Prince and wrought significant damage in the countryside. The scope of the damage was astounding by any measure. Port-au-Prince is slowly emerging from the ruins of what was almost certainly the single greatest urban catastrophe in modern history. The Haitian government estimates the official death toll to be 316,000, which would make the Haitian quake one of the ten deadliest natural disasters in history, just behind the 2004 Asian tsunami. Even lower estimates put the fatality rate at many tens of thousands. The Inter-American Development Bank (IDB) quickly calculated that the cost of rebuilding homes, schools, and infrastructure could cost as much as US$14 billion—more than double the country's annual GDP. The magnitude of the challenge mobilized the Obama administration to mount an unprecedented effort to help provide relief and assistance in the recovery of its badly damaged neighbor. The US government swiftly readied urban rescue units, medical ships, and military forces to aid the country in its time of crisis and played a key role in co-coordinating the support of the broader international community. The strong initial US response, backed by former presidents Bill Clinton and George W. Bush and endorsed by members from both parties in the Congress, was one of the few bright spots during an undeniably tragic moment.

The Haitian earthquake similarly provided an opportunity for the Haitian diaspora to reassert itself as a key partner in rebuilding the troubled country. The US government had long been deeply entangled in Haitian affairs, but the Haitian diaspora had only intermittently played an important role in conflict resolution and peace building in Haiti. The massive recovery effort required by the earthquake posed a new and uncertain challenge. While American officials charged with managing Haiti policy had, from time to time, sought the advice and analysis of Haitian actors in the United States, never before had there been a calamity of this magnitude. Of course, during the prior three decades, several dramatic events in Haiti had thrust Haitian issues onto the US policy agenda in a way that portended greater engagement between the Haitian diaspora and the US government. Salient examples included the fall of the Duvalier regime in 1986, Haiti's first free elections in 1990, and the subsequent military coup in 1991 that deposed the elected president Jean-Bertrand Aristide; the decision by US president Bill Clinton to authorize American military forces to restore Aristide to power in 1994; and the collapse of Aristide's second presidency in 2004, which led to greater US intervention once again. Indeed, given this track record of US government involvement in Haitian affairs, and the presence of a significant population of residents of Haitian descent in the United States, it was striking that, before the earthquake, communication and engagement between the US government (especially the executive branch) and the Haitian Diaspora had been largely episodic and had lacked the deeply woven interconnections that characterize other case studies such as Cuba, Iraq, Ireland, or Israel.

While there were many possible explanations for this, including the relative weakness of Haitian diaspora organizations and their tendency to reflect political divisions in Haiti in ways that undermined their impact, perhaps the most persuasive was that the US government had long diverged from the Haitian diaspora on many core issues. The Haitian diaspora, like many diasporas, wanted the United States to treat the plight of their home country as a top priority, but American policy for many years had been primarily geared toward making modest, as opposed to transformative, investments in Haiti. Haitians expatriates generally favored a more liberal US immigration policy for Haiti, but American policy planners had long held concerns that a "softer" stance on immigration would set off a wave of boat people seeking to leave Haiti and arrive on US shores. While a majority of the Haitian diaspora supported greater foreign aid for Haiti through the US government and multilateral development banks, an influential undercurrent of thought was protective of Haitian sovereignty and fearful of Haiti's evolution into a fully dependent client state that would rely on the United States to provide economic aid and internal security. American policy rhetoric toward Haiti increasingly highlighted the importance of the Haitian diaspora to the country's future, but US policy decisions were made without consulting the diaspora in any systematic way. This created a situation where Haiti's political difficulties created a diaspora that lacked the tools to help resolve the conflict and had little impact on shaping US policy responses.

The January 2010 earthquake and its aftermath changed this dynamic in several fundamental ways. The United States, motivated largely by humanitarian concerns, suddenly recast Haiti from a foreign policy afterthought to a central priority for foreign development assistance and began to set aside serious resources for rebuilding Haiti. Within a month of the quake, the amount of money mobilized or pledged by the US government totaled $636 million—including $250 million in US military support for humanitarian relief supplied by the Pentagon and an additional $380 million provided by USAID through the Office of Foreign Disaster Assistance. By the summer of 2010, the US State Department and USAID submitted a supplemental budget request totaling $1.6 billion—an eye-popping figure for a country that had regularly received less than a tenth of the amount annually from the United States. Within a week of the earthquake, the United States granted "Temporary Protected Status" (TPS) to undocumented Haitians already residing in the United States, thereby giving an estimated one hundred thousand Haitians the right to work legally and exempting them from deportation. This had been something the diaspora community had long been demanding, to no avail, prior to the earthquake.

The US government also supported the creation of the Interim Haiti Recovery Commission (IHRC), which was formed by Haitian authorities to oversee earthquake reconstruction. Cochaired by Haitian prime minister Jean-Max Bellerive and former US president Bill Clinton, the IHRC was composed of an equal number of Haitian and non-Haitian representatives, including international organizations, multilateral banks, the US government, and other major donors (Guyler Delva 2010). In a key breakthrough, the Haitian diaspora was formally represented on the IHRC by retired US Army major Joseph Bernadel, who was nominated by the Haitian Diaspora Federation, a new organization launched by an important diaspora conference hosted by the Organization of American States shortly after the earthquake. The magnitude of the Haitian earthquake had shaken old patterns of behavior that had long inhibited the development of close ties between the

US government and Haitian expatriates, creating new opportunities to build bridges in the aftermath of a major catastrophe.

Defining the Diaspora

The January 2010 earthquake was only the most severe of a long set of crises that had historically bedeviled the poorest country in the Western Hemisphere. Millions of Haitians have fled the country's chronic poverty and instability over the past two decades, and the vast majority have settled in the United States. However, the exact size of the Haitian American community in the United States is difficult to measure. Haitian American groups regularly claim a US-based population exceeding one million, with some estimates reaching as high as 1.5 million. However, data on the exact number of Haitian Americans in the United States are unreliable because of the high number of recent immigrants. The 2010 American Community Survey published by the US Census Bureau estimated that 830,000 people of Haitian ancestry live in the United States, with a population mainly concentrated in Florida and New York, which claimed 45.3 percent and 23 percent of the total Haitian population in the United States, respectively. (While there are anecdotal reports of an increase in Haitian migration to the United States following the 2010 earthquake, this has not been statistically verified.)

The demographics of the Haitian diaspora paint a mixed picture. In general, the Haitian American community in the United States is younger (by an average of seven years), earns less (by an average of $10,000 per capita per year), and has received less education than the average American. Thirty-seven percent of Haitian Americans speak English less than "very well," and 81.2 percent of households speak a language other than English at home. Still, the Census Bureau estimates that almost 325,000 Haitian Americans, or 40 percent of the total, were born in the United States. Of the almost 500,000 foreign-born Haitian Americans counted by the census, 45 percent entered the United States before Haiti's first democratic election took place in 1990. Many, therefore, have learned all they know about representative democracy in the United States. Nonetheless, the extent to which the Haitian diaspora has actually participated in US elections remains a question of great interest to politicians and diaspora leaders alike.

While there are no official figures on the total number of Haitian American voters in the United States, this population is estimated to number around 360,000 people. A state-level analysis reveals strong pockets of Haitian American influence in Florida, Massachusetts, and New York. Tens of thousands of Haitians could be registered to vote in both New York and Massachusetts, and Florida holds the largest bloc of potential Haitian American voters at about 150,000. The Haitian American vote is quite important in certain electoral districts in Florida. For example, prior to the 2012 redistricting, Haitian Americans accounted for 10 percent of all registered voters in Florida's Seventeenth District and nearly 7 percent of voters in the Twenty-Third District. Democrats Frederica Wilson and Alcee Hastings, who respectively represented the Seventeenth and Twenty-Third Districts, are African American members of Congress who have benefited directly from Haitian backing and who have promoted issues to support Haiti in Congress, although their positions are largely indistinguishable from those of other prominent members of the Congressional Black Caucus who have frequently advocated on behalf of Haiti. (After the 2012 redistricting, Representatives Wilson and Hastings now represent the Twenty-Fourth and Twentieth Districts, respectively, where they continue to draw on Haitian support.) Interestingly, the neighboring Twenty-Fifth and Twenty-Seventh Districts are home to two prominent Cuban American politicians, Republicans Mario Diaz-Balart and Ileana Ros-Lehtinen, who act as the gatekeepers on US-Cuba policy in the House of Representatives.

By contrast, in the United States, there are relatively few high-profile Haitian American politicians, despite the large number of accomplished Haitian professionals. There are no Haitian American members of the US Congress, in striking contrast to the Cuban diaspora, which has three US senators, four members of the House of Representatives, and several people who have served at the cabinet level. Even the Jamaican diaspora can claim Yvette Clarke, a New York congresswoman and the daughter of Jamaican immigrants, who was elected in 2006, as well as former secretary of state Colin Powell, who is also of Jamaican descent. Haitian Americans are only sparsely represented in state legislatures, although several cities in South Florida can claim Haitian American mayors. US policy toward Haiti lacks the direct link to electoral politics that strongly drives US policies toward regions with a strong domestic ethnic lobby. The size of the voting Haitian American population is a factor in determining whether and how the community makes its voice heard in the US government. On this count, the data reveal small but densely populated pockets of Haitian American voters that can play a role in deciding local elections but have not been decisive players in national politics. Members of the Haitian diaspora who wish to influence US policy, therefore, are forced to rely on tools other than shaping electoral outcomes to make an impact on US-Haitian relations. Before assessment of the nature of the interaction between the Haitian diaspora and the US government, however, it is useful to examine the convoluted nature of Haiti's conflicted politics and what has made it so difficult to sustain political progress.

In recent years, members of the Haitian diaspora have exhibited diverse reactions to the political travails of their home country, ranging from the "freedom fighters" who resisted the Duvalier dictatorship and later the excesses of the Aristide government; the "peacemakers," who called for greater reconciliation among all Haitians; and the "bystanders," who sought to keep a safe distance between their new lives in the United States and the poverty and violence that continued to bedevil Haiti. The January 2010 earthquake launched a new wave of activists and humanitarians engaged in Haiti, perhaps most famously Wyclef Jean, whose steady involvement in his home country deepened, became highly publicized, and even led to a quixotic presidential campaign. His support was later critical to the 2011 election victory of presidential candidate Michel Martelly, a prominent local musician and businessman.

Prior to the earthquake, however, many members of the Haitian diaspora had adopted a position of studied disengagement from the politics of their country of origin, while those calling for peace and reconciliation often lacked both the stature and the resources to bring together diverse Haitians into a common cause dedicated to the public good. As a result, the central dynamic that has shaped the diaspora's relation to the Haitian conflict has been vacillation between apathy and resistance, occasionally punctuated by spurts of hopeful and constructive engagement during brief periods of optimism, especially following the election of Aristide in 1990 and his return to Haiti in 1994. At this still early stage, the wave of renewed diaspora engagement in Haiti after the 2010 earthquake appears less likely to represent something fundamentally new and more likely to merely mark a more dramatic high in this cyclical trend. But the Haitian diaspora can hardly be faulted for lacking a consistent approach to Haiti's woes: a brief review of the country's past twenty years reveals how the complicated Haitian situation has become a case study of low-intensity conflict and resulting state fragility.

The Contours of the Haitian Conflict

The January 2010 earthquake changed Haiti's physical and political landscape but occurred against the backdrop of a country already teeming with problems. Few would dispute that Haiti is one of the most troubled countries in the world, but the precise causes of its seemingly never-ending political and economic turmoil defy easy classification. Haiti is not at war with its neighbors, nor does it face a violent insurgency from within. The Haitian military, once among the most repressive armed forces in the hemisphere, has been disbanded and replaced by a police force that is far from perfect but hardly a major force for state repression. The country is frequently described as a "weak state," but it shows no signs of breaking apart into separate territories and is arguably one of the most culturally cohesive nations in the Americas. All Haitians speak the common language of Haitian Creole, and the vast majority of Haitians are of African descent. Although there is a tiny, lighter skinned minority that wields a disproportionate amount of economic power, and most political and economic elites conduct business in French rather than Creole, the existing political divisions in Haiti do not break down along either racial or linguistic lines. Haiti's occasional paroxysms of dramatic political violence have created the widespread impression that Haiti is an unrelentingly violent country, but on a per capita basis Haiti's murder rate is actually quite a bit lower than that of many other countries in Latin America and the Caribbean. Given Haiti's weak institutions, deeply entrenched poverty, absent social safety nets, and prevalence of weapons flowing through the country, it is striking to note that Haiti has thus far avoided the kind of major conflagration and mass violence that has occurred in many countries in Africa.

Still, Haitian politics has been embroiled in conflict ever since the country gained independence in 1804. Since that time, there have been thirty-four coups d'état in Haiti, and the violent overthrow of government has been far more commonplace than the peaceful transition of power from one president to another. Indeed, a kaleidoscopic, multidimensional power struggle among an evolving array of competing groups has defined Haiti's contentious politics for more than two centuries. While the historical roots of conflict reach back to the country's founding, an analysis of Haiti's contemporary political landscape can usefully begin with the fall of the Duvalier regime in 1986. The ouster of Haitian dictator Jean-Claude "Baby Doc" Duvalier, who had succeeded his father "Papa Doc" Duvalier following the elder's death, was a cathartic moment that ushered Haiti into an unstable period of democratic transition, where it largely remains stalled nearly a quarter century later.

After Duvalier's exit, Haiti underwent several years of transitional civilian government that alternated with military rule until the country held its first democratic election in 1990, a historic event that remains the high-water mark in Haiti's democratic opening. In that election, Jean-Bertrand Aristide, a defrocked Catholic priest with a shy smile, a slight build, and galvanizing political rhetoric, swept to victory over Marc Bazin, a technocratic figure backed by the military and the country's elites. Aristide took power in February 1991 but was ousted in a military coup that September and fled into exile for the next three years as Haiti was governed by a military dictatorship headed by junta leader Raoul Cédras. In 1994, Aristide was restored to power in Haiti by a US military intervention conducted under the auspices of the United Nations, and he then handed power over to his elected successor Rene Préval in 1995. The first Préval administration presided over a gradual breakdown in constitutional government as political disputes led the president to disband the parliament and rule by decree. An attempt to remedy the situation by holding new parliamentary elections in May 2000 ended in failure when polling irregularities led the opposition to dispute the results, and the United States and other members of the international community cut off aid to Haiti until new elections were held and judged to be free and fair. In November 2000, Aristide was reelected in an election boycotted by the opposition and characterized by low turnout. After taking power again in 2001, the Aristide government became embroiled in a war of attrition with the opposition during negotiations about holding new parliamentary elections. Meanwhile, the international community continued to block development assistance to Haiti, and the country's already dire poverty became further exacerbated.

In February 2004, Haiti's simmering political situation exploded when an armed uprising against the government took place in the coastal city of Gonaives, led by youthful gang members who had become aggrieved with the government. Increasingly, scenes of desperation and violence emerged from Haiti, such as the burning of police stations and civilian casualties, which added to a general sense that chaos and lawlessness were sweeping the country. The United States, Canada, France, and other Western nations refused to send peacekeeping troops to Haiti to quell the violence unless

Aristide and the opposition could finally hammer out an agreement for establishing a government of national unity. The opposition, sensing Aristide's eroding position, refused to accept an agreement that left him in power, and the militant groups began to converge on the capital city of Port-au-Prince while threatening to execute the president. On February 29, 2004, American officials ushered Aristide onto a US-chartered jet and dispatched him to the distant outpost of the Central African Republic, where the United States had arranged for a temporary asylum. Upon landing, Aristide proclaimed his outrage at being forced to leave Haiti and announced that he had been the victim of a "modern kidnapping." He remained in exile, however, eventually moving to South Africa at the invitation of President Thabo Mbeki.

Back in Haiti, the next stage of the crisis was already unfolding, as Aristide's departure, together with the expiration of parliament, left the country devoid of any elected democratic apparatus whatsoever. The international community put together a tripartite committee consisting of representatives of the deposed government, the opposition, and the UNDP head, who then selected a seven-person "Conseil des Sages" (Council of Wise Men) who would be responsible for selecting an interim prime minister. The Conseil des Sages quickly settled on Gerard Latortue, a former Haitian foreign minister and semiretired UN official who won the job on a phone interview from his home in Boca Raton, Florida. Latortue then flew down to Port-au-Prince to assume the prime ministerial post, while Supreme Court Justice Boniface Alexandre was elevated to the presidency according to the procedure outlined in the Haitian constitution. (Haiti's political system calls for the elected president to appoint a prime minister who requires parliamentary ratification and is supposed to have greater authority to run the government. In fact, Haitian politics is inevitably presidentialist in nature, but during the transitional administration it was Latortue who acted as the chief decision maker.) During 2004, an emergency Multinational Interim Force that had been cobbled together by the United States, Canada, France, and Chile to provide stability in the wake of Aristide's departure gave way to a larger UN peacekeeping force in Haiti, which was led by Brazil and featured heavy Latin American participation.

Latortue, who led Haiti's government from March 2004 to May 2006, quickly assembled a cabinet of principally nonpartisan technocrats, although several opposition figures landed key posts, while Lavalas, the political organization founded by Aristide in 1991, went unrepresented. By the end of its mandate, the interim administration's technocratic credentials had become overshadowed by its penchant to become embroiled in messy political battles, such as sparring with member countries of the Caribbean Community, jailing dozens of prominent Lavalas supporters (including former prime minister Yvon Neptune, who had served on the tripartite committee that appointed the Conseil des Sages who selected Latortue), and later jumping into the presidential contest to bar prominent Haitian American candidates from participating. Latortue, who lacked a strong political base within the country, was hesitant to alienate the rebel leaders and the opposition figures that had pushed for Aristide's ouster. Thus he was reluctant to challenge a campaign against Lavalas orchestrated by Justice Minister Bernard Gousse and other cabinet officials that cut deeply into the government's international legitimacy. The interim government did have several key achievements. Its finance minister was widely respected, and the Latortue administration was seen to have tighter fiscal controls and a greater emphasis on minimizing state corruption. In addition, the pledge taken by Latortue and his top ministers not to compete in the elections enhanced the political credibility of both the government and the election process as a whole. To its credit, the interim government never wavered in its support for Haiti's return to a democratically elected government, and it played a constructive role in the negotiations following the 2006 presidential elections. The Latortue government made little headway in promoting national dialogue and political reconciliation, but its political legacy was relatively benign.

In February 2006, Haiti renewed the process of establishing a democratic government through three rounds of elections, for presidential, parliamentary, and municipal seats. But the democratic process has proceeded only in fits and starts. While the actors have changed, a standard set of problems continue to hamper the development of Haitian democracy. The political party system is weak, even anarchic, with new constellations forming and dissolving in rapid succession; this prevents the establishment of party norms and often means that parties are linked to the personality of a single leader. The Haitian constitution requires that the elected president select a prime minister to run the government, but the prime minister's appointment requires parliamentary approval. In recent years, this has been notoriously difficult to receive, as discord between the president and the parliament, and the lack of a political party system to help resolve their differences, often leave Haiti without a formal government for months at a time. Moreover, prime ministers rarely last more than a year or two, which means that this vital post undergoes frequent turnover during a five-year presidential term. Haitian elections rarely take place on time and are frequently heavily underwritten by and held at the behest of the international community, which requires that the Haitian government retain a patina of democratic legitimacy in order to justify continued development assistance.

The US Government and the Haitian Diaspora: Convergence or Divergence?

Since Haiti's first democratic election in 1990, US policy actions vis-à-vis Haiti have vacillated wildly, even though the premise of promoting democracy and economic sustainability has ostensibly been at the core of policy. US policy toward Haiti has included support for the democratic transition (1990–91); tough sanctions on the military government (1991–94); an armed intervention followed by an effort at nation building (1994–2000); political disengagement and a cutoff in aid to the elected government (2000–2004); another, briefer, armed intervention followed by support for a multilaterally managed transition back to a new government (2004–6); restoration of democratic rule and steady engagement (2006–10); and the current objective to "build a new Haiti" following the earthquake (2010–present).

Today, Haiti presents itself as an enduring concern for US policy makers for four principal reasons, which can be identified separately but are not mutually exclusive. The first stems from Haiti's deep poverty and ongoing humanitarian crisis, which were exacerbated by the earthquake and which manifest in high mortality rates, susceptibility to HIV, and widespread hunger. Haiti's fragility means that it lacks the political and economic shock absorbers to deal effectively with economic or environmental turbulence, such as the current spike in global food prices or the impact of tropical storm Jeanne in 2004, which killed more than four thousand people, and the storms of 2008, which killed another seven hundred at least. Haitian Americans generally share this concern, and the policy community and the diaspora mobilized their activities to never-before-seen levels following the 2010 earthquake.

The second reason is that Haiti remains a continuing source of out-migration and was, in the 1990s, at the center of a major refugee crisis when tens of thousands of Haitians took to the seas to escape the military dictatorship that ousted Aristide and ruled in his place from 1991 to 1994. Although it has been more than a decade since Haiti has produced a major wave of boat people heading to the United States, there is a steady stream to Florida, and hundreds of thousands of Haitians have fled elsewhere, principally to the Dominican Republic but also to the Bahamas, the Turks and Caicos, and Cuba. Immigration is a key area of divergence between the US government's views and those of the diaspora. US policy makers on both sides of the aisle have made avoiding a refugee crisis a top priority vis-à-vis Haiti and other Caribbean nations, which means the government has used language and action to limit the incentives for migration. The January 2010 decision to grant "Temporary Protected Status" to Haitians already in the United States was a positive step that was widely welcomed by Haitian diaspora groups, and it reflected the new humanitarian ethos guiding US policy to Haiti immediately following the earthquake.

Third, Haiti is an important transshipment point for Colombian cocaine and also is a hub of arms trafficking and human trafficking that has significant effects on the United States. From the US perspective, the war on drugs has spread from Colombia to Mexico, Central America, and the Caribbean, with Caribbean nations often arguing that the problems that they face from their link in the narco-trafficking chain are overlooked and underfunded. The US desire to stem the flow of drugs through the Caribbean is not one that dovetails significantly with the priorities of Haitian diaspora groups, who, like most of their counterparts in Latin America and the Caribbean, see the US-led "war on drugs" as unfairly punitive toward countries that are unlucky enough to be located between the drug-producing countries of South America and the insatiable consumer market for drugs that lies to their north.

Fourth, the establishment of democracy in Haiti, which has long been a principal goal of US policy, has been a long and winding road. Insofar as the United States has a stake in the consolidation of democracy in the Americas, Haiti is an important element in this agenda. The country has held semi-regular elections over the past twenty years, but these have mainly been organized by, and held at the behest of, the United States and the international community. Few can doubt that Haiti's electoral practices would decline precipitously and perhaps collapse altogether without continued foreign involvement. Moreover, Haiti still lacks a functioning democratic structure at most levels, and the parliament, civil service, judiciary, and national police all remain quite weak. The Haitian diaspora has been strongly supportive of Haitian democracy in theory, but in practice recent elections have unmasked underlying ideological and class tensions that have created a schism around certain leaders, most notably Jean-Bertrand Aristide, who was alternatively framed by diaspora leaders as a heroic figure on par with Nelson Mandela in South Africa or as a thuggish crook akin to Zimbabwe's Robert Mugabe. At these junctures, the US political system has reflected the political fissures in Haiti, and different factions within the US government have turned to the diaspora leaders who share their views as a way to make their case to support or spurn Haiti's elected leadership.

It is not surprising, therefore, that the United States has long been in a quandary about where exactly to place Haiti in the context of its overall foreign policy in the Americas. Other than those listed above, the US interests in Haiti are limited. Haiti is not a major supplier of commodities or manufactured goods to the US market, and there is little in the way of trade and investment. Haiti is not a major recipient of American tourists, and the US expatriate population in Haiti is small, consisting mainly of aid workers and Haitians who also claim US citizenship. Haiti is considered neither an important ally nor a strategic rival to the United States, nor is it effectively integrated into Latin American regional blocs. Haiti is a largely peripheral actor in hemispheric affairs, and its diplomacy abroad is mainly focused on winning more foreign aid. During the Cold War, Haiti's right-wing Duvalier dictatorship was considered to be an important, if unsavory, ally, but the geopolitical importance of Haiti declined precipitously in the 1990s, with the exception of US concerns about averting a major migration crisis. The robust US policy response to the Haitian earthquake suggests that humanitarian concerns will be put at the forefront of US-Haiti policy in the near term.

The Haitian diaspora has generally assumed an oppositional stance to US policy toward Haiti, which is rooted in the political dichotomy that emerged during the Cold War, when the United States initially supported, and later tolerated, the anticommunist Duvalier regime despite its crushing repression and reputation for corruption among the Haitian people. Haiti's deteriorating situation during those years prompted an ever-growing number of Haitians to flee to the United States, where they faced the dual problems of unequal treatment and a US policy at odds with what they perceived to be the Haitian national interest. An estimated one million people fled Haiti between 1957 and 1982, and during the 1970s and 1980s the flow of Haitian boat people to the United States increased dramatically. As a result, the early wave of diaspora mobilization during that time was linked to gaining refugee status for Haitians and protesting US support for the Duvalier regime. Following the regime's ouster and the subsequent election of Aristide in 1990, the Haitian diaspora briefly celebrated before it was confronted with the prospect of another authoritarian regime in control of its homeland, this time the military junta of Raoul Cédras.

When Aristide fled into exile (and thus became a de facto member of the diaspora himself), Haitians mobilized strong support for his restoration, but it was their alliance with powerful African American constituencies that gave Haiti more pronounced relevance for US policy makers. Following the election of US president Bill Clinton in 1992, African American interest groups, who tend to affiliate with the Democratic Party, had links to the new administration that allowed them to wield greater influence. Therefore, the fact that Haiti is a Creole-speaking black country (and one that has historically suffered a long line of injustices at the hands of Western powers) matters in terms of US policy making. The Haitian diaspora was able to effectively build coalitions in American domestic politics, which were principally channeled through the Congressional Black Caucus (CBC). In terms of immigration, in particular, the Haitian diaspora found the CBC to be sympathetic to their concerns that mistreatment or neglect of Haiti stemmed from a racial bias in areas such as migration policy. For example, Cubans who make it to US shores automatically get refugee status, even when they are economic migrants, but most Haitians are detained and deported without even an interview, even if they have credible claims as refugees.

In the wake of the January 2010 earthquake, the Haitian diaspora had a new opportunity to assert itself with respect to US policy making. Previously, outside of their links to the Congressional Black Caucus, the Haitian diaspora had had little impact on the US government and therefore had not done much to improve US policy responses to the various iterations of the Haitian conflict. Of course, some members of the diaspora have exercised significant influence at different junctures. Aristide was clearly an effective lobbyist for his own return to Haiti during his period of exile from 1991 to 1994, and a range of Haitian American community groups were actives in supporting the country in the late 1990s. Gerard Latortue was a member of the Haitian diaspora who became the interim prime minister of Haiti from 2004 to 2006. In more recent years, the Haitian rap artist Wyclef Jean has become a vocal spokesperson for increasing aid to Haiti, including performing at the World Bank, testifying before the US Congress, and launching an abortive run for the Haitian presidency after the earthquake in 2010. But in none of these cases did the individuals effectively represent a broader diaspora constituency. Setting aside the unique cases of Aristide in exile and Latortue's emergency recruitment into the Haitian government, most diaspora figures who have lobbied the US government or shaped its response were elite figures that were operating as policy entrepreneurs rather than as representatives of a broader diaspora interest group.

Since the Haitian earthquake, the US government has included the Haitian diaspora in its vision for improving the future of Haiti, and there are frequent appeals for members of the diaspora to give back to their country of origin. Indeed, the US government has been interested in harnessing the diaspora as a tool for Haiti's development ever since the country's 1990 election, and the severe circumstances of the earthquake played a critical role in overcoming the deep skepticism among Haitians who had been involved in previous such efforts with little to show for their sacrifices. In August 2009, former president Clinton, who had been recently appointed UN special envoy for Haiti, told a major summit of three hundred Haitian American leaders that "Haiti needs you now, and Haiti can take your help now" (Trenton 2009). Following the earthquake, Clinton emerged as one of the most passionate and persuasive spokesmen for Haiti, and he has consistently engaged with Haitian diaspora groups through his multifaceted roles with the United Nations, as chairman of the Clinton Global Initiative, and as cochair of the Interim Haiti Recovery Commission.

Prior to the earthquake, many Haitian diaspora groups pressed for preferential trade agreements for Haiti, such as the Haitian Hemispheric Opportunity through Partnership Encouragement Act (HOPE). To assist Haiti with rebuilding its economy by encouraging investment and job creation in the apparel sector, the 109th Congress passed HOPE I in December 2006. The act provided duty-free treatment for select apparel imports from Haiti, provided Haiti met eligibility criteria related to labor, human rights, and antiterrorism policies. However, the passing of the act did not result in dramatic growth in US textile imports from Haiti, and investments were inhibited by a limited time frame and complicated rules of origin. To enhance the effectiveness of the provisions, the 110th Congress expanded the provisions in June 2008 when it passed the Food, Conservation, and Energy Act of 2008—the Farm Bill, Title XV of which includes HOPE II Act. In essence, the new legislation extended tariff preferences for ten years, attempted to make the rules more flexible and simple, and expanded the duty-free treatment for US apparel imports wholly assembled or knit to shape in Haiti.[1] Critics of HOPE legislation, like Fondasyon Mapou, the Haitian Lawyers Leadership Network (HLLN), and Democracy for Haiti, reject the legislation because it fails to impose labor standards and "imposes patronizing and burdensome conditions on the Haitian people" (HLLN 2006). They feel that the HOPE legislation ignores sweatshop conditions, employer abuses, and exploitations of workers and that it benefits only wealthy Haitian employers. Diaspora leaders and experts recognize that job creation is integral to improving economic situations in Haiti, but they recommend that more rural, sustainable, and socially just development projects be supported by the US government as well (US Institute of Peace 2008). However, in the earthquake's aftermath, many of these doubts have been set aside in order to press ahead with job creation initiatives in Haiti.

In addition, the question of Temporary Protected Status (TPS) for Haitian migrants has emerged as a front-burner issue. TPS provides a safe haven for those aliens who may not meet the legal definition of refugee but are nonetheless fleeing—or reluctant to return to—potentially dangerous situations. There are three categories under which countries may qualify for TPS: ongoing armed conflict posing serious threat to personal safety; environmental disasters; or extraordinary and temporary conditions in a foreign state that prevent aliens from returning. The secretary of homeland security, in consultation with the secretary of state, can issue TPS for periods of six to eighteen months and can extend these periods if conditions do not change in the designated country (Wasem and Ester 2006).

Legislation that would provide TPS to Haitians was introduced in the 109th Congress, and Rep. Alcee Hastings has introduced similar legislation to the 110th Congress. Those opposed to granting TPS warn that any policy shift to provide immigration relief would prompt a mass exodus of Haitians, which would divert and strain homeland security resources. Proponents for TPS status for Haitians show that Haiti consistently meets the latter two criteria for approval and maintain that the Haitians are being singled out for more restrictive treatment. Furthermore, they challenge the view that Haitians pose a risk to national security.[2] As previously mentioned, the January 2010 earthquake fundamentally altered the political equation for TPS in the United States, and the Obama administration quickly granted, and later extended, this policy after treating it with little interest during Obama's first year in office.

Additionally, many members of the Haitian diaspora have been pressing their home country to settle the question of dual citizenship. The Haitian Constitution of 1987, the only legislation governing the issue of Haitian nationality, stipulates that Haitian nationality can be obtained by descent or naturalization, but being born in Haiti does not automatically confer citizenship. Dual citizenship does not exist under Haitian law, and Haitian citizenship is forfeited by naturalization in a foreign country, tenure of a political post in the service of a foreign government, or continuous residence abroad for three years without authorization. Furthermore, anyone who loses his or her nationality in these manners may not reacquire it. This issue is obviously of great import to the Haitian diaspora in the United States, who may one day hope to return to their home country. The issue of dual citizenship has also come up in Haitian politics. Musician Wyclef Jean was forced to abandon his campaign to be president of Haiti after election officials disqualified him for not meeting residency and citizenship requirements.

The Ebbs and Flows of Haitian American Lobbying

Haitian lobbying in the United States has a long history dating back more than a century, but the Haitian diaspora did not truly emerge as a cohesive ethnic bloc in American politics until the middle of the Cold War. At this time US support for the Duvalier regime and changes in US civil rights policies granting equal status to black citizens combined to provide a rallying point for Haitian American activism and opened sufficient political space in the United States for Haitians to engage in the political process. Recently, Haitian American lobbying in American politics has played a crucial role in episodes of US-Haitian relations, beginning with the Duvalier era ("Papa Doc" and "Baby Doc"), the post-Duvalier era (1986–91), the exile years of President Jean Bertrand Aristide (1991–94), the era leading up to Aristide's second ouster in 2004, and the period dating from 2004 until the present.

During the Duvalier era, government lobbyists and their paid American counterparts worked to muzzle the opposition from the Haitian diaspora, essentially providing damage control and political cover for the dictatorship. They had very little support or recognition from the Haitian American community, who for the most part demanded the removal of both Duvaliers from office, charging them with human rights abuses and other offenses (Laguerre 2006, 75). In the immediate post-Duvalier era, a prodemocracy coalition took shape, incorporating both grassroots organizations and formal lobbying organizations. Perhaps the period of greatest unity among the Haitian diaspora occurred with the election of President Aristide in 1990, which was thought to pose a moment in which Haiti could shake off the chains of dictatorship and build a better and more democratic future. This sense of "good and evil," with Aristide personifying the good, persisted following the coup against Aristide and the subsequent establishment of a tough, military dictatorship that prompted tens of thousands of refugees to flee in a migration wave. The 1994 restoration of Aristide and subsequent UN nation-building effort in the country was again a time when diaspora hopes for a better Haiti crested, and many Haitian Americans traveled back to Haiti to participate in the nation-building efforts. But the political squabbling and institutional unraveling that followed during the first term of Rene Préval (1996–2001) soured many expatriates on the prospects for Haiti, and the enthusiasm for the Haitian project dimmed. By the time that Aristide was ousted again in 2004, Haitian American opinion on Aristide was deeply split, with some sectors arguing that his government had been mistreated by the United States and others saying he had betrayed the democratic hopes of the Haitian people.

The dynamic between the Haitian diaspora and Haiti assumed new dimensions in the post-2004 period, when Gerard Latortue, a member of the Haitian diaspora himself, took the helm as the country's interim prime minister. A number of Haitians overseas moved to Port-au-Prince to play a role in the new government, but the lack of viable institutions was met with dismay. "I had a lot of big dreams for Haiti when I joined the interim government," one Haitian American adviser to the Planning Ministry once confided. "But nothing here works. It reminds me of those stories I used to read about flying a plane through the Bermuda triangle, where you have all of the controls in front of you but you can't get the instruments to respond and the plane just starts going down. The Haitian government today suffers from a kind of 'Bermuda triangle' syndrome." In the fall of 2005, Haitian American businessman Dumarsais Simeus declared himself a candidate for the president of Haiti, despite the fact that his US citizenship rendered him ineligible for public office under the Haitian constitution. (This law is erratically enforced in practice, and several prominent Haitian senators and deputies have US citizenship, as do many members of the Haitian business elite.) Latortue stepped in to block Simeus's candidacy, which was legally correct but politically awkward given that the prime minister's nephew, Youri Latortue, was serving in the Haitian parliament despite pervasive rumors that he also held American citizenship. Simeus's candidacy, and the 2006 presidential elections more broadly, also sparked a wide-ranging debate in the Haitian diaspora that pressed for the right of Haitians with dual nationality to participate in Haitian elective politics as candidates or voters, both of which options are currently prohibited. As a major contributor of remittances to Haiti, the diaspora population is eager to move beyond being simply a "cash cow" and to become a more engaged actor in Haiti. Many Haitians living in Haiti, however, rightly wonder whether there is a moral hazard in extending voting rights to a large and financially powerful (in relative terms) expatriate population that could influence election outcomes but not actually be forced to live with the results.

While the Haitian diaspora and the associated lobby have notched minor successes like HOPE legislation and other aid awards from the US government, other issues like TPS and broader development aid have frequently languished. In this regard, the lobbying efforts of the Haitian government and diaspora have fallen short. The reasons for this are myriad. The Haitian American diaspora is large, but not large enough to demand attention at the national level. The numbers game—whether diasporic population or potential lobbying dollars—is central to political decision making. It makes Haitian Americans particularly relevant only in New York City and South Florida; unfortunately for Haitian Americans, these are two regions where other diasporas have considerably more clout. Unlike Cuban Americans in Florida, Haitian Americans have been unable to parlay their presence in a pivotal swing state into disproportionate electoral power. Floridians point to Haitian immigration crises during the Elian Gonzalez debate as an instance of greater weight being assigned to Cuban issues than Haitian issues. This prompted the then executive director of the Haitian American Foundation, Leonie Hermantin, to say: "The policymakers have turned a blind eye on the plight of our children." In reference to the Cuban American lobby, however, she continued: "It's great to have that clout. I admire the Cuban community which has been able in such a short time to amass such power. They're my role model" (Associated Press 2000).

There are other inhibitors within the Haitian American community. From a strategic standpoint, Haitian American voters are courted only when they can shift electoral results on a local level, where foreign policy decisions are seldom made. Politicians elected to city and state posts typically seek to have a greater impact on Haitian Americans than on Haitians in their home country. For example, the Haitian American Political Action Group formed in 1994 in Brooklyn in order to mobilize Haitian Americans to advocate for their needs in the United States.

The limit of the Haitian diaspora's influence is more than a numbers problem. Historically, there has been remarkably little cohesion in how Haitian Americans view Haitian affairs, whether in times of conflict or times of relative stability. While a plurality of views certainly exists in other diasporas, what seems pronounced or perhaps unique about Haitian Americans is the uncertainty that belies many opinions. During debates about the United States invading Haiti in 1994 as well as during the violence and the departure of Aristide in 2004, many reporters interviewed Haitian Americans in Brooklyn and South Florida, trying to get a feel for the communities' views of the events on the island. While some did push a political agenda or argue against the current state of events, many of those interviewed expressed nervousness, disappointment, and uncertainty. After hosting a call-in show on Radio Nouveauté in March of 2004, owner Sylvane Simon summed up the mood in Boston's Haitian community: "The Haitians are afraid, they are afraid of what's next" (*Christian Science Monitor* 2004). Though many callers had expressed strong support for Aristide or frustration at yet another coup, the leap to forcefully lobbying the US government in order to achieve a goal did not naturally follow. Given the tumultuous history of legitimate and illegitimate governance, disillusionment in the diaspora with Haitian politics was not unfounded.

Another difficulty facing the Haitian American community was a lack of access to reliable information. While information generally traveled at a slower pace in 1994, by 2004 many countries had established infrastructure, through phones or the Internet, that allowed them to keep their families in the United States abreast of sudden developments. But as Daniella Henri of the Haitian Community Council in South Florida explained in 2004, there was significant confusion as to what exactly was going on in Haiti: "We don't know what's going on from one day to another" (*Boston Globe* 2004). Henri said she worried that the confusion and lack of information about Aristide's departure would lead those on the island to turn to violence: "I know my brothers and sisters. . . . They are just going to destroy the facilities. This is the way they express anger." Inconsistent reporting, limited contact with families back on the island, and rumors have combined to create a diaspora that is at times confused, unsure, or distrustful, but rarely cohesive and driven toward a common, reachable goal. For some it is a question of pride in Haiti, or a lack of interest in integrating into American society: "Deep down they think they are here for a just a little while to sit out the bad times; that when things get better politically or economically, they will go back home," says Leo Joseph, copublisher of the *Haiti Observateur* newspaper, published in Brooklyn (*Christian Science Monitor* 1994). Two decades later, many Haitian Americans remain dissatisfied with the quality of information about events in their home country. Today, the Haitian American community is growing deeper roots in the United States and carving out new and more sustainable ways to help through voluntary associations, religious outreach, and charitable contributions.

However, many Haitian Americans simply do not have the time or the money to lobby Congress, or to rent-seek on behalf of better policy actions from the US government vis-à-vis Haiti. Median income levels for Haitian Americans are well below the national average, and many work at several jobs so they can send money to family back in Haiti. They are more concerned with their immediate surroundings and quality of life within their US communities than with Haiti. Every diaspora includes people at risk for disenfranchisement, but the Haitian diaspora is particularly vulnerable because of continued poverty and lack of education. On these two fronts, Haitian Americans should have better opportunities in their adopted country than in Haiti, but they report facing ongoing struggles of marginalization in the United States.

The Haitian Diaspora and the US Government: The Road Ahead

In recent years, the US government has sought to build a constructive relationship with the Haitian diaspora in determining its policy approach, and the Haitian diaspora is moving beyond the classic tension between focusing on the crucial issues facing Haitians living in the United States and focusing on resolving the conflict in their homeland. Several conclusions and questions arise from this examination of the present era of lobbying by the Haitian diaspora or Haitian-based parties. First, most informal groups in the United States, though concerned with the civil, economic, and social issues in Haiti, are also advocating for the concerns and issues of Haitian American communities in the United States. Given that the largest populations of

Haitian immigrants are in New York and Miami, diaspora organizations in those settings are advocating for refugee and immigration rights, improved government representation, and better social and economic conditions in the host country. The two objectives are not disconnected, though, as improving Haitian status in the United States can translate into more influence on US policies toward Haiti as well as increased financial contributions and support to families back in Haiti.

One of the central questions that arises in relation to the Haitian diaspora is to what degree they are able to communicate with each another across regions and issues and present a unified case before government officials. The Haitian Diaspora Federation, created at a diaspora conference held by the Organization of American States in the spring of 2010, is emblematic of the new breed of diaspora mobilization following the Haitian earthquake. However, another concern that arises is which group or faction of the Haitian diaspora actually has access to and influence over US policies. With the Bush administration's disengaged stance toward Haiti, immigration issues, such as TPS, made little headway, and this remained true during the first year of the Obama administration. This is one policy issue where the January 2010 earthquake changed everything, and a policy that seemed reasonable but low priority beforehand was speedily implemented during a moment of high crisis.

In the 1990s, professional lobbying organizations were campaigning for US policies that had more direct links to potential and actual conflicts in Haitian politics, but formal lobbying organizations of the present era have focused primarily on promoting postearthquake revitalization or economic development for Haiti through legislation supporting trade preferences. Today, the need for investment and economic development in Haiti is undeniable, and it appears that most informal lobbying organizations have these concerns and can serve as a voice of accountability.

Finally, as diaspora groups seek to explore ways they can contribute to Haiti's recovery from the 2010 earthquake, the possibilities for deeper collaboration with Haiti may also help smooth over latent tensions between the country's expatriate and domestic populations. The diaspora can offer much-needed assistance through professional expertise, investment, and a policy perspective that is enriched by the deep cultural and personal connections to their home country. The Haitian diaspora has historically achieved its greatest successes by adopting strategies of resistance, whether to the crimes of the Duvalier regime, the excesses of the Aristide era, or US policy makers' indifference to the plight of Haitian refugees. The diaspora has struggled, however, to present itself as a force for political reconciliation in Haiti or as an agent of the country's broader development. Moreover, the Haitian diaspora has to date been too fragmented to mobilize much support around a specific policy agenda. Too frequently, the Haitian diaspora has merely stood by during the US foreign policy debates that have had such a dramatic impact on the country.

If any single lesson can be gleaned from the experience of the past twenty years or so, it is that the United States cannot achieve lasting results with short-term interventions. The most important role of the Haitian diaspora is to keep the US government engaged in political and economic development in Haiti over the long run. In this sense, the Haitian earthquake has galvanized an unprecedented level of resource mobilization for Haiti and has forced a degree of convergence between US policy makers and Haitian diaspora groups that would have been almost unthinkable in a different context. Though tragic, the earthquake may have also made possible a long-term US engagement with Haiti in a supportive multilateral environment that will be required to move the country forward. If this comes to pass, the Haitian diaspora will have an important role in enabling Haiti to embrace a more promising future.

Notes to Chapter 8

I wrote this essay while I was senior associate for US policy and director of Caribbean programs at the Inter-American Dialogue, before I accepted a position at the State Department's Bureau of Western Hemisphere Affairs. It is based on independent analysis and does not reflect the views of the US government. I am grateful to Ana Karim, Greta Levy, and Paul Wander for their research assistance.

1. See Seelke and Hornbeck (2008) for a full description.

2. TPS, of course, is part of a broader issue regarding US immigration policies toward Haiti. For example, in 1998, Congress enacted the Haitian Refugee Immigration Fairness Act (HRIFA; S. 1504/H.R. 3049), which enabled Haitians who filed asylum claims or who were paroled into the United States before December 31, 1995, to adjust to legal permanent residence.

References

Associated Press. 2000. "Elian Saga: Florida's Cuban-Americans Flex Their Political Muscle." April 1.

Boston Globe. 2004. "Unrest Continues in Haiti/Miami; A Community at Odds over Aristide's Departure." March 2.

Christian Science Monitor. 1994. "Long Isolated, Haitians in the US May Enter Local, National Politics." September 22.

———. 2004. "Haiti's Chaos Reverberates for Expatriates in American Cities." March 3.

Guyler Delva, Joseph. 2010. "Haiti Approves Key Post-quake Reconstruction Body." Reuters, April 16.

Haitian Lawyers Leadership Network. 2006. "Statement of Haitian Activists on the HOPE Legislation Passed by Congress, December 16, 2006." Press release, December 16. Text reproduced in "Haitian Activists on New US Legislation to 'Help Haitians': Enriching the Few at the Expense of the Many Is Not 'Hope,'" *Ezílí Dantò*, December 16. www.margueritelaurent. com/pressclips/activist.html#nothope.

Laguerre, Michel S. 2006. *Diaspora, Politics, and Globalization*. Gordonsville, VA: Palgrave Macmillan.

Seelke, Clare Ribando, and J. F. Hornbeck. 2008. "Haiti: Legislative Responses to the Food Crisis and Related Development Challenges." CRS Report, July 7. http://nationalaglawcenter.org/wp-content/uploads/ assets/crs/RS22879.pdf.

Trenton, Daniel. 2009. "Bill Clinton Tells Diaspora: 'Haiti Needs You Now.'" *Miami Herald*, August 9.

US Institute of Peace. 2008. "Haiti after the Storms: Weather and Conflict." Panel discussion, October 28. Audio at www.usip.org/events/ haiti-after-the-storms-weather-and-conflict.

Wasem, Ruth, and Karma Ester. 2006. "Temporary Protected Status: Current Immigration Policy and Issues." CRS Report for Congress, January 27. https://www.fas.org/sgp/crs/homesec/RS20844.pdf.

Diaspora-Government Convergence in Policy Making

CHAPTER NINE

The Iraqi Diaspora and the US Invasion of Iraq

Walt Vanderbush

In my opinion, any future defense secretary who advises the president to again send a big American land army into Asia or into the Middle East or Africa should have his head examined.
—Defense Secretary Robert Gates

Many insiders on both sides of the debate agree on this: without Chalabi, there would have been no war.
—Aram Roston

We will never be entirely sure whether Ahmed Chalabi was essential to the invasion of Iraq in 2003, one of the two wars during the George W. Bush administration that together prompted the above statement made in 2011 by Secretary Gates to future army officers at West Point. But given the nearly nine years the US military spent at war in Iraq, an assessment of the role played by members of the Iraqi diaspora in the foreign policy process that led to this "war of choice" would certainly seem worthwhile. Given their numerically small size in comparison to other prominent ethnic interest groups such as Cuban or Jewish Americans, Iraqi exiles' influence on the debate about policy toward their homeland is all the more surprising. Even if the Iraqi diaspora in the United States voted as a bloc or coordinated their financial support toward sympathetic politicians, it is unlikely that they could successfully influence very many elections. But by developing a range of relationships over time with officials in the executive and legislative branches, a small group of Iraqi Americans were able to help produce an explicit US policy goal of overthrowing the Hussein government in Iraq; and in the post-9/11 period they played important, and perhaps essential, roles throughout the foreign policy process that led to the US invasion and occupation of Iraq.

Given a consensus that Arab Americans in general have not been particularly effective historically as a lobbying force, an influential role played by members of the Iraqi diaspora is noteworthy. Of course, some of the perceived weakness of Arab Americans is rooted in the comparative strength of the Jewish American lobby, with whom they are seen to be frequently competing. As Mearsheimer and Walt noted in their work on the Israeli lobby, "Although Arab Americans are a significant minority, they are neither as wealthy, well organized, numerous, or politically active as Jewish Americans" (2007, 141). John Sununu, himself of Palestinian descent and the chief of staff for President George H. W. Bush, realized in 1989 that "there had never been a significant meeting of Arab Americans in the White House with a sitting president," so he put together a group of fifteen, including one Iraqi American. After that meeting did not go very well, Sununu offers it as an example of "years of the worst, least constructive, most counterproductive involvement in the political process of any group in the United States" (2006, 148). At that time, the foreign policy goals of many Arab Americans would have generally been at odds with those of the well-organized Jewish American lobby. In the particular case of Iraqi American exiles at the end of the 1980s, US support for the Hussein government in the Iran-Iraq War and the Israeli interest in a weakened Iranian government made it unlikely that that the Iraqi diaspora could influence or be influenced by the US government. With the Iraqi invasion of Kuwait, the divergence between US government and Iraqi exile goals began to fade. From that point on, there were opportunities for members of the Iraqi diaspora to find common ground with officials in different branches of the government, as well as among influential foreign policy analysts out of the government. Individual political entrepreneurs within the diaspora developed alliances with like-minded officials, and they were able to use each other to further political and policy goals.

Iraqi Emigration

The first modern wave of Iraqi emigration took place in the late 1950s and was largely drawn from the socioeconomic elite who left in the wake of the coup that overthrew the Hashemite monarchy. The teenaged Chalabi left at the time with the rest of his family; the Chalabi family was as wealthy as any in Iraq. Ahmed Chalabi went on to receive degrees from MIT and the University of Chicago in the 1960s, and then he spent quite a bit of time over the next couple of decades in Jordan and Lebanon. A banking scandal in Jordan prompted Chalabi to flee that country, and he was largely based in the United Kingdom or the United States from then until shortly before the 2003 US invasion of Iraq. Other Iraqis, such as Kanan Makiya, left after Saddam Hussein's Ba'th Party seized power in 1968. Makiya was studying at MIT at the time of the overthrow, and he decided not to return to his homeland. After getting his degree he moved to the United Kingdom and then later returned to the United States as a professor at Brandeis University. Adnan Pachachi also left in the late 1960s, but he spent most of his exile in the United Arab Emirates, where he advised that government. Pachachi was a member of one of Iraq's elite Sunni families. Ayad Allawi left Iraq a few years after Pachachi and Makiya, and he moved to the United Kingdom to pursue an education in medicine; in the mid-1970s he formally left the Ba'th Party and became part of the exile opposition. Soon after his split from the Ba'th Party, he survived an assassination attempt in the United Kingdom. Shi'ite religious leaders also sought refuge outside Iraq in the wake of the 1968 change in government; large numbers of Shi'ites followed over the next several years, whether leaving "voluntarily" or being deported. Much of that group ended up in Iran.

The Iran-Iraq War in the 1980s produced another surge of Iraqi emigration, and by the start of the first Gulf War some 1.5 million of a population estimated to be about 18 million had gone into exile. Revolts after the end of the war that were put down by the Hussein government produced yet another large exodus, and by the mid-1990s there were likely at least two million Iraqis outside the country (Marr 2004, 273). The growing Iraqi diaspora was considerably fragmented by class, religion, ethnicity, and ideology, so it was difficult for them to form strong exile organizations. Their dispersion throughout the Middle East, Europe, and to a lesser extent the United States complicated things as well. The largest single concentration was in Iran, where at least five hundred thousand and perhaps as many as one million had fled; other significant communities were in Jordan, Syria, and elsewhere in the Gulf region. The largest part of the European-based diaspora found its way to the United Kingdom: "hundreds of thousands," by one estimate (Marr 2004, 273). Even the Kurds were divided into competing organizations such as the Kurdish Democratic Party (KDP) and the Patriotic Union of Kurdistan (PUK). Other small Iraqi Shi'ite exile groups were scattered around the region. An attempt to unite some of them under the umbrella of the Supreme Council for the Islamic Revolution in Iraq (SCIRI) in Tehran did bring several Shiʻa parties together, but they were left somewhat dependent on the Iranians. Another group, the Iraqi National Accord (INA), was founded by Ayad Allawi and largely made up of defectors from the country's military and security forces; the group became publicly known in 1990–91.

Divided and dispersed, the Iraqi diaspora does not seem to have had any significant political presence in the US foreign policy arena before the 1990s. As of the 1990 census, there were only an estimated forty-five thousand people of Iraqi descent living in this country. That number began to increase after the first Gulf War, but even the census of 2000 indicated that fewer than ninety thousand people born in Iraq were US residents. Approximately one-third of those lived in the area around Detroit, Michigan. Chicago also had a significant Iraqi population, and other small communities were scattered across the United States. The numbers certainly did not suggest potential electoral bloc strength. London itself had far more influential Iraqi exiles at the time than all of the United States. It seems likely that Iraqi exiles would need allies outside the diaspora community if they wanted to affect US policy toward their homeland.

The US government's relations with Iraq in the period before the first Gulf War suggested a divergence from the views of most of the exile community. When Saddam Hussein became president in 1979, the State Department did put Iraq on its list of countries supporting terrorist groups, even as the Carter administration was dealing with the hostage crisis in neighboring Iran. But when the Iran-Iraq War began the following year, a shift in US policy toward Hussein's government began to take place. A 1982 National Security Decision Directive made the Reagan administration's support for Iraq in the war with its neighbor official US policy. Iraq was taken off the list of sponsors of terrorism and began to receive financial and military resources from the United States. Donald Rumsfeld visited Baghdad at the end of 1983, and the picture of him shaking hands with President Hussein at the time has been widely circulated. For the next couple of years, US support for Iraq continued, including satellite photography to assist Iraqi bombers (Woodward 1986). The Reagan administration challenged congressional attempts to limit US support for Iraq and instead authorized dual-technology exports at the same time that evidence of Iraqi use of chemical weapons was becoming clear. In the 1980s, while the United States maintained a strategic alliance with Iraq during their war with Iran, anti-Hussein exiles were not likely to agree with that choice. Chalabi himself was "openly rooting for Iran" (Roston 2008, 36).

As late as October 1989, official US policy stated: "Normal relations between the United States and Iraq would serve our longer-term interests and promote stability in both the Gulf and the Middle East" (White House 1989).

At the end of the war with Iran, individual Iraqi exiles began to gain political visibility in the United States. In 1989, Kanan Makiya published his book *Republic of Fear* under a pseudonym to protect members of his family still in Iraq. When Saddam Hussein invaded Kuwait in August 1990, the book grew more popular among a US population that was not particularly knowledgeable about Iraq. In response to that Iraqi occupation of Kuwait, the first President Bush condemned the Iraqi action, supported economic sanctions, and built up the US military presence in the region. In January 1991 heavy bombing began, and at the end of February the one-hundred-hour ground campaign was undertaken. The Bush administration encountered significant opposition at home leading up to the invasion, as war opponents advocated negotiations and economic sanctions instead of war. Although there would have been a convergence of interests at the time between anti-Hussein exiles and the Bush administration, there is no evidence of coordination between the government and members of the Iraq diaspora to build support for the war.

As President Bush deployed troops to the Middle East, Chalabi's words also appeared in print: he was first quoted by name in a *New York Times* article in January 1991, and his *Wall Street Journal* op-ed "A Democratic Future for Iraq" appeared the following month (Roston 2008, 69). The decision by the Bush administration to call a cease-fire after the one-hundred-hour ground war and not continue on to Baghdad disappointed many in the Iraqi diaspora who had hoped for at least the removal of Hussein from power, if not a significant move toward democracy. The exiles' desire to see Hussein leave office was shared by a good many people in the Bush administration. President Bush himself directed the CIA to begin operations to facilitate the Iraqi president's demise, including the authorization to spend $100 million. Iraqi exiles would have seemed an obvious ally in that effort, but the fragmentation of the community continued to limit their effectiveness. As a means of increasing the Iraqi diaspora's influence, Chalabi and a few others began forming the Iraqi National Congress (INC) in a process that somewhat resembled the development of the Cuban American National Foundation under the leadership of Jorge Mas Canosa a decade earlier. There was also a similar debate about the relative roles of the US government and exiles in its formation. Like

Mas Canosa, Chalabi took credit for the idea of an umbrella organization that would bring disparate exiles together in order to better coordinate their efforts. In a 2003 interview, Chalabi argued: "No one suggested the INC to me. I suggested the INC to people." Some analysts have contended, however, that the initiative came from the US government rather than the exile leader. Laura Miller (2004), for example, has written: "Working with the CIA, the Rendon Group [a public relations firm] created an umbrella organization for Iraqi dissidents, naming it the Iraqi National Congress." According to a report to the Senate by the Select Committee on Intelligence (2006, 6), the CIA approached Chalabi in May 1991, and the June 1992 creation of the INC was the eventual product of their collaboration.

Regardless of the exact origins of the INC, it is clear that by the last year of the first Bush presidency, Iraqi exile groups, the CIA and other government officials, and the Rendon Group were at least tentatively working together to remove Saddam Hussein from power. Neither the commitment to removing Hussein from power nor total support for Chalabi and the INC was universal across the US government at the time. But Chalabi did have enough support that he was soon able to access government funding—both directly from the CIA and funneled through Rendon—and solidify his position as the leader of the INC. During President Clinton's first term, however, the INC's relations with the US government, including the CIA, were somewhat strained. Others in the exile community, including Kurdish groups and the Iraqi National Accord (INA), established bases outside the INC. A failed coup attempt by the INC in 1995 and a similar failure for the INA in 1996 left the exile community weakened and further divided. By the end of President Clinton's first term, the strained relationship between members of his administration, including the CIA, and the INC had deteriorated even further. Finally, in February 1997, the CIA formally ended its relationship with both Chalabi and the INC (Select Committee on Intelligence 2006, 25). The intelligence agency also had an existing relationship with Allawi at the time, and they effectively seemed to be choosing the former Ba'th Party member over Chalabi (Brinkley 2004). Although the Iraqi exiles had limited influence within the Clinton administration, individuals such as Makiya and Chalabi were becoming better known in Washington circles. In the updated edition of *Republic of Fear* that was published under Makiya's own name in 1998, the author uses the introduction to attack US policy toward Iraq, speaking of "a bungling United States" and the "clumsy, unprincipled, hands-on/

hands-off policy of a musclebound superpower" (Makiya 1998, xix). He goes on to note "how little the United States understood about the country" and complains about "the failure of the American political imagination" (xx, xxi). That rhetoric would strike a chord with Clinton's neoconservative critics.

Rebuffed by the Clinton administration, Chalabi and the INC pursued a two-part strategy going forward. First, they sought support from US neoconservatives who were critically observing Clinton's foreign policy from Washington think tanks and other positions outside the government. Following the first President Bush's defeat in the 1992 election, a number of analysts experienced in Cold War foreign policy making migrated toward think tanks and other organizations from which they attempted to influence both elected officials and public opinion in general on global issues. A consensus among these neoconservatives, as some of them were identified, was that the United States needed to more firmly assert its global leadership in the post–Cold War period than some in the Clinton administration seemed to believe. For Chalabi, their support could give him the opportunity to strengthen his claim to be the most important spokesperson for the exile community, even though there were clearly others who had bases of support as well. Some of those neoconservatives were involved with the Project for the New American Century (PNAC), a think tank dedicated to "global leadership," which in part meant challenging "regimes hostile to our interests and values" (PNAC 1997). Among those working with PNAC and linked to Chalabi were former Reagan administration officials such as Paul Wolfowitz and Richard Perle. Neoconservative academic Albert Wohlstetter had introduced Chalabi to Perle and Wolfowitz back in the mid-1980s. One can reasonably speculate that these Reagan administration officials' favorable experience with Jorge Mas Canosa and the CANF during the 1980s would have influenced them to see the potential for a strategic alliance with Chalabi and the INC.

The second part of the INC strategy was to target Congress as potentially more receptive than the executive branch, as long as it was headed by President Clinton. PNAC members and the INC worked together effectively to get Congress to pass the Iraq Liberation Act (ILA) in 1998. Chalabi was described as the "star witness" at a March 1998 hearing called "Iraq: Can Saddam Be Overthrown?" In addition to answering the question affirmatively, Chalabi suggested that those in the Clinton State Department who did not agree with his position on Saddam Hussein were "racist" in the sense that they did not believe Iraqis were capable of a self-governing democracy

(Roston 2008, 151). Here, then, is an early sign of the future marketing campaign to promote an invasion of Iraq: an Iraqi exile, and therefore presumed expert, discrediting those who did not support the military overthrow of Saddam Hussein as somehow lacking confidence in the capacities of Arab people to live under democracy. That argument about promoting democracy in Iraq as a justification for changing US policy may have been enough to produce a congressional expenditure of $97 million to support some opposition activity, but more would be necessary to sell an invasion of the country. Still, when President Clinton signed the ILA at the end of 1998, the overthrow of Saddam Hussein had become the official policy goal of the United States.

Nearly $100 million more was to be committed to the effort to remove Hussein from power, and much of that money was expected to go to the INC. Perhaps more importantly, the ILA made efforts to remove Hussein from power—"regime change"—the official US policy toward Iraq. Less than a decade after his middle-of-the-night flight from Jordan to avoid responsibility for the crash of his Petra Bank, a large amount of US taxpayer money was being put at Chalabi's disposal to facilitate the overthrow of Saddam Hussein. Chalabi's background suggests one of the potential credibility problems faced by a diaspora group. If the individuals appear to be motivated by narrow or selfish interests such as regaining personal property or settling old scores, the US public is likely to view their policy advocacy with considerable skepticism. But if the exile community is able to frame its policy promotion on the basis of interests collectively held by non-Iraqi Americans as well, then the general public is likely to be more receptive to their presumed expertise based on experiences in or links to their homeland. In the case of the 2003 invasion of Iraq, we do see a convergence between the aims of some activists in the Iraqi diaspora and the basic foreign policy goals of many in the US government and society as a whole.

Iraqi Americans Make the Case for War

When George W. Bush became president in January 2001, the climate improved considerably for both neoconservative policy advocates and hardliners in the Iraqi exile community. During his debate with Democratic vice presidential candidate Joseph Lieberman, Dick Cheney had suggested that the new Republican administration might "have to take military action to forcibly remove Saddam from power" (CATO Institute 2000). One of the first Bush administration officials to publish a memoir, former Treasury secretary Paul O'Neill, claimed that the president had ideas of taking out Saddam Hussein as soon as he took office: "From the very beginning, there was a conviction that Saddam Hussein was a bad person and that he needed to go" (Leung 2009). At least ten of the original twenty-five PNAC members moved into government positions, and there was clearly interest on their part in reversing what they saw as the Clinton administration's weak policy on Iraq. In effect, as the PNAC signees moved into important foreign policy positions in the Bush administration, the door that some Iraqi Americans had been pushing on was held wide open for those in the Iraqi exile community who advocated aggressive action against the Hussein government.

With the events of September 11, 2001, some Bush administration officials saw an opportunity to convince others in the government and the US public of the need to invade Iraq in order to remove Saddam Hussein from power. To make that case, individuals in the Iraqi diaspora would play a prominent role. Diaspora members certainly continued to engage in some of the lobbying of executive and legislative branch officials that we might see as expected behavior from any sort of interest group; but more importantly, some representatives worked almost from inside the government with like-minded officials to promote a specific policy. That relationship was of considerable mutual benefit—the exiles got funding, legitimacy, and the likelihood of influence over post-Saddam Iraq; and the presumed expertise of the exiles lent support or even authenticity to the claims made by that group of government policy makers.

The events of September 11, 2001, changed the foreign policy–making context in ways that favored the advocates of military action against Iraq. President Bush's address the night of 9/11 made it clear that the response to that attack would include any countries that harbored terrorists; and, according to Richard Clarke (2004, 32), the president instructed Clarke and a few others to look for any possible links of the attackers to Saddam Hussein.

As it played out, of course, the first US response to the events of September 11 would be the invasion of Afghanistan. But some Bush administration officials were focused on preparing the nation for war with Iraq. Working in their favor was the general lack of information about Hussein and Iraq beyond the country's invasion of Kuwait, which had led to the first Gulf War. Iraq was not exactly a blank slate, but the relative lack of access to the country by media, academics, and even UN observers after 1998 provided an opening for Iraqi exiles and their allies in the government to paint a picture of Hussein and the country that warranted an attack by the US military. The Iraqi National Congress Support Foundation (INCSF) was set up as a tax-exempt corporation in 1999 as a way for the State Department to fund activities that included collection and dissemination of information about the activities of the Hussein regime. Discussions between State and the INC produced an agreement as to where the exile organization could operate and maintain offices for its Information Collection Program (ICP). An October 2001 report to the Department of State from the exiles about the ICP activities to that point stated that the organization was "collect[ing] sensitive information that reveal[s] Iraq's link with September 11th aftermath and anthrax exposures in USA" and that it was "contacting defected Iraqi officers and [had] held a meeting with them for coordination" (Select Committee on Intelligence 2006, 27–28). A Senate Select Committee on Intelligence Report from a few years after the invasion noted that the goals of the ICP had been to contact Iraqi dissidents, collect information from them, and then circulate that information as widely as possible. According to interviews the committee did with INC officials, including Chalabi, "The ICP used a 'publicity campaign' to bring sources to the attention of 'anyone who would listen,' which included the media, Congress, members of the Intelligence Community and other government agencies, think-tanks, and other interested parties" (Select Committee on Intelligence 2006, 37). Some in the State Department were uncomfortable with the connection to the ICP; and by the summer of 2002, the program was moved over to Defense.

At the same time that the INC was helping to disseminate information collected from dissidents, several officials from the civilian side of the Pentagon were trying to shape public opinion on Iraq. Douglas Feith argues that many war critics (he names Seymour Hersh in particular) overstated and confused the activities of these advocates of invasion within the Defense Department, referring to the "mythology" around the Office of Special Plans (2008, 117, 293–94). But clearly Vice President Cheney, Paul Wolfowitz, Douglas Feith, and others were not satisfied with the intelligence on Iraq or the analysis of that intelligence by some in the State Department and the CIA. In response, they sought to develop other sources of information, including that which could be supplied by Iraqi "externals."

No one can doubt the important role played by these individuals within the Bush administration in promoting the invasion of Iraq, but it is also important to see the ways that their work was supplemented by US government-funded activities of allies in the Iraqi diaspora. When talking about issues such as the existence of weapons programs and links to terrorist organizations, US government officials start off with a clear advantage over journalists who do not have direct access to the raw intelligence gathered by national and foreign agencies, much less the ability to take their own satellite photos. In the case of a relatively closed country such as Iraq, where few members of the media had much experience or their own sources in the country, journalists depended even more on US government sources for information. Alternatively, they could talk to Iraqi exiles, particularly those who had been in the country recently or were at least in regular contact with those still in Iraq. The potential problem, of course, with relying on dissidents or exiles is that their analysis of the situation in the country they left may be affected by the nature of their departure. If we assume that those who flee a country are among the most aggrieved, we have a selection bias at the very least. And the problem becomes even greater if a dissident exile perceives a potential benefit from embellishing the harshness of life left behind or the threat posed by the oppressive government to others.

Beginning soon after September 11, 2001, the INC accelerated its efforts to get information about the threat posed by the Hussein government into the public arena. In a memo sent to Congress to explain its work, the INC claimed some of the credit for more than one hundred articles published between October 2001 and May 2002 in publications such as the *New York Times*, the *Washington Post*, *Vanity Fair*, and the *Times* of London (Landay and Wells 2004). An early example of INC success appeared under Jim Hoagland's byline in the *Washington Post*. He credits the INC for providing a photograph to Washington of Abdul Rahman Yasin, wanted for his role in the 1993 World Trade Center bombing, living in Baghdad. Hoagland goes on to write of two defectors who provided him with information about how training had been given for airliner hijacking in the Salman Pak area of Baghdad. The article concludes with "The mounting evidence of Iraqi involvement in the brand of terror practiced by al Qaeda can no longer be swept under the rug or minimized. Abdul Rahman Yasin's presence in Baghdad makes Iraq part and parcel of this war on killers and their protectors" (Hoagland 2001). In the media echo chamber, the defectors' story bounced to the *New York Times*, the *Wall St. Journal*, and other mainstream media outlets. A couple of days later the public television program *Frontline* conducted an interview with one of the defectors supplied by the INC to Hoagland, and he claimed that the events of 9/11 were "conducted by people who were trained by Saddam" (Khodada 2001). A week later the executive director of PNAC, in an article advocating the invasion of Iraq, wrote: "There are Iraqi defectors who claim to have seen radical Muslims at a special terrorist training site in Iraq where trainees learn, among other things, to hijack airplanes. None of this should be a surprise. Iraq can offer bin Laden money and technical expertise, and in exchange al Qaeda can provide the manpower to strike at the United States without exposing Baghdad's hand" (Schmitt 2001). The US population was predisposed to believe that there had been Iraqi involvement—a September 13, 2001, Pew survey found that 78 percent of respondents suspected involvement by the Hussein government. Nearly two years later 69 percent of Americans still thought it was likely that Hussein was involved in the World Trade Center and Pentagon plane attacks. Clearly, this belief cannot be entirely attributed to the stories told by Iraqi defectors. But defectors' quick reinforcement of an immediate popular assumption helps explain how the nonexistent Hussein link held up for so long. Vice President Cheney's insistence that Mohammed Atta had met with an Iraqi agent in Prague, as well as President Bush's practice of mentioning Iraq and al-Qaeda in close proximity, were clearly also important.

In promoting the idea that Saddam Hussein posed a security threat to the United States, Iraq's possession of weapons of mass destruction played a prominent role. Here again, the role of the INC and defectors was central to the invasion advocates' attempts to shape public opinion. During a *Frontline* interview several months after the invasion of Iraq, Chalabi explained how the organization was able to maximize the impact of dissident "expertise." In the case of Adnan Ihsan al-Haieri, a defector whose claims have since been shown to be false, Chalabi (2003) described the process: "He told us, we told Judy Miller, she interviewed him, then we give him to the US government." That process, of course, was susceptible to a number of problems. First, it was likely that the INC debriefing of an exile would include at the very least leading questions and some degree of coaching about what sort of information would serve their purposes. Second, the defector was supplied to a *New York Times* writer before any government intelligence had a chance to verify the source's credibility. Although journalists certainly have some experience at judging credibility of their sources, they do not generally have the information, skills, and background that one would expect in the Iraq division at the CIA. Regardless of what the government intelligence ultimately concluded about the veracity of the source, the defector's story was already in the "paper of record" and circulating throughout the media, serving the purposes of those who wanted the public to see Saddam Hussein as a threat to US security.

Miller has been heavily criticized since the March 2003 invasion for her personal role as a conduit between the INC and the US public. In an e-mail to the *Washington Post* that became public, she wrote: "I've been covering Chalabi for about 10 years, and have done most of the stories about him for our paper, including the long takeout we recently did on him. He has provided most of the front page exclusives on WMD to our paper" (Kurtz 2003). Miller also got information from Chalabi's allies in the government, such as Wolfowitz, Perle, and Feith. While the activities of the Office of Special Plans (OSP) remain contested, it seems that the group supplied favored journalists such as Miller with information as part of its policy promotion. As Franklin Foer (2004) suggested, that put the journalist in an "almost irresistible cycle"—as long as what she wrote continued to serve the party line, she got more stories and quotes from the war proponents around the OSP. Miller makes an easy target, given that her history suggests both excessive ambition and ideological sympathy with war proponents, but she was certainly not the only journalist to consider Chalabi and other Iraqi exiles as experts worth consulting and quoting at length. The important point here, however, is what this tells us about the role of exiles in the marketing of foreign policy. The selective leaking of information to the press by people in the government as a means to strengthen a position in a policy debate would not be new or surprising, but here we see a government-sponsored private organization attempting to influence the policy debate by obtaining its own "intelligence" and "leaking" it to the media before it got passed on to the government. Government officials could then use the media report itself—the product of a defector not yet debriefed by government intelligence officials—as "evidence" to support a particular policy preference.

Michael Massing (2004) has provided an example of how this process worked in the case of Iraq's interest in nuclear weapons. In an article in the Sunday *New York Times* of September 8, 2002, Judith Miller and Michael Gordon wrote: "Mr. Hussein's dogged insistence on pursuing his nuclear ambitions, along with what defectors described in interviews as Iraq's push to improve and expand Baghdad's chemical and biological arsenals, have brought

Iraq and the United States to the brink of war." Massing then notes that on that Sunday morning's talk shows, "Dick Cheney, Colin Powell, Donald Rumsfeld, and Condoleezza Rice all referred to the information in the *Times* story." In the case of Rice, he notes that her statement "We don't want the smoking gun to be a mushroom cloud" was taken directly from the newspaper article.

Not all of the defectors used by the Bush administration to make its case came through the same process. The story told by an Iraqi informant code-named "Curveball," who ended up in the hands of German intelligence, was a primary source for the US accusation about biological weapons in Iraq. As a former top CIA official wrote: "As a result of his [Curveball's] reporting . . . the estimate of October 2002 changed our earlier assessment that Saddam could have a mobile biological weapon to describe our 'high confidence' that he in fact had one" (Drumheller 2006, 78). Finally, his information ended up in Colin Powell's infamous preinvasion defense of the war before the United Nations. There was speculation that Curveball too had been coached by Chalabi—a relative of Curveball was said to be a Chalabi bodyguard—but no evidence of their being in contact has ever been found. But it is true that of the three sources who were supposed to have corroborated his story, two had ties to the INC. Curveball, whose actual name is Rafid Ahmed Alwan al-Janabi, openly admitted to a British newspaper in early 2011 that he had deliberately lied about weapons of mass destruction in Iraq in the hopes that it would lead to the "liberation" of Iraq (Pidd 2011). Chalabi had been a little more subtle in offering a similar comment to a reporter from the *Telegraph* several years before that: "We are heroes in error. . . . That tyrant is gone and the Americans are in Baghdad. What was said before is not important" (Fairweather and LaGuardia 2004).

Beyond the main arguments that Iraq posed security threats to the United States because of its weapons of mass destruction and links to terrorists, another justification for the invasion was that we would be welcomed as liberators by the Iraqi population, who would embrace the opportunity to live under democracy. There was absolutely no way for either the media or US public to know what sort of welcome US troops would receive in Iraq. Historians might think about the reception that the British occupiers got in the early twentieth century to try to predict what the United States would get in the twenty-first, and political scientists might ruminate on what academic work on democratization suggested for the Iraq case. But for the most part, the only academics whose work was referenced by the Bush administration were those whose homeland was Iraq or perhaps elsewhere in the Middle East. And even those choices were selective. Clearly, social scientists who had studied the region in which they had been born should have been among the sources consulted as the United States prepared for the invasion and occupation of Iraq. But the problem was that their presumed special expertise due to ethnicity and heritage seemed to effectively exclude nonexile voices from the debate. In a *Meet the Press* interview only days before the invasion, Vice President Dick Cheney (2003) explained that he had met with people

> like Kanan Makiya who's a professor from Brandeis, but an Iraqi. He's written great books about the subject, knows the country intimately, and is part of the democratic opposition and resistance. The read we get on the people of Iraq is there is no question but what they want to get rid of Saddam Hussein and they will welcome as liberators the United States when we come to do that.

Professor Makiya, speaking the next day at the National Press Club along with Richard Perle, repeated his oft-quoted promise to President Bush that the US forces would be "greeted with sweets and flowers" in Iraq (Perle and Makiya 2003). Makiya had written widely on Iraq, and he was welcome to take that position about the likely reception for the US troops in Iraq. But the MIT graduate had not spent significant time in Iraq for decades, and Cheney's assertion that this professor born in Iraq "knows the country intimately" suggests an attempt to claim credibility by birth rather than from the scholarship that Makiya produced while teaching in a US institution.

Makiya presents an interesting case, given that unlike Chalabi he never gave any indication of seeking power for himself in Iraq. His voice was that of an intellectual whose publications on Iraq over the years had been well received by many in academia. The former leftist professor did not participate in the advocacy of invasion based on Saddam Hussein's supposed weapons of mass destruction, or the claim that the Iraqi leader was linked to al-Qaeda. Rather, he argued that taking down an evil dictator and liberating oppressed Iraqis was an obligation of the United States and others in the West. As George Packer argues in his work on the war, "The Americans wanted the imprimatur of Iraq's leading intellectual on their war" (2005, 74). According to Douglas Feith, Makiya was particularly active behind the scenes, advising "many administration officials on constitutional and political considerations for post-Saddam Iraq—at State, the White House, and the Pentagon, including my Policy office" (2008, 375). Unlike Chalabi, who seems almost proud of his role in promoting information that turned out to be false, Makiya has spent considerable time trying to figure out what went wrong. Still, even though events have proved him wrong about how US troops would be received in Iraq, and he concedes that he is pained by the violence that took place in the aftermath, he refuses to repudiate his support for the US invasion (Filkins 2007). Makiya and Chalabi are the two individual exiles whose influence in selling the Iraq invasion to government officials and to the general public seem to be most significant; Makiya provided intellectual credibility, while Chalabi's INC "seemed to produce an inexhaustible supply of defectors with top-secret information about Saddam's efforts to rebuild his unconventional weapons programs and his terrorist training camps" (Packer 2005, 78). Policy makers in the vice president's office and the Department of Defense found that exile support very helpful.

Donald Rumsfeld has written since about the divisions that existed within the US government over the role Iraqi expatriates should play once the war began, and he professes to be unsure why State and the CIA resisted the efforts by the Defense Department. His position on the diaspora was that "these Iraqi 'externals,' many living in the United States or London, included some highly educated and skilled professionals. . . . While by no means monolithic in their politics or their views, they shared an interest in Iraq's freedom and success" (2011, 488–89). He goes on to blame State Department wariness for not including the externals more in the planning for the postwar period (490). Of course, given the easy transition promised by the external allies of the Bush administration, it is hard to blame State or anyone else in the government for not worrying more about the post-Hussein situation in Iraq.

The Iraqi diaspora overall was far from monolithic in its prewar view of US policy toward their homeland and what might happen after an invasion. Several weeks before the invasion, Kanan Makiya was attacked in the left-leaning *Nation* magazine, which quoted a reference to him on an independent Iraq information site as "the American paper tiger." The Iraqi-born author of the *Nation* article, Sinan Antoon, conceded that most Iraqis in the diaspora agreed with Makiya on the "necessity of ending the Saddam's tyranny" but pointed out that hundreds of prominent exiles from different ethnic and political backgrounds had signed a "No to war on Iraq . . . No to dictatorship" petition. That list was headed by London-based Saadi Yousif, "the greatest living Iraqi poet and a longtime dissident." The problem according to Antoon was that many of the signatories either wrote mostly for Arabic-speaking audiences or at least lacked access to mainstream US media. Written more than a month before the invasion, the article quoted multiple exiles who offered predictions of the Iraqi response to the US military's arrival in Iraq that diverged wildly from that of Makiya, who Antoon suggested had "become a Bush regime intellectual of sorts—even an empire intellectual" (2003, 6). The problem was that a single article in the *Nation*, whose circulation at the time was little more than 150,000 subscribers who largely opposed the war anyway, could not begin to counter the marketing campaign waged by the Bush administration and prowar Iraqi exiles. For the mainstream media, which had already framed the debate as one between those who wanted to get rid of Saddam Hussein and the appeasers, anti-Saddam exiles who opposed invasion would pose a dilemma. By and large, the mainstream media chose not to include in their reporting Iraqi externals who opposed the war.

The Return of the Diaspora

The role of expatriates after the military's mission was "accomplished" in Iraq continued to be controversial. The State Department and the CIA were said to be more worried than Defense about the likely conflicts between internals and externals, who would be seen as lacking legitimacy after their years of easy exile (Feith 2008, 252). But Wolfowitz, in the Defense Department, had speculated to the press that the exiled opposition would return to Baghdad and assume power, just as General Charles de Gaulle and the Free French had returned triumphantly to postwar France (Rubin 2003). Chalabi was flown into Nasiriyah and then escorted to Baghdad along with members of the Free Iraqi Forces by the US military in mid-April 2003. As Paul Wolfowitz argued, "It's an enormously valuable asset to have people who share our values, understand what we're about as a country, and are in most cases citizens of this country, but who also speak the language, share the culture and know their way around Iraq" (Jehl 2003). On the other hand, there was the potential for a backlash against those who had been comfortably living out of the country for so long. At the end of April 2003, one mainstream US journalist wrote that many in Iraq viewed Chalabi as "an opportunist who is living large, out of touch with Iraqis who stayed in Iraq and weathered fallen president Saddam Hussein's brutality for three decades." That same writer went on to quote Saad Jawad, a British-educated professor at Baghdad University who was identified as part of the internal opposition to Hussein, as saying that neither he nor any of the other anti-Ba'thist intellectuals he knew had been consulted or asked to participate in the post-Saddam governing process (Chandrasekan 2003).

In July 2003 Paul Bremer approved the formation of an Iraqi Governing Council that included such prominent members of the Iraqi diaspora as Chalabi, Allawi, and Abdul Aziz al-Hakim, the brother of the head of SCIRI. The dominant role played by exiles on the Governing Council may have made it an "easy target for the likes of Muqtada al-Sadr, who denounced it as an arm of the American occupation" (Diamond 2005, 43). Among the members of the Iraqi Governing Council were a number of exiles who had actually opposed the US invasion in 2003. Nearly all of the other divisions among the Iraqi diaspora that existed during the years of exile were present on the council as well. One of Bremer's first acts upon arrival in Iraq was the controversial de-Ba'thification order, and he appointed Chalabi to head the commission charged with implementation. That process would make it more difficult for at least some of the internals to potentially serve in the new Iraqi government. Externals continued to be highly visible in the US media as representatives of the new Iraq. When Hussein was captured, two of the four Iraqi Governing Council members who met the prisoner of war first were Chalabi and Adnan Pachachi. The same two exiles were given prime seating at President Bush's 2004 State of the Union address—Pachachi sitting next to Laura Bush and Chalabi just behind them. Pachachi's return to Iraq from the United Arab Emirates may have given him some advantages in his homeland over Chalabi. While Pachachi was a beneficiary of the US invasion, no one in Iraq saw him as a favorite of the Pentagon (Ajami 2006, 220–21).

Chalabi's star began to fade soon after his State of the Union appearance sitting just behind the first lady. By May Iraqi police had raided Chalabi's house; the monthly payments to the INC's information collection program were halted; and mainstream media articles were reporting that Chalabi's US government allies had severed their ties with the INC leader (Slavin 2004). His popularity among the Iraqi people was called into question as well. A survey done early in 2004 asked respondents which national leader they trusted the most, and Chalabi was the choice of 0.2 percent of all those surveyed; but when asked which leaders, if any, on a list of twenty-eight they did not trust at all, 10.2 percent of all respondents selected Chalabi. Coming in second was Saddam Hussein, who was not trusted at all by 3.3 percent

(Oxford Research 2004). But at the end of 2005, Chalabi was still getting audiences with old allies, including Cheney, Rumsfeld, and Rice during a visit to Washington. Ayad Allawi, who did serve as prime minister in 2004–5, may not have been as popular in those Washington circles as Chalabi; but he has fared somewhat better in Baghdad. Succeeding Allawi as prime minister was Ibrahim al-Jaafari, who worked with SCIRI in Iran and later was based in the United Kingdom; in exile, he played an important role in the larger anti-Hussein movement, but he opposed the US invasion in 2003. Nouri al-Maliki, who became prime minister after al-Jaafari, spent most of his more than two decades of exile in Syria and Iran.

Clearly, recent exiles or those who have maintained relationships with their home countries may be able to provide the sort of information that helps the US public, Congress, and members of the executive branch to make better decisions about foreign policy preferences. But if policy advocates promote selected exile voices as part of a campaign to sell their own position, there is a danger that the debate will become distorted rather than enriched. Those of us following congressional hearings and mainstream media coverage in the United States during the period leading up the invasion of Iraq might have easily been left with the impression that the Iraqi exile community was of a single mind in supporting the impending war. But that was certainly not the case, even in the United States. In the media of the United Kingdom, the country that provided the second-largest contingent of troops for the invasion, anti-war Iraqi exiles seemed a little more visible than in the United States. When Downing Street published a letter from an Iraqi exile group supporting Prime Minster Blair's position in February 2003, for example, the presence of exiles on the other side was clearly noted in the *Guardian* (Mahdi 2003; Steele 2003). While there is no way to know the exact numbers, significant blocs of the diaspora in the United Kingdom and throughout the Middle East did not support a US invasion to remove Hussein. That perspective was very difficult to find in the US media. That omission in the US media does not mean that the Iraqi diaspora in this country was of a single mind. It does suggest that the US media, caught up in the post-9/11 atmosphere, generally preferred to cite the perspectives of exiles who supported the war and offered assurances that the venture would not be a difficult one.

This chapter, like many of the analyses critical of the US invasion of Iraq, has focused considerable attention on the role of Ahmed Chalabi and the

INC within the larger Iraqi exile community in the United States. In the process, Iraqi American war supporters who may have been less well connected to Judith Miller at the *New York Times* or in as frequent contact with invasion advocates in the executive branch have received less attention than perhaps is warranted. Even if their audiences were local media or public broadcasting outlets, Iraqi Americans who could assure the general public in the United States that our troops would be well received by an Iraqi population oppressed by a tyrannical Saddam Hussein contributed to the war support. Other groups in opposition to Hussein were less visible or less appealing to US audiences than Chalabi and his close allies. Hamid al-Bayati, the London representative from 1992 to 2003 for the Supreme Council for the Islamic Revolution in Iraq (SCIRI), one of the most important opposition groups historically, recognized that his organization's lack of a Washington office diminished their influence in the United States. In a book that provides plenty of insights about the US government's selective use of the Iraqi exile community, al-Bayati noted that only the INC and the Kurds of the main opposition groups among the Iraqi diaspora "were present in Washington" (al-Bayati 2011, 141). Other members of the diaspora, such as Adnan Pachachi, whose position on Israel or apprehension about a US-led regime change in Iraq diverged from Washington, were marginalized until they were needed in the occupation phase. Even a number of those who had once been aligned to Chalabi and the INC efforts became disillusioned and gradually distanced themselves from both Chalabi and his neoconservative allies in Washington. Today they seem in many cases to be politically engaged largely in their homelands, rather than lobbying US officials. The reaction of Iraqis inside Iraq to the expatriates who have returned has been mixed, and this, combined with splits among the returning members of the diaspora, has limited their contribution. Similarly, the role of Iraqi Americans in US foreign policy decision making has diminished; on the one hand, Iraq is no longer the black box that it was during the Hussein era, and expatriates relying on friends and family members or their own decades-ago experience in the country no longer can claim more authentic or exclusive knowledge about the country. But also, those who predicted that Iraqis would welcome the US invasion and move easily toward democracy have had to reconsider their position. Some have retreated into academia, others have returned to Iraq, and a few have argued that the problem was not in their analyses but in the errors by the United States in the postinvasion period of occupation.

With the benefit of the several years since the occupation of Iraq began, the memoirs of Bush administration officials, self-criticism by some in the media, and congressional reports, there is plenty of evidence of mistakes made in the lead-up to and conduct of the war with Iraq. The argument here has been that in the marketing of this invasion and occupation, select members of the Iraqi diaspora allied with like-minded government officials were able to frame the debate about Iraq in ways that sidelined opposition voices, including alternative perspectives in the diaspora itself. Media that generally lacked significant background in the region and had almost no language skills for the most part uncritically accepted claims by Bush administration officials and their exile allies as they sold the US public on the need to invade Iraq. The most important organization of Iraqi externals working with the US government was the INC, which was initially formed with the support of executive branch officials. When the Clinton administration did not fully support the Iraqi American group, they turned their sights on Congress, where they were able to get both government funding and the passage of an act making the overthrow of Saddam Hussein the official US policy toward Iraq. Their final success came with a new president, whose administration included a number of officials with goals that converged with those of the INC. The ethnic group returned through an "open door" in the executive branch to work closely with members of the Bush administration to persuade the US population that the overthrow of Saddam Hussein was worth the financial and human costs associated with the March 2003 invasion.

What the analysis of the Iraqi diaspora case here suggests is that the convergence between a group of Iraqi exiles and their allies in the US government at the very least facilitated the US invasion of Iraq in 2003. Iraqi exiles gave credibility and perhaps even substance to advocates for invasion in the Bush administration, even if it is hard to imagine that Paul Wolfowitz or Dick Cheney changed his position on Saddam Hussein under the influence of Kanan Makiya, much less Ahmed Chalabi. But an alliance that included Makiya and Chalabi was certainly stronger than one made up of only Cheney, Wolfowitz, and Feith. That implies a quite different relationship between ethnic interest groups and the government than many have described. While some ethnic interest groups certainly still compete with elected officials to change public views toward foreign policy, the greatest impact that these groups may have is when their interests converge with those of at least some government officials. From that convergence they may subsequently be able to sell the public on policies up to and including, in the case of Iraq, a military invasion.

On the basis of developments in Iraq since the invasion, including suspicions on the part of internals toward externals who did not pay their dues during either the war years of the 1980s or the period of sanctions on Iraq in the next decade, there is good reason to be skeptical of future diasporic claims in support of an easy invasion and transition in any of their homelands. Nor should we assume that members of the diaspora will easily slide into leadership roles upon return to those countries. Cheney and many in the Pentagon were expecting power to be handed over rather rapidly and easily to Chalabi; the CIA favored Allawi, and State was rumored to be behind Pachachi (Diamond 2005, 28–29). In the end, though, Chalabi's effectiveness in Washington, D.C., did not mean that he would be as successful in Baghdad. Chalabi's former allies in the US government are mostly trying to sell their memoirs now, and the Obama administration has struggled to deal not just with postwar Iraq but with a number of its neighbors as well. While the experiences and perspectives of Iranian or Syrian exiles might be useful to foreign policy debates in the United States, the Iraq experience suggests that skepticism about claims made to support future foreign interventions by a like-minded alliance of government officials and exile experts from the target country would be justified.

Note

The first epigraph's quote from Robert Gates can be found in Shanker (2011). The second epigraph is from Roston (2008, xi).

References

Ajami, Fouad. 2006. *The Foreigner's Gift: The Americans, the Arabs, and the Iraqis in Iraq.* New York: Free Press.

Antoon, Sinan. 2003. "Dissident or Apologist." *Nation*, February 3. www.thenation.com/article/dissident-or-apologist#axzz2ePBnmxih.

al-Bayati, Hamid. 2011. *From Dictatorship to Democracy: An Insider's Account of the Iraqi Opposition to Saddam.* Philadelphia: University of Pennsylvania Press.

Brinkley, Joel. 2004. "Ex-C.I.A. Aides Say Iraq Leader Helped Agency in 90's Attacks." *New York Times*, June 9. www.nytimes.com/2004/06/09/

world/reach-war-new-premier-ex-cia-aides-say-iraq-leader-helped-agency-90–s-attacks.html.

CATO Institute. 2000. *CATO Daily Dispatch*, October 6. www.cato.org/dispatch/10-06-00d.html.

Chalabi, Ahmed. 2003. "Truth, War, and Consequences." *Frontline*, October 9. www.pbs.org/wgbh/pages/frontline/shows/truth/interviews/chalabi.html.

Chandrasekaran, Rijav. 2003. "Exile Finds Ties to US a Boon and a Barrier." *Washington Post*, April 27, A01.

Cheney, Dick. 2003. Interview by NBC News, *Meet the Press*, March 16. https://www.mtholyoke.edu/acad/intrel/bush/cheneymeetthepress.htm.

Clarke, Richard A. 2004. *Against All Enemies: Inside America's War on Terror.* New York: Free Press.

Diamond, Larry. 2005. *Squandered Victory: The American Occupation and the Bungled Effort to Bring Democracy to Iraq.* New York: Times Books.

Drumheller, Tyler. 2006. *On the Brink: An Insider's Account of How the White House Compromised American Intelligence.* New York: Carroll and Graf.

Fairweather, Jack, and Anton La Guardia. 2004. "Chalabi Stands by Faulty Intelligence That Toppled Saddam's Regime." *Telegraph* (London), February 19. www.telegraph.co.uk/news/worldnews/northamerica/usa/1454831/Chalabi-stands-by-faulty-intelligence-that-toppled-Saddams-regime.html.

Feith, Douglas J. 2008. *War and Decision: Inside the Pentagon at the Dawn of the War on Terrorism.* New York: Harper Collins.

Filkins, Dexter. 2007. "Regrets Only." *New York Times*, October 7. www.nytimes.com/2007/10/07/magazine/07MAKIYA-t.htm.

Foer, Franklin. 2004. "The Source of Trouble." *New York Magazine*, June 7. http://nymag.com/nymetro/news/media/features/9226/.

Hoagland, Jim. 2001. "What about Iraq." *Washington Post*, October 12, A33.

Jehl, Douglas. 2003. "Aftereffects: The Advisers; Iraqi Exiles, Backed by U.S., Return to Reinvent a Country." *New York Times*, May 4. www.nytimes.com/2003/05/04/world/aftereffects-the-advisers-iraqi-exiles-backed-by-us-return-to-reinvent-a-country.html.

Khodada, Sabah. 2001. "Gunning for Saddam." *Frontline*, November 6. www.pbs.org/wgbh/pages/frontline/shows/gunning/interviews/.

Kurtz, Howard. 2003. "Intra-Times Battle over Iraqi Weapons." *Washington Post*, May 26, C01.

Landay, Jonathan, and Tish Wells. 2004. "Iraqi Exile Group Fed False Information to News Media." Knight Ridder, March 15. www.mcclatchydc. com/2004/03/15/10176/iraqi-exile-group-fed-false-information.html.

Leung, Rebecca. 2009. "Bush Sought 'Way' to Invade Iraq?" *CBS News*, February 11. www.cbsnews.com/stories/2004/01/09/60minutes/main592330. shtml.

Mahdi, Kamil. 2003. "Iraqis Will Not Be Pawns in Bush and Blair's War Game: An American Attack on My Country Would Bring Disaster, Not Liberation." *Guardian*, February 20. www.guardian.com.uk/politics/2003/feb/20/foreignpolicy.iraq1.

Makiya, Kanan. 1998. *Republic of Fear: The Politics of Modern Iraq*. Berkeley: University of California Press.

Marr, Phebe. 2004. *The Modern History of Iraq*. 2nd ed. Boulder, CO: Westview Press.

Massing, Michael. 2004. "Now They Tell Us." *New York Review of Books*, February 26.

Mearsheimer, John J., and Stephen M. Walt. 2007. *The Israel Lobby and U.S. Foreign Policy*. New York: Farrar, Straus and Giroux.

Miller, Laura. 2004. "Our Man in Iraq: The Rise and Fall of Ahmed Chalabi." *PR Watch*, 11 (2). www.sourcewatch.org/index. php?title=The_Rise_and_Fall_of_Ahmed_Chalabi.

Oxford Research International Poll. 2004. "National Survey of Iraq." February. http://news.bbc.co.uk/nol/shared/bsp/hi/pdfs/15_03_04_iraqsurvey. pdf.

Packer, George. 2005. *The Assassins' Gate: America in Iraq*. New York: Farrar, Straus and Giroux.

Perle, Richard, and Kanan Makiya. 2003. Iraq Seminar, National Press Club, Washington, DC, March 17. Transcript no longer available.

Pidd, Helen. 2011. "Curveball Deserves Permanent Exile for WMD Lies, Say Iraq Politicians." *Guardian* (London), February 16. www.guardian. com.uk/world/2011/feb/16/curveball-exile-wmd-lies-iraq-politicians.

Project for the New American Century. 1997. "Statement of Principles." www.newamericancentury.org/statementofprinciples.htm.

Roston, Aram. 2008. *The Man Who Pushed America to War: The Extraordinary Life, Adventures, and Obsessions of Ahmad Chalabi*. New York: Nation Books.

Rubin, Trudy. 2003. "Bush Never Made Serious Postwar Plans: Litany of Problems in Iraq Is the Result." *Philadelphia Inquirer*, June 26. http://articles.philly.com/2003-06-26/news/25448395_1_jay-garner-postwar-plans-iraq-war.

Rumsfeld, Donald. 2011. *Known and Unknown: A Memoir.* New York: Sentinel.

Schmitt, Gary. 2001. "Why Iraq?" *Weekly Standard*, October 29, 13.

Select Committee on Intelligence. 2006. "The Use by the Intelligence Community of Information Provided by the Iraqi National Congress." S. Rep. September 8. 109th Cong., 2nd sess. www.intelligence.senate.gov/phaseiiinc.pdf.

Shanker, Thomas. 2011. "Gates Ratchets Up His Campaign of Candor." *New York Times*, March 4. www.nytimes.com/2011/03/05/world/05gates.html?partner=rss&emc=rss.

Slavin, Barbara. 2004. "Former Exile's U.S. Supporters Seem to Have Cut Him Loose." *USA Today*, May 21. www.usatoday.com/news/world/iraq/2004-05-20-chalabi-analysis_x.htm?loc=interstitialskip.

Steele, Jonathan. 2003. "Independent Iraqis Oppose Bush's War." *Guardian*, March 5. www.guardian.co.uk/politics/2003/mar/05/iraq.world.

Sununu, John. 2006. "Being Part of the Solution." In *American Arabs and Political Participation*, edited by Philippa Strum. Washington, DC: Woodrow Wilson International Center for Scholars.

White House. 1989. "U.S. Policy toward the Persian Gulf." National Security Directive No. 26. October 2. www.fas.org/irp/offdocs/nsd/nsd26.pdf.

Woodward, Bob. 1986. "CIA Aiding Iraq in Gulf War: Target Data from U.S. Satellites Supplied for Nearly 2 Years." *Washington Post*, December 15, A1.

Historical Perspective

Convergence and Divergence Yesterday and Today in Diaspora–National Government Relations

Tony Smith

The editors of this volume have called on its contributors to focus on a difficult but critical topic: the convergence and divergence of American governmental foreign policy goals and those of diasporas (or ethnic groups) in the United States regarding US foreign policy toward their ancestral homelands. Where government and civil society constituencies *converge,* each actor presumably multiplies the force of the other (the example of President Ronald Reagan might be cited, working with Polish Americans and the Vatican to free Poland from communist rule, or the Reagan administration's role in creating the Cuban American National Foundation [CANF], since then the chief lobbying organization of the Cuban community). But when the diasporic community and the government *diverge* with respect to policy objectives (as when President Reagan wanted to sell advanced AWACS aircraft to Saudi Arabia over Israeli and Israel lobby objections), more difficult analytical questions arise: Who influences whom, how, and with what results?

Framing the problem in terms of the correspondence between governmental and ethnic objectives is in general a more promising line of investigation than asking about the relation between diasporic efforts and "the national interest." The character of the national interest is usually inherently so debatable that whether civic actors serve the common good is often impossible to determine. Focusing instead on the question of ethnic group activism in relation to government goals allows us to analyze concrete policy outcomes and thus is more manageable and may offer more fruitful insights. Such an approach underscores the importance of social forces in state policy formation, for it requires that we study diasporic political mobilization, the process of governmental policy making, and the intersection of the two in a way that sheds light on the domestic sources of US involvement in world affairs—a difficult undertaking but one that is portable to a wide range of questions, many of them beyond the intersection of ethnic and governmental interaction and involving especially economic actors.

But there are problems with this approach as well. Framing the question as if it were the study of the intersection between two autonomous actors encourages us to think that government policy or social ambitions exist independently of each other's reciprocal influence, which is seldom the case when important decisions are involved in a democracy. Like other special interest groups (particularly those that are economic), diasporic constituencies are active in the selection of national political leaders (usually beginning when possible with the primaries), and through their multiple means of access to decision makers they are also involved in agenda setting once elected officials take office, thereby influencing governmental objectives long before they are publicly declared (the influence of the Congressional Black Caucus and TransAfrica on President Bill Clinton's policy toward Haiti is an example). More, it is a two-way street. The government may also shape the character of diasporic organizations (President Woodrow Wilson organized Polish and Czechoslovak Americans for war with Germany in 1917, for example, as for a time the administration of President George W. Bush supported the Iraqi National Congress of Ahmad Chalabi). As a result of what are often protracted negotiations between civil actors and government officials, clear-cut public cases of sharp divergences are relatively rare. One divergence that is of special importance, however, pits the opposition of an unbroken succession of American presidents of both parties since 1967 to Jewish settlements in the occupied Arab territories, an Israeli policy consistently backed by most, but not all, of the major organizations of the Israel lobby in this country. More usually, however, divergence is publicly muted and some form of mutual accommodation is reached, what might be labeled "negotiated convergence," although as we shall see what most stands out is the vigor of civil action groups in American democracy, which in the cases covered here after the end of the Cold War means that an ethnic community more often than not finds its essential demands are met by policy set in Washington. Whatever the case, divergence and convergence on policy preferences are seldom as clear-cut as these two words suggest they might be; notions of "negotiated convergence" or "negotiated divergence" often better convey the intricacy of political intercourse.

Divergence and Convergence Historically Considered

Reviewing the historical record can help orient us toward contemporary issues in terms of the complicated interaction between government and actors in civil society. Let us start with a case in which divergence and convergence are somewhat difficult to identify: Irish American use of armed force in 1866, and again in 1870, under the auspices of the Fenian Brotherhood, to invade Canada so as to bring pressure on Britain to emancipate Ireland. Given that the horror of the potato famine that had devastated Ireland beginning in 1847 was fresh in the minds of the some 150,000 Irish Americans who during the Civil War were mustered into the Union and Confederate armies (often in Irish-only regiments), in addition to perhaps 50,000 Irish who came to the United States to fight in response to invitations from both northern and southern commanders, the Fenian initiative (counting on thousands of trained and hardened men) just after this epic struggle had to be taken seriously in Washington. Britain was the world's greatest power, its ability to threaten East Coast cities with its navy remained as real in 1866 as it had proved to be in 1812, and it was by far America's most important trading and investment partner. Yet there was a wide populist base to Anglophobia (American Anglophilia based on feelings of ethnic or racial kinship has always been an exaggerated concept), and in the North simmering resentment remained over London's failure to support the Union during the Civil War (linked to a range of issues, from British anger at the blockade of southern ports that prevented the export of cotton, to the hope of limiting the growth of American power by finding counterweights to Washington in areas such as Texas). Ultimately, Washington opposed the Fenian raids but treated their perpetrators rather well, confiscating such weapons as they could but sending Fenians away from the Canadian border at public expense and later returning seized weapons upon a pledge that their owners would no longer engage in such wildcat actions (Kelly 2006; Walker 1969).

Stage 1: 1900–1941
Only in the twentieth century did the play of diasporic communities in the United States become a truly pressing issue in American foreign policy.

Between 1900 and 1914 some 13.4 million persons immigrated to the United States in the greatest wave of newcomers relative to the established population in the country's history. As Europe moved toward war after 1912, ethnic constituencies rather naturally divided, some favoring American involvement in Europe's struggles, others (which were much better organized) calling for a policy of neutrality. Americans of German, Scandinavian, and Irish ancestry tended to favor American neutrality in the war—and isolationism thereafter. Americans of British, Russian, Polish, Yugoslav, and Czechoslovak descent tended to favor American participation in the war on the side of the Allies and were supportive of efforts to join the League of Nations thereafter. Even before the United States entered the war in the spring of 1917, forty thousand Greek Americans fought in the Balkan Wars that had broken out before 1914, and some thirty thousand Polish Americans fought under French command (Smith 2000, ch. 2).

The strains of "hyphenation" were therefore acute, first as the country moved toward war, then as it tried to organize the peace that followed. German Americans tended to oppose war with Germany, but they called for neutrality in preference to outright alignment with Berlin. Most Irish Americans opposed an alliance with Britain, citing its brutal control of Ireland. Initially, Jewish and Scandinavian Americans opposed alliance with Russia, the former with memories of pogroms, the latter remembering Czarist expansionism. By contrast, President Woodrow Wilson's decision to call for war made him an honorary founding father of the Polish, Czechoslovak, Yugoslav, and Albanian republics that emerged from the conflict, and he was saluted for his eventual support for a Jewish homeland in Palestine and his consideration of an American mandate for Armenia, which did not materialize. Divergence as well as convergence among diasporic communities and between these and Washington thus marked America's march toward war (Luebke 1974; DeConde 1992).

Demographic statistics make Wilson's dilemma clear. Of a total US population of 92 million in 1910, 13.5 million were foreign born, of whom some 12 million came from belligerent or strongly partisan countries in the Great War—including 1.2 million Americans born in Great Britain, 1.4 million in Ireland, 1.3 million in Scandinavia, 2.3 million in Germany, 1 million in Poland, 1.3 million in the Austro-Hungarian Empire (perhaps half of whom were of subject Czech, Slovak, Romanian, and Yugoslav stock), 1.4 million in Russia (including some 200,000 Balts), and 1.3 million in Italy. Nor was this all. Approximately 17 million Americans had been born here of at least one foreign-born parent from a country involved in the war or with decided sympathies in the struggle. To make matters more acute, these immigrants had not dispersed uniformly across America but were concentrated in specific geographic regions, increasing the likelihood of strong ethnic identification and giving them more electoral clout. Thus, of the 24.5 million whites in the Northeast in 1910, 6.6 million were foreign born (26 percent); of 29.3 million in the North Central states, 4.7 million were foreign born (16 percent) (US Bureau of the Census 1975, 116-17; Small 1996; DeConde 1971).

Walter Lippmann believed that Wilson's proposals for multilateral institutions after the war reflected in part America's need to satisfy all its diasporic communities with the peace in Europe. Because an alliance system based on a traditional balance of power would favor some Americans' countries of ancestry over others, the domestic sources of US foreign policy preconditioned American leaders to think in terms of organizing European politics in a way that would ease the tensions of governing a multiethnic America (Small 1996, 43). Given the repeated efforts of foreign governments to influence Washington through their kinfolk here, Wilson expressed his concern in 1914 that "we definitely have to be neutral since otherwise our mixed populations would wage war on each other" (quoted in Small 1996, 43).

Acting on these same premises, the German government not only made promises to Mexico City to restore territory that country had lost to the United States in 1848 should Mexico back Germany in the war but appealed as well to German American communities to act on its behalf. The British were well aware of these forces and also concerned that American Jews (whose strength London overestimated) were, like the Irish, opposed to working with Great Britain. In issuing the Balfour Declaration late in 1917, with its promise of a Jewish homeland in Palestine, London had its eyes at least in part on Jewish American sympathies, as well as on the presumed thinking of Jews in Russia who had participated in the Bolshevik Revolution that year and who were talking about pulling out of the war against Germany.

During the interwar period, ethnic tensions continued. German Americans moved toward the Republican Party. Irish Americans opposed the League of Nations (so President Wilson repeatedly declared that "hyphens are the knives that are being struck into" the peace treaty) (quoted in DeConde 1992, 82ff.). Somewhat later, Italian Americans, many of them proud of Mussolini, who had come to power in 1922, contributed to the isolationism of the

1930s (DeConde 1971). By the 1940 election, Republican isolationists looked forward to picking up votes from Italian and German Americans while Democrats could look to East European and Baltic American preferences for their party so far as world affairs mattered.

As Lippmann observed in 1937, although the United States needed to become intimately involved in European affairs, the dilemma was that Americans could not "fuse as a nation if they are not secure against the divisive passions of their European ancestors. . . . Our dealings with the European nations instantly raise issues which divide us at home" (quoted in Tucker, Keely, and Wrigley 1990, 8). One must be careful not to exaggerate the power of these sentiments. Yet their existence bedeviled American involvement in European affairs from the 1910s through the 1930s to an extent that still today too often passes unnoticed (Tucker, Keely, and Wrigley 1990, 8).

Stage 2: 1941–89

We might call the period from 1900 to 1941 a first stage in the involvement of American diasporas in world affairs, a period typified by conflict among these groups and divergence between the demands of important ethnic actors and the government. Convergence came to typify a second, contrasting stage: that of the Cold War. For after 1945, the divisive impact of European affairs on American domestic politics changed completely, from divergence and stalemate to convergence and action. Not simply the national unity created by World War II, but even more importantly the struggle with the Soviet Union that broke out thereafter served to blur distinctions between ethnic and national identity and to fuse European Americans in a common national identity. American encouragement of European integration, which began with the Marshall Plan in 1947 and continued with the creation of the North Atlantic Treaty Organization (NATO) in 1949, meant that internationalism, not neutrality or isolationism, became the hallmark of this new stage of ethnic involvement in world affairs, providing a firm domestic underpinning to US steadfastness in containing Soviet communism.

Of course, not all problems were settled by this sea change. During the war Ireland had remained neutral, despite the efforts of a group of prominent Irish Americans who visited the island to persuade Dublin to change its policy now that it was an independent country. Nor was the problem of Northern Ireland successfully settled, so Anglo-American differences remained on this score, not to be ameliorated by cooperation against the Soviet Union.

Moreover, just how to be internationalist could be a matter of bitter partisan debate. The Republican charge that President Franklin Roosevelt had "given away" or "sold out" Eastern Europe to the Soviets at Tehran and Yalta succeeded in moving large numbers of these diasporic communities, which previously had voted solidly for the Democrats, the party of their hero Woodrow Wilson, to vote for the Republicans, who promised to "roll back" Soviet control of their ancestral homelands. In the 1950s, President Eisenhower faced serious objections from the right wing of his party when he would not confront the Soviets more aggressively over their control of Eastern Europe, particularly with his refusal to support the Hungarian uprising of 1956. In 1959, the Congress passed a "captive nations resolution," although in due course it went unobserved until resurrected in 1982 by President Reagan, to the satisfaction of those East European Americans who had never stopped pushing for the liberation of their former homelands from communist rule (Gerson 1964).

Whatever the burden of these tensions, they were substantially outweighed by the benefits that flowed to Washington from diasporic involvement in world affairs. For example, the Truman administration, aided by the Catholic Church, encouraged tens of thousands of letters from Italian Americans to their relatives in Italy warning of the danger of communism and urging a vote for the Christian Democrats. Again, in the Truman Doctrine of 1947, many Greek Americans could see a defense of Greek independence free of communism, which most wholeheartedly supported. For their part, many Jewish Americans saw Truman as a hero for going against the advice of several of his closest advisers and recognizing the new state of Israel in 1948. All three of these constituencies voted for Truman in 1948 partly because of these issues. By contrast, the Republicans were slow to address diasporic constituencies. For example, although the Republicans, in an effort to pander to the Italian vote, said they would work for the return of Italy's African colonies to that country, they failed to appreciate both that African Americans would take offense at this pledge and that Italy itself was not interested in such an offer. It was during the Reagan years, with the appeal of that president to the Cuban and East European American communities, that the Republicans most self-consciously exploited the opportunity to work for a convergence of government policy with the ambitions of diasporic groups.

The role of Polish Americans in the eventual breakup of the Soviet empire in Eastern Europe deserves special attention. At an early date, this community became involved in helping Washington in a difficult and delicate process of engaging the Polish government. The essential strategy was one of rewarding Warsaw when it was independent of Moscow but withholding approval if the communist government or Moscow moved to diminish whatever margin of freedom the Poles enjoyed. At the same time, the strategy dictated covertly helping those sectors of Polish society—the Catholic Church, and later Solidarity—that were slowly creating a new social contract and basis for state power in Poland (Kovrig 1991; Neier 2003).

During the Cold War, American liberals typically lamented the visceral anticommunism of the East European diaspora as an impediment to better relations with Moscow. And not only liberals: the efforts of national security adviser (later secretary of state) Henry Kissinger to establish détente with the Soviet Union in the early 1970s by finally accepting the division of Europe decided at Yalta go a good way to explain why he had so little influence over Reagan's wing of the Republican Party after 1981. In the event, it was the Reagan years that saw the closest convergence of Washington's ambitions and those of politically active East European Americans.

A major legacy of World War II for international affairs was the revelation of the Holocaust. The result was widespread sympathy in the United States for the creation of Israel in 1948 and a new commitment to Zionism on the part of the American Jewish community. Prior to 1939, Zionism had been opposed by segments of this community in favor of stressing integration into American life. But the lessons of the war, the birth of Israel, and the challenges the new country faced from hostile neighbors underscored the need for active involvement on behalf of the Jewish state.

Like other diasporas in relation to their ancestral homelands, American Jews found that the Cold War permitted them to be at once both patriotic Americans and outspoken proponents of aid to Israel. During its early years, Israel's leaders were unsure how to react to the increasing tension between Moscow and Washington. Many Israelis were socialists, millions of Jews still lived in the Soviet Union, and neutrality in any case seemed prudent. But by 1951 Israel had decided to seek its security by aligning with the United States. For the American Jewish community, then, to defend Israel was not just to work against Arab efforts to undermine the Jewish state but to counter Soviet efforts as well, a conviction that increased after the 1967 War, when American Jewry could see that a dimension of the conflict had been the superiority of American over Soviet arms (and thus influence) just as they were becoming more concerned about the oppression of Jews within the Soviet Union itself (Bialer 1990; Halperin 1961; Novick 1999).

Still, divergence as well as convergence existed between the Jewish diaspora and Washington. In 1974, Senator Henry Jackson and Representative Charles Vanik managed to get Congress to deny the Soviet Union's most-favored-nation trade status so long as it restricted the emigration of Jews and certain other categories of Soviet dissidents. Kissinger complained mightily that this kind of public censure only complicated a Jewish exodus from Soviet control and wrecked the spirit of détente he had labored so mightily to engender. But to no avail. Again in 1977, President Jimmy Carter could complain that Jewish Americans acting in league with Israel had derailed US-Soviet efforts to establish a joint framework for a Middle East settlement between Israel and the Arabs, with Israel claiming that this would be an "imposed solution" of the sort it had always opposed. Again, the Israel lobby was successful. By contrast, in 1981 when President Reagan wanted to sell early warning AWACS aircraft to Saudi Arabia, he succeeded despite opposition from both the lobby and Israel.

An unanswerable question is the extent to which the confluence of ethnic group commitment to the Cold War fueled Washington's determination to stay the course, driving the competition to a successful conclusion that made impossible a global condominium with Moscow of the sort that Kissinger sought through détente. Surely many factors other than ethnic considerations were involved in prolonging the superpower contest, including the basic dissimilarities between Soviet and American economic, social, and political systems; the stakes in world affairs ranging from the nuclear balance to regional conflicts (Poland and Afghanistan, for example); and a Soviet unwillingness to try to make détente workable in the 1970s. However, Moscow also had ethnic communities under domestic or imperial control whose resentments it surely feared. The influence of American diasporic groups—the Poles, Czechoslovaks, Balts, Hungarians, Jews, Greeks, Armenians, and Cubans—is underappreciated in the literature on this period. These communities put pressure on the American government to stand firm against Moscow, while they reached out to their kinfolk abroad to take part in the global struggle on the side of the United States, with consequences that need to be recognized.

The one significant diasporic constituency that stood outside this Cold War consensus was the black community, whose hopes for US foreign policy did not meld with geopolitical thinking in Washington as easily as did the concerns of groups of European descent. Here divergence, not convergence, is most to be noted. For many blacks, the problems of racism and white rule in Africa outweighed alarm about the dangers of communist and Soviet (or Cuban) expansion in that region. Similarly, it proved difficult to see the Vietnam War as only a struggle against communism as the disproportionate number of black combat casualties rose (Plummer 1996, 2003; Von Eschen 1997; Krenn 1998).

The Cold War was far from the first time the African American community felt concern about world affairs. In 1898, black Americans supported the United States in its war with Spain for the sake of emancipating blacks in Cuba. During World War I, Marcus Garvey and W. E. B. DuBois emerged as black anticolonial internationalists, although Wilson turned a deaf ear to their appeals despite his call for national self-determination. In 1935, black leaders deplored the Italian invasion of Ethiopia. In 1945, DuBois became president of the Pan-African Congress (headquartered in Manchester, England). DuBois's internationalism was such that Martin Luther King Jr. could claim in 1967 (in a salute to DuBois on the centennial of his birth) that the black diaspora could "readily see the parallel between American support of the corrupt and despised Thieu-Ky regime [in South Vietnam] and northern support to the southern slave-masters in 1876" (quoted in Von Eschen 1997, 189). True, many black leaders deplored King's attacks on President Lyndon Johnson's decision to expand the Vietnam War, for they feared the negative impact this stand might have on the domestic goals of the civil rights movement. But in short order, King's position found favor with most in the diaspora, giving us the clearest example of divergence of an ethnic group from Washington's official policy during the Cold War.

The United States was fortunate that the difference between white and black perspectives on the Cold War did not greatly disturb domestic politics. Part of the reason was the growing willingness of the American political system to accommodate black demands of the civil rights movement; part of it was that the Cold War never exploded in Africa with the force that it did in East and Southeast Asia and (to a lesser extent) in Latin America. By 1969 Charles Diggs had become head of the House Foreign Affairs Subcommittee on Africa, and two years later he created the Congressional Black Caucus (CBC). By 1972 divestment from South Africa began to be discussed in Congress, and in 1974 Democrats in the Ninety-Fourth Congress held repeated hearings on human rights violations in countries friendly to the United States, including those in Africa.

The willingness of mainstream black leaders to work through the system to influence foreign policy was rewarded with the inauguration of Jimmy Carter in 1977. For the first time, African Americans had direct access to the White House for foreign policy deliberations. Andrew Young became US ambassador to the United Nations, Randall Robinson founded TransAfrica, and Vice President Walter Mondale was in South Africa declaring that the United States looked forward to a regime there based on the principle of "one man, one vote" and communicating "the profound commitment that my nation has to human rights, to the elimination of discrimination, and to full political participation. . . . We believe that perpetuating an unjust system is the surest incentive to increased Soviet influence. . . . They know we will not defend such a system" (quoted in Smith 1994, 246).

The convergence that marked the Carter years in the relationship between the black diaspora and government objectives turned to divergence again during the Reagan presidency. African Americans felt that Washington was dragging its heels in opposing apartheid and called for economic sanctions on South Africa. And many opposed the American coup in 1983 against the communist government of Grenada. Still, by the end of the Cold War, blacks had become fully integrated into the political process, allowing a potential convergence of viewpoints that could be recognized in a new era.

Stage 3: Since 1989

If the period of 1900–1941 was a first significant stage of ethnic group involvement in international relations, one marked most noticeably by divergences both among diasporic groups and between some of these and government policy, and if the second stage, which lasted from 1941 to 1989, was marked most by convergence on both counts, what we might call the third stage emerged as the United States became the sole superpower in the 1990s, following the disintegration of first the Soviet empire and then the Soviet Union itself. At the same time, following a domestic trajectory, multiculturalism (which, though related to an earlier period of pluralism, existed in its own right with the civil rights movement of the 1960s) had come of age, making it legitimate morally to organize ethnically (as well as religiously and racially) on foreign policy agendas. The conjunction of world and domestic events— the intersection of a mature multiculturalism with America's unchallenged dominance of world affairs—thus spelled a significant change in the United

States politically. The first man to turn this conjunction to account was Bill Clinton, who in 1993 became the fortieth president of the United States.

Irish Americans were apparently the first to make Clinton aware of the potential power of ethnic concerns in his race for the presidency. During the 1992 Connecticut primary for the Democratic nomination, the explanation for why Jerry Brown edged Clinton out was that he appealed to the Catholic (especially Irish Catholic) electorate because of his time in a Catholic seminary. Clinton learned from his defeat, promising to initiate a peace process in Northern Ireland if elected. In doing so, he was heeding the advice given him by Irish American senators Daniel Patrick Moynihan and Edward Kennedy (O'Grady 1996).

Moynihan and Kennedy had been deeply involved in the problems of Northern Ireland for some two decades. In 1968 "the Troubles" began in Northern Ireland as police attacked a Catholic civil rights march; in 1969 British troops were called in; and by 1970 the Irish Republican Army had split and the Provisional IRA (PIRA) was using the threat of force to get Britain out of the six provinces of Ulster so as to reunify the island (Coogan 1996). PIRA efforts found backing in the United States from Noraid, the Irish Northern Aid Committee. Kennedy and Moynihan opposed violence but called for the withdrawal of British troops and the eventual unification of the island if approved by a popular vote. Moreover, they pointed out to Clinton that he should look for other opportunities to work for the return of so-called Reagan Democrats (largely blue-collar, white Catholics) to the Democratic Party from which they had first defected in 1980. The result of this convergence of interests was positive. Well before the signing of the Good Friday Peace Agreement of April 1998, there was general agreement— even among those British who at first had deplored Clinton's invitation to Sinn Fein leader Gerry Adams to visit the United States and Clinton's fol- low-up trip to Ireland in 1995—that the American role in the peace process, under George Mitchell's leadership, had been substantive and effective. And in the 1992 election, Clinton received more Catholic votes than his opponent George H. W. Bush, marking the return of this traditionally Democratic electorate to the party for the first time since 1976.

Working along the same lines, Clinton also promised during the cam- paign to expand NATO, a pledge that appealed to the East European Amer- ican electorate, which was also largely Catholic. It should thus come as no surprise that President Clinton delivered all his major addresses in 1996–97 on NATO enlargement in cities like Detroit, Chicago, and Milwaukee, where large ethno-religious communities would be attentive to the message and likely to rally in support. The independence of the Baltic peoples, Poland, Hungary, and Czechoslovakia had not ended the serious challenges to these lands, so the prospect of NATO's expansion, coupled with that of the European Union, promised to consolidate the gains made by the collapse of the Soviet Empire in 1989.

President Clinton also associated himself with the effort of Jewish Americans to bring an end to the Arab-Israeli conflict through the Oslo peace process. With the eclipse of Soviet power and the defeat of Iraq in the Gulf War in 1991, radical Arab rejectionists had been weakened to such a point that bold new initiatives could be contemplated, ideas that seemed to be coming to fruition in negotiations between Israeli prime minister Yitzak Rabin and Palestinian leader Yassir Arafat that culminated in their famous handshake on the White House lawn in the fall of 1993.

The end of the Cold War also facilitated efforts by the World Jewish Congress, in alliance with the US government and the state of New York, to pursue claims on behalf of victims of the Holocaust against the Swiss banking system. Tens of millions of dollars in accounts once belonging to European Jews had in effect been confiscated by Swiss banks when they went unclaimed after 1945. Prominent Jewish Americans like Stuart Eizenstadt (under President Kennedy first in the Treasury Department, then the State Department) assembled the evidence, which was brought to the Senate floor by the head of the Banking Committee, New York's Alfonse D'Amato, with the implied threat that Swiss banks in the United States might be closed if the matter were not satisfactorily addressed (a threat first exercised in October 1997 when the Union Bank of Switzerland was barred from participation in a New York state bond project because of its opposition to investigation) (Independent Committee of Eminent Persons 1999).

An equally impressive example of diasporic lobbying to use economic sanctions as a political weapon came when the Cuban American National Foundation persuaded Congress to pass, and Clinton to sign, the Helms-Burton bill in 1996, extending the jurisdiction of American courts over suits brought by American citizens (including naturalized Cubans) to honor property rights that the Castro government had nullified after 1959. The Cuban American sponsors of this bill worked closely with powerful Cold Warriors like Senate Foreign Relations chairman Jesse Helms, who were determined to complete the American triumph over the Soviet Union by destroying the Castro government. (The CANF was fortunate that Castro once again proved to be his own worst enemy by shooting down unarmed Cuban American planes dropping anti-Fidelista pamphlets over Cuba at the same time a Cuban human rights organization in Havana was holding its first meeting, which Castro shut down.)

This exercise of diasporic power faced formidable obstacles, for Helms-Burton occasioned a major row in US relations with its best trading partners, including not only all members of the European Union but Mexico and Canada as well. Like most liberal Americans, representatives of these governments felt that Castro could be "killed with kindness" if its isolation were ended. Clinton himself was likely of much the same mind. But the reality of the CANF's power was such that the president moved to conciliate it.

The end of the Cold War resulted in the birth of Armenia and the emergence of the Armenian American diaspora as a player in foreign policy. It is widely agreed that the high level of US aid to Armenia (second in per capita only to Israel) and the nearly decade-long embargo of official assistance to Azerbaijan (which sits alongside massive energy deposits in the Caspian Sea) would have been inconceivable were it not for this diaspora's influence and its determination that the Armenian population of Nagorno Karabakh, a province of Azerbaijan, be given home rule if not united with Armenia proper. By Section 907 of the Freedom Support Act of 1992, Armenian American lobbyists managed to exclude Azerbaijan from receiving aid intended to support newly independent former Soviet states, even though the Armenian government was authoritarian, was an aggressor state, and was friendly with Iran and Russia, whose influence Washington was trying to limit in this region. (A congressional waiver late in 2001 allowed the president to lift the ban on aid to Azerbaijan, as President George W. Bush then did.)

The success of the Armenian American lobby reflected as well the support of the Greek American lobby with its long-standing opposition to relatively high levels of military aid from the United States for Turkey. Ancient enmities between the Turks and the Greeks (today focused for the most part on Cyprus) combined with Armenian insistence that Ankara recognize the Armenian genocide of the era of World War I (during which the Turks killed some one million Armenians) seriously complicated American policy in this region. The appeals of these diasporic communities had to be weighed against the critical geostrategic position of Turkey, amplified by the discovery of vast oil and gas reserves in the Caspian Sea (making the area second only to the Persian Gulf in proven deposits), and what was then by Jerusalem's relatively close relationship with Ankara.

In 1998, the dilemmas of making government policy in this region were illustrated by a conflict that pitted then secretary of state Madeleine Albright, fourteen oil companies with interests in Caspian Sea energy (and so in Azerbaijan), an impressive collection of Jewish organizations, and a segment of the Republican leadership in the House against the Armenian lobby. Eventually a trade-off was reached that allowed the construction of an oil pipeline from Azerbaijan through Georgia and Turkey bypassing Armenia but that continued the cutoff of official aid to Azerbaijan and that increased aid to Armenia as well as to Nagorno Karabakh.

The ongoing struggle among interest groups in the United States was illustrated on November 8, 1998, when the American Jewish Committee, the American Jewish Congress, and the Anti-Defamation League published the following statement in the *New York Times:*

> Congratulations! Mazeltov! Tebrinkler! As Americans and Jews, we join in celebrating the 75th anniversary of the Turkish Republic. We especially applaud Turkey for: its democratic and secular values; its close and mutually beneficial ties with the United States; its invaluable strategic role as a NATO partner; its ever deepening relations with the State of Israel; its historic tradition dating back more than 500 years as a haven for Jews fleeing persecution. We join with the Turkish people in celebrating this milestone and we look forward to continued flourishing ties in the years ahead among Turkey, the United States, and Israel.

Within days, Greek American associations had made public their displeasure with this statement—not speaking as representatives of anything that might be construed as American national interests or congruent with official government policy but instead rehearsing the long list of Greek complaints about Turkey. Months later, as the United States bombed Serbia over its actions in Kosovo, Greek Americans again expressed their dissatisfaction with US foreign policy in the Balkans and with respect to Turkey, this time in terms that made the matter essentially religious: "President Clinton, why do you ignore the suffering of Orthodox Christians?" ran a full-page ad in the *New York Times* on May 2, 1999, recounting oppression against the Orthodox in Cyprus, Albania, Croatia, and Turkey before concluding: "Why is Washington more tolerant when the victims are Orthodox Christians? Why is American foreign policy slanted against Orthodox Christians wherever we turn?"

African American leaders were also active following the Cold War and especially during the years when Clinton, for whom the black electorate had voted massively in 1992 and 1996, was president. Perhaps Washington would have decided to occupy Haiti militarily in 1994 without the Congressional Black Caucus's and TransAfrica's insistence in the face of the human rights outrages of the military government of Raoul Cedras, who had deposed the duly elected president Jean-Baptiste Aristide. Concern over a tide of refugees from Haiti if Washington did not act combined with Cedras's repeated reneging on public commitments to Washington. But polls showed that 80 percent of the public opposed military intervention in this country, so the role of black leaders on policy must be seen as a fundamental reason Clinton decided to act (Singh 1998).

Subsequently, black Americans became leaders in defining administration policy toward sub-Saharan Africa. A particular ambition of TransAfrica was the restoration of democratic government in Nigeria as well as the promotion of human rights elsewhere on the continent. Jesse Jackson visited Kenya in 1997 to foster the consolidation of democratic process there. And the CBC and black entrepreneurs were influential in pushing for new initiatives for trade and investment in this region, which eventually passed the House in 1998 as the Africa Growth and Opportunity Bill.

This recital of events should not obscure the difficulties of black involvement in American foreign policy, problems that arose not so much from a lack of convergence between administration and diasporic goals as from divergences in the ranks of the latter. Thus Nigerian pressure eventually forced TransAfrica to back off its involvement in African affairs, just as disagreements between the CBC and TransAfrica ultimately stymied legislation for trade and aid to Africa. Still, the importance of promoting the participation of African Americans in the making of US foreign policy—and not only toward the Caribbean and Africa—can be understood if we juxtapose the mainstream leaders of this diaspora against Minister Louis Farrakhan's attacks on America's role in world affairs. In a trip through the Middle East and Africa in 1996, Farrakhan was reported to have called for the destruction of this country by agents of the Muslim world and to have accepted $1 billion from the Libyan leader Muammar Gaddafi for his political activities within the United States. Better by far the role played by Reverend Jackson in world affairs, most Americans would agree, than that played by Minister Farra-khan (Singh 1997; Sanford 1997).

If we consider immigration law an aspect of foreign policy (and I think we should), then convergence and divergence of Hispanic and East Asian Americans' goals for public policy with those of official Washington also call for attention. Here the appeals of foreign governments (particularly of Mexico) for relaxed immigration controls collided in 1994 with measures like Proposition 187, which sought to end the right of undocumented foreigners to have access to public facilities like schools and hospitals (the law was declared unconstitutional in 1997). Unlike Canada, which has relatively clear laws on immigration that are enforced, the United States still today lacks a coherent public policy on who can immigrate and under what terms. The growth of Hispanic populations, from California through Texas (and also in New York and Florida), combined with the concerns of this electorate with the politics of the countries from which they are descended (the Cubans in particular), means that these diasporic groups will be ever more involved in national poli-tics in the years to come (Yzaguirre 1995; Skerry 1993).

Something of the same may be said for Asian Americans in their many varieties. At present, the most contentious issues pit Indian and Pakistani Americans against one another for military and economic assistance in South Asia. But the rise of China along with the immigration of Chinese, Taiwan-ese, Vietnamese, Korean, Japanese, Thais, and Filipinos to the United States suggests that foreign policy concerns may eventually mobilize these diaspo-ras more actively into American political life, perhaps with seriously divisive consequences, both internally (among Asian Americans) and between these groups and official Washington (Paul and Paul 2009, chs. 4–5).

The model for all of these groups—whether Asian, European, Hispanic, or African—is the Israel lobby. The American Israel Public Affairs Com-mittee (AIPAC) has been cited by the *New York Times* as "the most impor-tant organization affecting America's relationship with Israel," and ranked by *Fortune* as the second most effective lobbying organization in Washington (after the AARP) and the most powerful in terms of American foreign policy (Rosenson, Oldmixon, and Wald 2009). After the Cold War, and especially after the assassination of Prime Minister Yitzak Rabin in November 1995, convergence gave place to increasing divergence concerning principally the expansion of Jewish settlements in the occupied Arab territories that some Israelis called Judea and Samaria. The American Jewish community was far from one mind on how Israel should negotiate with the Palestinians who lived on land Jerusalem controlled. Yet whatever the internal debates, the community generally found unity in seconding whatever the Israeli government ultimately decided. To be "pro-Israel," which was what most of the major organizations of the diaspora expected of American policy, in effect meant a blank check for Jerusalem. Only in recent years have a more assertive series of organized Jewish American pressure groups appeared—including Americans for Peace Now, the Israel Policy Forum, Tikkun, and J Street—to argue that it is in Israel's interest, as well as that of the United States, to bring pressure on Jerusalem to evacuate most (but not all) of its settlements beyond the 1967 borders and to recognize a sovereign Palestinian state based on the consent of the governed. The administration of President Barack Obama, with Hillary Clinton as secretary of state, at first appeared to be working with this growing force among American Jewry, but any such efforts immediately came up against the determination of the Israeli government of Prime Minister Benjamin Netanyahu to maintain a position that contradicted these ambitions. In the stand-off, the hard-line Israeli position carried the day.

The Rights and Responsibilities of Diasporic Communities in a Democratic Polity

The preceding pages have sought to give an overview of convergences and divergences in what diasporic communities want in American foreign policy and what official Washington aims to achieve. More often than not, the result can be called "negotiated convergence." That is, it is likely that if diasporic lobbying were absent government policy would often be different from what it ultimately becomes. But thanks to the structure of American politics—private financing of political campaigns from primaries to general elections, the weak structure of the party system, the way congressional committees allow public access to their proceedings—well-organized ethnic communities, like special interests in general, rather easily find voice in our democracy and are able to translate their influence in meaningful ways into policy (Smith 2000, ch. 3; Paul and Paul 2009, ch. 3).

At times, to be sure, convergence seems to happen almost of itself. As we have seen, during the Cold War the anticommunism of a wide spectrum of American ethnic sentiment coincided closely with mainstream thinking among both Republicans and Democrats in general (even if party appeals to these communities varied). A similar virtually spontaneous convergence might be seen after the Cold War among East European Americans on the policy of the Clinton administration in expanding NATO. By contrast, on occasion diasporic constituencies succeed in setting the major terms of the agenda (as with the Israel lobby), and at times the government organizes the ethnic constituency (as the Reagan team did the Cubans) only to gradually find that the strength of the diaspora has grown to be relatively independent of government influence. Or if not a negotiated consensus, then a "controlled incoherence" may emerge, as on immigration policy, where the strength of diasporic constituencies is such that a coherent policy of reform is unlikely to materialize.

In a word, no clear general pattern emerges. One may salute this state of affairs as showing the vigor of American democratic life, especially the right of civil society to influence the policies determined by government, or one may regret that special interests (including not only diasporas but also, indeed especially, a wide variety of economic groups that place maximizing of profit before the national interest) have the power that they do over public decision making, often to the detriment of the common good. Whatever one's judgment, it is rare that an outright divergence occurs between official policy and what a politically consolidated diasporic community insists is an essential demand to such a point that the government rides rough-shod over ethnic concerns.

None of this is surprising. Struggles among interest groups and between organized sectors of civil society and the government are intrinsic to democratic life. In certain respects, to be sure, demands on public policy made by diasporic constituencies are unique. Given the organization of these communities around what we today call "identity politics" and "the right to be different," and seeing that the considerations of these groups involves foreign peoples who quite clearly are not Americans, the emotional element of dealing with ethnic group influence on foreign policy made in Washington is particularly salient. Nevertheless, the problem of reconciling ethnically based preferences for America's role in world affairs with other considerations is inherent in the life of an immigrant country like the United States. As the eminent observer of American political life Robert Dahl observes,

> In a political system as large as a country, the plurality of relatively independent organizations is necessary . . . for the democratic process. . . . Yet a problem

arises—which I have called the dilemma of democratic pluralism—because while necessary, desirable, and inevitable in a democratic order, organizational pluralism may also play a part in stabilizing inequalities, deforming civic consciousness, distorting the public agenda, and alienating final control over the public agenda by the citizen body. . . . Organizations may use the opportunity to increase or perpetuate injustice rather than reduce it, to foster the narrow egotism of their members at the expense of concerns for a broader public good, and even to weaken or destroy democracy itself. (1982, 1).

Examples that could be cited from contemporary American policy include not only (and certainly not primarily) ethnic constituencies but also the numerous vested economic interests blocking basic reforms that clear majorities of the American public favor, including the pharmaceutical, insurance, agricultural, mining, military-related, and banking industries, among others, whose financial contributions often speak more loudly that the will of the voters.

Dahl's "democratic dilemma" is fated to endure. The lifeblood of democracy is the right of the citizenry to organize in defense of its interests, and perhaps in no democracy is this more apparent than the United States, where the government has historically been weak relative to organized civil actors, and where the system is maintained in place most basically by an entrenched two-party system that has weak party discipline internally, private financing for elections, and a congressional system wide open to penetration by popular forces. Before we take satisfaction in this being "the American way," we must recall Dahl's warning that the success of special interests may endanger the republic by exposing it to dangers abroad or undermining its strength at home.

Two essential questions thus arise that the study of diasporic relations with the government necessarily involves. First, when is the relationship synergistically positive both for the ethnic community and for Washington's policy to such an extent it can be said to serve the national interest, and when, by contrast, is government policy made so subservient to diasporic influence that one can reasonably argue that the national interest is in peril? Second, and in a related sense, what are the rights and the obligations of a diasporic constituency with respect to fellow citizens in a democracy and more especially to a reasonable construction of the common good? While the two questions are related, they are nonetheless distinct. The first asks us to evaluate in practical terms the impact of ethnic group activism on the quality of American foreign policy. The second investigates in theoretical terms the nature of responsible citizenship in the democratic process.

Neither question is open to easy, authoritative, or final judgment. Ethnic communities always are able to fashion arguments that make their goals for America in world affairs congruent with the national interest and thus to portray themselves as acting responsibly and not simply in a self-interested manner, even if their critics will argue the opposite. Given that the character of the country's place globally as well as the nature of democratic citizenship is at issue, sharp debates over divergence between ethnic group preferences and announced public policy are likely to remain with us so long as United States continues to hold its status as the world's sole superpower.

A better understanding of these complicated matters is not aided by what seems to me to be the moribund character of so much writing on domestic political matters, which is where the analysis of ethnic group influence on world affairs must start. Part of the problem is specialization, which means that interest groups are too often studied apart from parties, which in turn are studied apart from congressional and presidential actions. The result is a fragmented field, one in which the trees are appreciated much more than the forest in which they find themselves. Another part of the problem is the frequent insistence on quantitative methods, which, while often laudable in itself, can lead too frequently to questions of methodology trumping the analysis of substantive issues.

In these circumstances, debating a divergence between government policy and diasporic preferences, especially when arguments over the national interest can be invoked, rapidly becomes emotive, especially when questions of "dual" or "divided" allegiance give rise to charges of "racism" from a diaspora being criticized, and charges of being "un-American," or disloyal to the nation, from their critics. Yet the topic is critical because it is much more evident today, after the Cold War, when ethnic and national interests were largely convergent, that the lobbying of ethnic communities for policies that they believe favor their kinfolk abroad often badly needs to be debated in national politics. If American power is in decline after Iraq and the financial meltdown that began in earnest in the last quarter of 2008, then the country's room for maneuver in international relations is becoming more constrained, and there may be instances—such as concerns of domestic health, banking, agricultural, or energy interests—where diasporic communities may find their preferences questioned in the name of the greater national good. Can we find a way, then, to respect the right of ethnic constituencies to make their voices heard while at the same time insisting that the obligations of these groups to the greater nation to which they belong gives their fellow citizens the right to debate diasporic preferences and, on occasion, to reject them?

A case in point arose with the publication in September 2007 of Stephen Walt and John Mearsheimer's *The Israel Lobby and American Foreign Policy*. Although this lobby had always prided itself on its influence in Washington, its attitude changed dramatically when the sinews of power it possessed were clearly laid out by this study for all to see, and when responsibility was assigned to it for getting the American government to march in lockstep with Israeli foreign policy, to the detriment of American national security with respect not only to the 2003 invasion of Iraq but also to Syria, the Palestinians, and Iran. As a consequence, charges of "anti-Semitism" (usually implicit, sometimes explicit) against the authors rained down from virtually every public forum in the country. As it happened, the publication of this book coincided with attacks by part of the American Jewish community on others who questioned the moral correctness and practical efficacy of Washington's relationship with Jerusalem. Among the targets were George Soros (for criticizing AIPAC's adherence to an Israeli policy of Greater Israel), Jimmy Carter (for asking whether Israel's control over the Palestinians was similar to what apartheid had been in South Africa), Tony Judt (for suggesting that Israel might become a binational state), and Human Rights Watch (for reporting on human rights abuses by the Israeli military in the Palestinian territory and in Lebanon) (Walt and Mearsheimer 2007).

Arguing the practical impact of ethnic group lobbying on American foreign policy is critical to arguing its moral standing. For if it can be reasonably maintained that a special interest group in pursuing its own ambitions is a threat to the common good, then the question of the balance of rights and responsibilities of citizenship in a democracy naturally comes to the fore. As in the 1920s, the question of the impact of "divided loyalties" on the national interest is bound to resurface. In the case of the Walt and Mearsheimer volume, the emotional dimension underlying debates over ethnic group preferences has been vividly revealed.

One of the most outstanding features of the demands of various diasporic groups on American foreign policy is how little attention is paid to national security interests. We are told of what Armenia, or Cuba, or Israel, or Poland, or Haiti may need in terms of US support, but the analysis of what America can expect in return is typically incomplete and self-serving. Indeed, we often hear that the United States should be considered the "host country" of these diasporas, whereas their "home country" is that where their ancestral kinfolk reside, terminology that implies that members of ethnic communities have a right to favor what they consider to be the needs of the ancestral homeland over those of America (Sheffer 1986; Shain 1999).

During the 1920s, the arguments in favor of "pluralism" had never doubted the superiority of loyalty to the United States over the ties of affection that might bind many American citizens to their kinfolk abroad. The right to be ethnically (or racially or religiously) distinct never superseded the right and the obligation to be American. Indeed, the former flowed from the latter. To be sure, in practice such a distinction could be difficult to make; for many ethnic activists, especially in the years before World War I, loyalties to their foreign attachments more than to the United States largely determined their orientation toward world affairs. But in theory, the "right side of the hyphen" was nonetheless seen as the more powerful: if one were Irish American, for example, one was properly American first and Irish second.

With multiculturalism after the 1960s this was to change. A primary loyalty to the United States no longer was mandatory. Thus the *Armenian International Magazine* dedicated its July 31, 1998, edition to rallying the Armenian diaspora to the defense of the homeland. As one contributor to the issue declared in terms implicitly echoed throughout the journal, "We in the Armenian Diaspora have a unique opportunity to exercise our dual allegiance to our host country and to Armenia. We should take advantage of our rights as citizens of the host country to gain its support of Armenia" (quoted in Smith 2000, 14).

Theoretical justification for this position could be found in the writing of a leading contemporary American political philosopher, Michael Walzer, a Zionist: "In the case of hyphenated Americans, it doesn't matter whether the first or the second name is dominant. . . . An ethnic American is someone who in principle lives his spiritual life as he chooses, *on either side of the hyphen*. In this sense, American citizenship is indeed anonymous, for it doesn't require a full commitment to American (or any other) nationality" (Walzer 1992, 45). Irish Americans, for example, are not "culturally Irish and politically American. . . . Rather they are culturally Irish American and politically Irish American. . . . Their politics is still, both in style and substance, significantly ethnic" (45). Walzer is crystal clear: "*E pluribus unum* is an alchemist's promise; out of liberal pluralism no oneness can come. . . . For support and comfort and a sense of belonging, men and women look to their groups; for freedom and mobility they look to the state" (97ff.).

The danger of a position such as Walzer's should be apparent: it sanctions privileging the sentiments of allegiance to "the home country," that is, where one's foreign kinfolk live, over loyalty to the "host country," the United States, where the members of these groups are citizens. His argument is explicit: "The United States isn't a 'homeland' (where a national family might dwell), not, at least, as other countries are, in casual conversation and unreflective feeling. It is a country of immigrants who, however grateful they are for this new place, still remember the old places. . . . Their children . . . no doubt are native born, but some awkward sense of newness here, of distant oldness, keeps the tongue from calling this land 'home'" (Walzer 1992, 100). Here we encounter the worm in the fruit of diasporic arguments based on celebrating the rights and powers of an ethnic community while omitting any corresponding discussion of their obligations as citizens of democratic states. Yet the members of this community, or those from whom they are descended, are part of a social contract that should make their primary allegiance unquestionably to the democratic national community to which they belong. (An exception might be made for many members of the African American community, whose ancestors arrived as slaves and who thus are technically not bound to put American national interests before all others.) Do those who came voluntarily forget the terms sworn to by themselves or by their ancestors at the moment of their naturalization? "I hereby declare, on oath, that I absolutely and entirely renounce and abjure all allegiance and fidelity to any foreign prince, potentate, state or sovereignty, to whom or which I have heretofore been a subject or citizen; that I will support and defend the Constitution and laws of the United States against all enemies, foreign and domestic; that I will bear arms on behalf of the United States when required by the law . . . and that I take this obligation freely without any mental reservation or purpose; so help me God" (US Oath of Allegiance 1991). The concern to make the national motto—*e pluribus unum*, out of many, one—a living reality has concerned American leaders since the founding of the republic. The case against what he called "factionalism" was first made by George Washington toward the close of his second term as president. Washington was concerned by the tendency of many Americans to value their geographic (or state-centered) interests and loyalties above those that were national. He was also alarmed by what he saw as partisan divisions between those who favored France and those who supported Great Britain in the war that broke out between these two countries in 1793, divisions in which what was best for the United States (noninvolvement in the struggle, in Washington's opinion) often went ignored. As he put it in his famous Farewell Address of 1796:

> Against the insidious wiles of foreign influence, (I conjure you to believe me, fellow citizens) the jealousy of a free people ought to be constantly awake; since history and experience prove that foreign influence is one of the most baneful foes of Republican Government. . . . Nothing is more essential than that permanent, inveterate antipathies against particular nations, and passionate attachments for others, should be excluded; and that in place of them just and amicable feelings towards all should be cultivated. The nation, which indulges towards another a habitual hatred, or a habitual fondness, is in some degree a slave. It is a slave to its animosity or to its affection, either of which is sufficient to lead it astray from its duty and its interest. (Washington 1796)

Washington's warning has proved unpersuasive in a multicultural age to diasporic spokespersons. Instead, their priority concern has more often than not been to serve the needs of their "home country" while paying little more than lip service to the national security of the United States, their "host country." Foreign governments have been quick to realize the advantages they might gain from rousing their American kinfolk to work on their behalf, to the extent that special attention is paid to the organization of diasporic communities by Jerusalem, Warsaw, Athens, and Mexico City, among others.

There can be no denying that on occasion diasporic networks have converged with official American policy and have served what may reasonably be construed as the national interest. Yet only to celebrate these ties, as if they almost never raised serious practical problems for American foreign policy by their divergence from official goals, and as if they posed no ethical dilemmas for theories of democratic citizenship, is all too common among multiculturalist writers today and those who speak on behalf of diasporic constituencies. Moreover, when these are special interests without organized opposition, what seems like a convergence of national and ethnic goals far too often is the consequence of diasporas writing legislation in Washington. Not much has changed since George Kennan, in 1977, reaffirmed Alexis de Tocqueville's concerns about foreign policy making in a democracy. In Kennan's words:

> Our actions in the field of foreign affairs are the convulsive reactions of politicians to an internal political life dominated by vocal minorities. . . . No one who thinks back over the annals of just these postwar decades will have difficulty bringing to mind a number of prominent instances in which ethnic minorities have brought pressures with a view to influencing foreign policy on behalf of what they perceive as the interests of their former mother countries—interests which of course may or may not be identical with those of the United States. . . . What has been most remarkable about these pressures has been not so much their existence, for they are in the nature of things, as the degree of their success. Example after example springs to mind where [diasporas] have proven more powerful and effective as influences on Congressional decision in matters of foreign policy than the views of highly competent persons of the Executive Branch who, in contrast to the lobbyists, had exclusively the national interest at heart. (1977, 4–5)

Such a judgment applies, of course, not just to diasporic constituencies but to special interests in general. To cite Robert Dahl once again:

> Whenever democratic processes are employed on a scale as large as the nation-state, autonomous organizations are bound to come into existence. . . . They are also necessary to the functioning of the democratic process itself, to minimizing government coercion, to political liberty, and to human well-being. Yet as with individuals, so with organizations: independence or autonomy . . . creates an opportunity to do harm. Organizations may use the opportunity to increase or perpetuate injustice rather than to reduce it, to foster the narrow egotism of their members at the expense of concerns for a broader public good, and even to weaken or destroy democracy itself. (Dahl 1982, 1)

Nowhere do these observations apply more clearly than to the convergence and divergence of diasporic agendas and those of the American national government. The task today is for citizens of the United States to argue the aims sought by ethnic communities in the making of foreign policy with respect for the rights of these constituencies as citizens but with due regard to their responsibilities to the nation and its interests as well. Multicultural arguments of the sort that permit a stronger allegiance to an ancestral "homeland" than to an American "host country"—the position taken by Michael Walzer, cited above, for example—must be challenged every bit as vigorously as the arguments of those who would erase completely the richness of subnational ethnic identities in the name of a monolithic sense of what it means to be American. As the post–Cold War era moves toward what seems for many reasons to be an era of America's decline, the room for maneuver in terms of national security becomes tighter and the need for reasoned debate grows daily stronger.

Note

Material for this chapter is based on my previous work, in particular *Foreign Attachments* (Cambridge, MA: Harvard University Press, 2005).

References

Bialer, Uri. 1990. *Between East and West: Israel's Foreign Policy Orientation, 1948–1956*. New York: Cambridge University Press,

Coogan, Tim Pat. 1996. *The Troubles: Ireland's Ordeal 1966–1996 and the Search for Peace*. Boulder, CO: Roberts Rinehart.

Dahl, Robert A. 1982. *Dilemmas of Pluralist Democracy: Autonomy vs. Control*. New Haven, CT: Yale University Press.

DeConde, Alexander. 1971. *Half Bitter, Half Sweet: An Excursion into Italian American History*. New York: Scribner.

———. 1992. *Ethnicity, Race and American Foreign Policy: A History*. Boston: Northeastern University Press.

Gerson, Louis L. Gerson. 1964. *The Hyphenate in Recent American Politics and Diplomacy*. Lawrence: University of Kansas Press.

Halperin, Samuel. 1961. *The Political World of American Zionism*. Detroit, MI: Wayne State University Press.

Independent Committee of Eminent Persons. 1999. *Report on Dormant Accounts of Victims of Nazi Persecution in Swiss Banks*. Berne: Staempfli. www.crt-ii.org/ICEP/ICEP_Report_english.pdf.

Kelly, M. J. 2006. *The Fenian Ideal and Irish Nationalism, 1882–1916*. Woodbridge: Boydell.

Kennan, George. 1977. *The Cloud of Danger: Current Realities of American Foreign Policy*. Boston: Little, Brown.

Kovrig, Bennett. 1991. *Of Walls and Bridges: The United States and Eastern Europe.* New York: New York University Press.

Krenn, Michael J., ed. 1998. *Race and U.S. Foreign Policy: From the Colonial Period to the Present.* Vols. 4 and 5. New York: Garland.

Luebke, Frederick C. 1974. *Bonds of Loyalty: German-Americans and World War I.* De Kalb: Northern Illinois University Press.

Neier, Aryeh. 2003. *Taking Liberties: Four Decades in the Struggle for Rights.* New York: Public Affairs.

Novick, Peter. 1999. *The Holocaust in American Life.* Boston: Houghton Mifflin.

O'Grady, Joseph. 1996. "An Irish Policy Born in the USA." *Foreign Affairs* 75 (3): 2–7.

Paul, David M., and Rachel Anderson Paul. 2009. *Ethnic Lobbies and U.S. Foreign Policy.* Boulder, CO: Lynne Rienner.

Plummer, Brenda. 1996. *Rising Wind: Black Americans and U.S. Foreign Affairs, 1935–1960.* Chapel Hill: University of North Carolina Press.

———, ed. 2003. *Window on Freedom: Race, Civil Rights, and Foreign Affairs, 1945–1988.* Chapel Hill: University of North Carolina Press.

Rosenson, Beth A., Elizabeth A. Oldmixon, and Kenneth D. Wald. 2009. "U.S. Senators' Support for Israel Examined through Sponsorship/Cosponsorship Decisions, 1993–2002: The Influence of Elite and Constituent Factors." *Foreign Policy Analysis* 5 (1): 73–91.

Sanford, Karin L. 1997. *Beyond the Boundaries: Reverend Jesse Jackson in International Affairs.* Albany: State University of New York Press.

Shain, Yossi. 1999. *Marketing the American Creed Abroad: Diasporas in the U.S. and Their Homelands.* Cambridge: Cambridge University Press.

Sheffer, Gabriel, ed. 1996. *Modern Diasporas in International Politics.* New York: St. Martin's Press.

Singh, Robert. 1997. *The Farrakhan Phenomenon: Race, Reaction, and the Paranoid Style in American Politics.* Washington, DC: Georgetown University Press.

———. 1998. *The Congressional Black Caucus: Racial Politics in the U.S. Congress.* Thousand Oaks, CA: Sage Publications.

Skerry, Peter. 1993. *Mexican Americans: The Ambivalent Minority.* Cambridge, MA: Harvard University Press.

Small, Melvin. 1996. *Democracy and Diplomacy: The Impact of Domestic Politics on U.S. Foreign Policy, 1789–1994.* Baltimore: Johns Hopkins University Press.

Smith, Tony. 1994. *America's Mission: The United States and the Worldwide Struggle for Democracy in the Twentieth Century.* Princeton, NJ: Princeton University Press.

———. 2000. *Foreign Attachments: The Power of Ethnic Groups in the Making of American Foreign Policy.* Cambridge, MA: Harvard University Press.

Tucker, Robert W., Charles B. Keely, and Linda Wrigley. 1990. *Immigration and U.S. Foreign Policy.* Boulder, CO: Westview Press.

US Bureau of the Census. 1975. *Historical Statistics of the United States: Colonial Times to 1970.* Washington, DC: Government Printing Office.

US Oath of Allegiance. 8 C.F.R. § 337.1 (1991).

Von Eschen, Penny M. 1997. *Race against Empire: Black Americans and Anticolonialism, 1937–1957.* Ithaca, NY: Cornell University Press.

Walker, Mabel Gregory. 1969. *The Fenian Movement.* Colorado Springs, CO: Ralph Myles.

Walt, Stephen, and John Mearsheimer, 2007. *The Israel Lobby and American Foreign Policy.* New York: Farrar, Straus and Giroux.

Walzer, Michael. 1992. *What It Means to Be an American.* New York: Marsilio.

Washington, George. 1796. "Farewell Address." September 19. American Presidency Project. www.presidency.ucsb.edu/ws/?pid=65539.

Yzaguirre, Raul. 1995. "Statement before the Subcommittee on Immigration, Committee of the Judiciary, US House of Representatives, June 29." http://judiciary.house.gov/legacy/610.htm.

Contributors

MOHAMMED A. BAMYEH is a Professor of Sociology at the University of Pittsburgh and editor of *International Sociology Reviews*. He is the author of *Anarchy as Order* (2009), *Of Death and Dominion* (2007), *The Ends of Globalization* (2000), and *The Social Origins of Islam* (1999). He has edited *Intellectuals and Civil Society in the Middle East* (2012) and *Palestine America* (2003).

JOSH DEWIND is Director of the Migration Program and the Dissertation Proposal Development Fellowship Program at the Social Science Research Council. Since receiving his PhD in anthropology from Columbia University in 1977, his research and publications have focused largely on migration, as related to theoretical and comparative approaches, social integration, transnationalism, religion, internal and international mobility, development, and other topics. With Charles Hirschman and Philip Kasinitz, he is editor of *The Handbook of International Migration: The American Experience* (1999).

DANIEL P. ERIKSON is Senior Adviser for Policy in the Bureau of Western Hemisphere Affairs at the US Department of State. He previously served as Senior Associate for US Policy and Director of Caribbean Programs at the Inter-American Dialogue, the Washington, D.C.–based think tank, where he directed the Haiti project. He is the author of *The Cuba Wars: Fidel Castro, the United States, and the Next Revolution* (2008) and has contributed chapters to numerous books, including *Coping with the Collapse of the Old Order: CARICOM's New External Agenda* (ed. Kenneth O. Hall and Myrtle Chuck-a-Sang,

2013), *China Engages Latin America: Tracing the Trajectory* (ed. Adrian H. Hearn and José Luis Leon Manriquez, 2011), *Inter-American Cooperation at a Crossroads* (ed. Gordon Mace et al., 2011), and *Shifting the Balance: Obama and the Americas* (ed. Abraham F. Lowenthal et al., 2010). His chapter was written before he joined the State Department and does not reflect the views of the US government.

TERRENCE LYONS is Associate Professor at the School for Conflict Analysis and Resolution, George Mason University. He received his doctorate in international relations from the Johns Hopkins University School for Advanced International Studies. His publications include *Politics from Afar: Transnational Diasporas and Networks* (2012), "Conflict-Generated Diasporas and Transnational Politics in Ethiopia" (2007), *Avoiding Conflict in the Horn of Africa: U.S. Policy toward Ethiopia and Eritrea* (2006), and *Demilitarizing Politics: Elections on the Uncertain Road to Peace* (2005).

LISANDRO PÉREZ is Professor and Chair of the Department of Latin American and Latina/o Studies at John Jay College of Criminal Justice, City University of New York. He previously served for twenty-five years on the faculty of Florida International University in Miami, where he established and directed FIU's Cuban Research Institute (CRI). He was the editor of the journal *Cuban Studies* from 1998 to 2003. Pérez holds a PhD in sociology from the University of Florida.

NEIL ROGACHEVSKY is a PhD candidate in history at Sidney Sussex College, University of Cambridge, and a former visiting fellow in the Abba Eban Program on Diplomacy at Tel Aviv University.

RENATA SEGURA is the Associate Director of the Conflict Prevention and Peace Forum of the Social Science Research Council. As such, she has overseen dozens of research projects and workshops on challenges to democratic governance and peace in Latin America and the Caribbean, and on topics ranging from drug policy and food security to gender policies in the continent. She received her PhD in political science from the New School for Social Research.

YOSSI SHAIN is Romulo Betancourt Professor and Chair, Department of Political Science, Tel Aviv University, and Professor of Government and Diaspora Politics at Georgetown University. His books on diasporas include *Kinship and Diasporas in International Affairs* (2007), *The Frontier of Loyalty: Political Exiles in* the *Age of the Nation-State* (2005), *Marketing the American Creed Abroad: Diasporas in the US and Their Homelands* (1999), and *Governments-in-Exile in Contemporary World Politics* (1991). Shain is now writing a book titled *The Israelization of Judaism*.

GABRIEL (GABI) SHEFFER is Professor in the Political Science Department of the Hebrew University of Jerusalem, Israel. His research focus is ethnic politics, with special emphasis on ethno-national-religious diasporas. He has published numerous books, edited volumes, journal articles, and chapters in edited volumes. Among his recent relevant books are *Middle Eastern Minorities and Diasporas* (2002), *Diaspora Politics: At Home Abroad* (2003), *Who Leads? Israeli-Diaspora Relations* (in Hebrew, 2006), and *The Jewish Diaspora and the Jerusalem Issue* (in Hebrew, 2012).

TONY SMITH is the Cornelia M. Jackson Professor of Political Science at Tufts University. He is currently working on a book about the origins of American human rights and democracy promotion abroad in the thought of Woodrow Wilson, the president whose tradition of "Wilsonianism" became a synonym for American liberal internationalism. Its object is to show how the Wilsonian tradition has changed over time, in some ways with results that Woodrow Wilson himself might well have deplored.

JOSEPH E. THOMPSON is a Professor in Villanova University's Graduate Theology Department. He received his PhD in political science from Catholic University of America in 1977. He is the author of *American Policy and Northern Ireland* (2001) and *American Policy and African Famine* (1990). His articles have appeared in the *Brown Journal of World Affairs*, *L'Irlande: Politique et sociale*, *World Affairs*, the *National Social Science Association Journal*, and the *Journal for the Study of Peace and Conflict*. He has also reviewed numerous books in American and European publications.

WALT VANDERBUSH is Associate Professor of Political Science at Miami University in Oxford, Ohio. Prior to his work on the role of the Iraqi diaspora in shaping US intervention in Iraq, his scholarship focused on the similar influence of Cuban American lobbying on US policy toward the island nation and on the political economy of US–Latin American relations, including a coauthored book, *The Cuban Embargo: The Domestic Politics of an American Foreign Policy* (with Patrick Haney; 2005) and articles in *International Studies Quarterly*, *New Political Science*, and *Foreign Policy Analysis*, among others.

Index

Clinton, Hillary, 72, 126, 256

Clinton Foundation, Ethiopian diaspora's pressure on, 178

Clinton Global Initiative, 199

Coalition for Unity and Democracy (CUD), 170, 171, 172, 175, 177

coalition-building as strategy, 38, 42, 54

Cold War: Cuba and, 18, 91–92, 133–34, 143–49; diaspora populations and, 8, 244–49, 256–57; Ethiopia and, 173; Haiti and, 201; US priorities during, 7–8, 25, 84, 239, 244–49

Colombian diaspora, 37

Commission for Assistance to a Free Cuba (CAFC), 151

Committees. See Ad Hoc Congressional Committee for Irish Affairs; American Committee of Irish Studies; American Israel Public Affairs Committee (AIPAC); American Jewish Committee; Arab American Anti-Discrimination Committee (ADC); Irish Northern Aid Committee; National Committee on American Foreign Policy; Select Committee on Intelligence

common good, subordination of interests to, 7, 8–9, 14, 258–65

communalism as strategy, 38

communications. See media campaigns as influence mechanism

Conference of Presidents, 65

Congressional Black Caucus (CBC): creation of, 248; Haitian interests and, 22, 189, 198, 240, 254; sub-Saharan African policies, 254

Congressional Research Service (CRS), 108–9

Conte, Silvio, 113

convergence of interests: diaspora influence and, 5–7, 11, 13–14, 24, 25, 32–33, 90–93; examples of, 16–19, 22–24, 50–51, 72–73, 239, 256–57; historical considerations, 239–65; homeland conflicts and, 42–45, 218–27, 231–32, 261–65; negotiated, 19. *See also specific ethnic groups*

Coogan, Tim Pat, 111

corporatism as strategy, 38

Corzine, Jon, 150

Council on American-Islamic Relations (CAIR), 86

counterterrorism efforts, Horn of Africa and, 25, 163, 165, 166, 173–74, 177, 179, 180

criminal activities of diasporans, 33, 45–50, 56

Cuba: annexationist movement, 140, 141, 142; Carter administration's normalization efforts, 144–45; Castro's revolution in, 44, 132–33, 140–41, 142; Cold War policies toward, 18, 91–92, 133–34, 143–49; as divided nation, 133–34; economic sanctions against, 5, 19, 151, 251–52; exhaustion of model for, 154–55; independence struggle, 1868, 135–36; post-Cold War policies toward, 150–57; post-revolution emigration, 136–39, 153; Powell Report and, 150–54; pre-revolution emigration, 134–36, 140, 142; rupture scenario for, 152, 154–55; Spanish-American War and, 141, 142,

Devlin, Bernadette, 106–7

Diálogo (1978), 144–45

diaspora populations: arenas and mechanism of government relations, 24–27, 50–56; categorization of, 38; criminal or terrorist activities, 33, 111, 118, 130, 175; divergence and convergence with US policies, 1900–1941, 241–44; divergence and convergence with US policies, 1941–1989, 244–49; divergence and convergence with US policies, since 1989, 249–56; divergence and convergence with US policies in nineteenth century, 241; early twentieth-century immigrants, 242; effects of nature, types, and goals on hostland foreign policies, 31–56, 261–65; ethno-national-religious, 12–13, 24; generational differences, 4, 152–54, 156–57, 168; growth of, 31, 255; heterogeneity of, 56; hybridizing and globalizing trends, 34, 36, 40; identity politics and, 257–58; influence success factors, 52–55; integration of, 51; lobbying groups, 14; multiplicity of views, 33; nature of, 11–14; perceived comparative influence on US foreign policies, 10–11, 15–16, 52–55, 239–40; peripheral members of, 56; "political entrepreneurs" in, 164; pressure groups contrasted with, 92–93; pre-World War I, 242–43; problems troubling, 56; recent vs. more established groups, 3–4, 25; research on, 31–32; rights and responsibilities of, 256–65; selection bias in, 221, 224, 225; social, political, and economic power of, 41; stigmatization avoidance, 56;

stigmatization of, 49–50; in the United States, 40–42. *See also specific ethnic groups*

Díaz-Balart, Lincoln, 149, 150

Díaz-Balart, Mario, 150, 156, 189

Diggs, Charles, 248

Ditchley Conference, 116–17

divergence of interests: diaspora influence and, 5–7, 9–10, 11, 13–14, 24, 32–33, 177–78, 180, 186–87; examples of, 19–22, 76, 87–89, 239; historical considerations, 239–65; homeland conflicts and, 42–45, 165, 261–65; stateless diasporas and, 13. *See also specific ethnic groups*

Diversity Visa program, 167–68

DLA Piper, 176–77

Dobriansky, Paula, 126

Donaldson, Jeffrey, 125

donations. *See* campaign donations as influence mechanism; charitable contributions and organizations; economic activities of diasporas

drug trafficking, 49

DuBois, W. E. B., 248

Duvalier, François "Papa Doc," 192, 201

Duvalier, Jean-Claude "Baby Doc," 191–92, 201

Duvalier rule, 186, 190, 191–92, 197, 201, 206

Eagleburger, Lawrence, 121

economic activities of diasporas, 45; 2, 179; charitable contributions, 67, 80, 82, 167, 205; circulatory migration and, 81–82; fund-raising, 38, 56, 65, 68, 80, 141–42, 147, 165, 168–69, 170, 175; US government protection mechanisms, 52

economic interests, vested, 258

economic sanctions as conflict type: against Cuba, 5, 19, 155, 251–52; against Haiti, 195; against Iran, 260; against Iraq, 215, 232; against South Africa, 249

Egyptian revolution, 91

Eilber, Joshua, 108

Eisenhower, Dwight D., and administration, 133, 245

Eizenstadt, Stuart, 251

elections. *See* electoral power; *specific cities and states*

electoral power: of Cuban diaspora, 17, 18, 54, 149, 155–56, 203; of Haitian diaspora, 188–89, 203–4, 206; as influence mechanism, 26, 45, 51, 54, 240, 243; of Irish diaspora, 18, 121–22, 250

Erikson, Daniel P., 21–22

Eritrea, 173, 178

Eritrean diaspora, 168

Ethiopia: conflict in, 178–79; election of 2005 and post-election crackdown, 165, 169–72, 174, 179, 180; Italian invasion of, 248; request for diaspora groups to be classified as terrorist, 166, 172, 175; US's changing relationship with, 20, 163, 173–74, 179–80

Ethiopian American Council, 176

Ethiopian Democracy and Accountability Act (2007), 20, 166, 176–79

Ethiopian diaspora: active involvement in homeland, 163–64, 170–72; anti-government groups, 20, 44, 166, 175; as conflict-generated, 164–65, 167–68; discrimination as issue, 44; divergence of interests from US foreign policies, 163, 165, 166, 173–75, 179–80; as ethno-national-religious diaspora, 37; goals and strategies of, 42, 165; identity markers, 168; influence on US foreign policies, 4, 19–21, 25, 51, 163–80; lobbying activities, 165, 176–80; media campaigns of, 55; non-lobbying activities, 20–21, 165, 177–78; organizations and cultural activities, 166–67; population and distribution, 166

Ethiopian North American Health Professionals Association, 167

Ethiopian Orthodox church, 167

Ethiopian People's Revolutionary Democratic Front (EPRDF), 20, 167, 168, 169, 170, 172, 173, 175

Ethiopian People's Revolutionary Party (EPRP), 167

Ethiopian Sports Federation of North America, 167

ethno-national-religious diasporas, 12–13; assimilation resisted by, 12–13; criminal activities, 48–50; effectiveness factors of, 24; features of, 37–40; homeland connectedness and, 12, 34–35, 39, 168, 261–65; homeland-linked vs. stateless, 13, 24, 44; hybridization theories, 34; identity reawakening, 37–38; integration strategies, 38; irredentist groups contrasted with, 37; migration reasons, 37; nature of, 12; overlapping identities in, 33–34; persistence of, 35; repatriation and, 39–40; solidarity of, 38–39; terrorism and, 48, 111, 118, 130, 175; transnational communities contrasted with, 12, 33–35, 36, 46–47; transnational links, 56

Euskadi Ta Askatasuna, 43

executive arena of diaspora engagement, 26, 240; Cubans' access to, 141–42, 145–46, 149–50, 189, 239; elected officials, 41; Haitians' lack of access to, 189; Iraqis' access to, 211, 220–27, 231–32; personal contacts, 14, 54–55, 84

Fair Employment Act (1989), 119

Farrakhan, Louis, 254–55

Farrelly, Patrick, 121

Fascell, Dante, 147

Federalist Papers, 7

Feith, Douglas, 220, 223, 225

Fenian Brotherhood, 241

Filipino diaspora, 255

Fish, Hamilton, 142

Flannery, Michael, 107

Florida: Cuban diaspora in, 17, 18–19, 132, 134, 135, 136, 149, 154; Haitian diaspora in, 188, 189, 203, 204, 206; Hispanic population growth, 255; Ybor City cigar factories, 136

Florida International University Cuba Poll, 154, 155

Flynn, Raymond, 121, 124

Flynn, William, 122–23

Foer, Franklin, 223

Foley, Thomas, 122

Fondasyon Mapou, 200

Food, Conservation, and Energy Act (2008), 199–200

foreign attachments and loyalty: "mischief of factions" concept, 7–11, 262–63; national security concerns about, 3, 6–7, 13–14, 39, 41, 258–65; post-Revolutionary War concerns, 7

Franklin, Ben, 97

Frazer, Jendayi, 175, 179

Free French, 227

Free Iraqi Forces, 227

Freeh, Louis, 122

freedom and democracy interests in foreign policies, 8–9, 20–22, 42; Cuba and, 152, 155; Ethiopia and, 20–21, 163, 170–71, 176–77, 179; Haiti and, 195, 196, 200, 201–2, 2122

Freedom Support Act (1992), 252

Freeman, Charles, 77

Friends of Ireland, 18, 116, 117

Frontline television show, 221, 222

funding. *See* campaign donations as influence mechanism; charitable contributions and organizations; economic activities of diasporas

Gaddafi, Muammar, 254

Garvey, Marcus, 248

Gates, Robert, 211

Gavin, Martin, 121

Gaza Strip, 71, 77, 89–90

Georgia, 253

German diaspora, 242, 243

Germany, World Wars and, 243

Gerson, Louis L., 8

Ginbot 7, 166, 175

Giuliani, Rudolph, 177

globalization, diaspora populations and, 34, 36, 40

Gonzalez, Elian, 203

Good Friday Agreement, 18, 50, 99, 125–26, 164, 250

Gordon, Michael, 223–24

Gousse, Bernard, 194

Islamic Jihad, 37

isolation as strategy, 38

Israel: 1967 War, 246; anti-Palestinian policies, 86; conversion bill debate, 69–70; establishment of, 245, 246–47; as fulcrum of Jewish affairs, 66–67; government influence on US foreign policies, 53, 63–65, 239; "Law of Return" debate, 70; Orthodox Jews in, 68, 70; perceived as Western implant, 85–86; right-wing government in, 77

Israel lobby: Cold War and, 7–8, 15, 84; influence on US foreign policies, 7–8, 10, 15–16, 50–51, 62–64, 77–78, 83, 86–93, 212, 239, 247, 255–56; Israeli-Palestinian conflict and, 61–63, 240, 247, 260; as model for Cuban lobby, 146; as model for other diaspora lobbies, 255–56; success of, 8, 55, 257, 260; "theory of everything" and, 61–63, 72–73

Israel Policy Forum, 256

Israeli criminal networks, 49

Israeli-Palestinian conflict, 5; 1967 War, 78; first Intifada, 78; Gaza War, 77, 89–90; post–Cold War US policies, 89–90, 251; right of return goal of Palestinians, 79, 80; second Intifada, 64–65; two-state solution, 61, 70–71, 83; US foreign policy interest in, 43, 50–51, 54, 71–73, 86–93, 260; West Bank settlements and, 77, 88, 240, 255–56

Italian diaspora, 38, 48, 49, 243–44, 245

Italy, African colonies of, 245, 248

Jackson, Henry, 247

Jackson, Jesse, 254–55

Jacksonville, Palestinian diaspora in, 81

Japanese diaspora, 39, 255

Jawad, Saad, 227–28

JDate, 68–69

Jean, Wyclef, 190, 198–99, 201

Jerusalem Fund for Education and Community Development, 80

Jewish diaspora: assimilation and intermarriage of, 66; campaign donations, 45; Cold War and, 247; connections with Israel, 24, 63–65, 66–67, 246–47; criminal activities, 49; as ethno-national-religious diaspora, 37, 38; goals and strategies of, 40–42, 61–73; as historical diaspora, 38; homeland investments, 45; influence on US foreign policies, 4, 7–8, 15–16, 25, 53, 54, 211, 212; liberal views in, 61, 62, 65–73; media campaigns of, 55; multiplicity of views in, 16, 54; Orthodox, 67–68, 69; pre-Israel, 44, 47; repatriation of, 39; revival of ethnic interests, 3; solidarity of, 39; Truman's stance on Israel and, 245; World War I and, 242, 243. See also Israel lobby

Johnson, Lyndon, and administration, 248

Johnson, Ralph, 121

Joseph, Leo, 205

J Street, 16, 54, 62, 68–69, 70, 83, 256

Judt, Tony, 69, 260

Keane, John "Jack," 110

Kennan, George, 264

Kennedy, John F., and administration: Cuba relations, 133, 143; Irish heritage, 100

Kennedy, Robert, 123

pressure groups, diaspora groups
contrasted with, 92–93
Préval, Rene, 192, 202
Project for the New American Century
(PNAC), 23, 217, 219, 222
Proposition 187, 255
Provisional Irish Republican Army (Provo
IRA), 101–2, 109, 111, 115–16, 250
public opinion polls, 62–63, 154–56, 254

Rabin, Yitzak, 71, 251, 255
radio. *See* media campaigns as influence
mechanism; *specific stations*
Radio Martí, 148, 152, 155
Radio Nouveauté, 204
Raei, Lamia, 81
Rafter Crisis, 1994, 138
Ramsbotham, Sir Peter, 108
Rawlins, John, 142
Reagan, Ronald, and administration:
African Americans and, 249; "captive
nations resolution" and, 245; Cold
War and, 239, 245–46; Cuban policies,
18, 145–47, 217, 239, 257; diaspora
population outreach, 245; Ethiopian
policies, 173; Iraq policies, 214; Irish
roots, 100; Northern Ireland conflict,
116–20; sale of AWACS aircraft to
Saudi Arabia, 76, 87–88, 239, 247
Reich, Otto, 150, 151
Reid, Father Alex, 123
Reiss, Mitchell, 126
remittances, sending, 20–21, 45, 164
Rendon Group, 216
Reno, Janet, 122
Republicans. *See* executive arena of
diaspora engagement; legislative

arena of diaspora engagement; *specific
presidential administrations and specific
names*
Rice, Condoleezza, 224, 229
Robinson, Randall, 249
Rogachevsky, Neil, 16
Rogers, William, 105
Roma diaspora, 38
Romney, Mitt, 63, 156
Roosevelt, Franklin D., 245
Rosen, Jonathan, 64
Rosenthal, Steven, 64
Ros-Lehtinen, Ileana, 149, 189
Ross, Marc, 98
Roston, Aram, 211
Rotem, David, 69
Rove, Karl, 132
Royal Ulster Constabulary (RUC), 105
Rumsfeld, Donald, 214, 224, 225, 229
Russian criminal networks, 49

Sadat, Anwar, 71
Said, Edward, 78
San Francisco, Palestinian diaspora in, 81
Sands, Bobby, 115–16
Sasson, Theodore, 66–67
Saudi Arabia, sale of AWACS aircraft to,
76, 87–88, 239, 247
Scandinavian diaspora, 242
Schlesinger, Arthur, Jr., 9
Schneerson, Menachem Mendel, 70
Schorsch, Ismar, 70
Selassie, Haile, 167
Select Committee on Intelligence, 216, 220
September 11 terrorist attacks: Iraq War
and, 23, 219, 220, 221–22, 229–30;
Israeli-Palestinian conflict and, 64–65